I0866734

"*Highway Robbery* offers a sophisticated account of the long struggle to create a federal no-fault auto insurance system, explaining why passing a reform that promises to lower premiums, reduce administrative costs, and enhance benefits has proven so elusive. Along the way, Kinzler shows how the US policy-making system actually works and the difficulties of navigating political obstacles inside the Beltway. This crisply written book is ideal for courses on American politics and policymaking, offering an invaluable contrast to the standard 'how-a-bill-becomes-a-law' texts in the field."

Jeb Barnes, professor of political science, University of Southern California

"I highly recommend Peter Kinzler's book. Having worked with Peter on the public policy issue, which is the basis of this book, I believe readers will find it to be both fascinating and informative as to how public policy issues are pursued in the US Congress."

Herman Brandau, associate general counsel, retired, of State Farm Insurance

"Peter Kinzler navigates through political and legislative gridlock that, underwritten for decades by the US insurance industry, has kept American citizens and motorists from reaching the destination of nationwide, no-fault insurance. Whether you take this historical excursion for academic purposes or simply to educate yourself on the bumps along the long-haul journey, rest assured Kinzler's style will keep you on course and fully alert behind the wheel."

Peter George Markwith, adjunct faculty, Bentley University, and owner, Unified Business Technologies, LLC

"Peter Kinzler's masterful book provides an instructive, scholarly insider's analysis of two central issues confronting the American system of lawmaking: how to weigh the costs and benefits of proposed major social legislation and how the forces of competing interest groups combine to resolve—or not resolve—such proposals. Because Kinzler examines these general issues in the concrete setting of the decades long efforts to enact national no-fault auto insurance legislation, his analysis is particularly deep and rich."

Thomas G. Krattenmaker, former professor of law, Georgetown University Law Center

"Everyone who drives a car—and thus pays auto insurance—must wonder if there is a cheaper way. In this terrific book, Peter Kinzler tells the inside story of why no-fault auto insurance, that better and cheaper way, has yet to become widely available in this country. This book is that rare combination of excellent policy analysis and real-world politics, from a former insider, that can hopefully one day impel legislative reform to make no-fault auto insurance a reality."

Robert Litan, nonresident senior fellow and former director of the Economic Studies program at the Brookings Institution

"Peter Kinzler provides a vivid and revealing account of his decades-long quest to enhance the value provided to automobile insurance consumers. The story accurately recounts his work to help consumers over the efforts of those who profit handsomely off of the liability system. A compelling read for those interested in congressional advocacy, true consumerism, liability system inefficiencies, and the $300 billion automobile insurance industry."

Steve McManus, senior vice president and general counsel, State Farm Mutual Automobile Insurance Company

"Peter Kinzler's modern history of the effort to enact no-fault automobile insurance is a must-read book. He brings his considerable intelligence and his compelling judgments to bear. He makes a powerful argument for real reform, making it clear that the beneficiaries of a no-fault style reform are American car owners. They would save billions, not just in lower premiums, but also in better and fairer claim service. His case for reform is overwhelming, and though Peter is no longer on Capitol Hill, he continues to be a tireless advocate for this essential reform."

William Mattea, retired chief of staff to Senator Carol Moseley Braun

"'How the Sausage Fails to Get Made.' That would be my subtitle for this worthy volume. It is the definitive history of the auto-insurance insanity; the engaging story of an idealistic lawyer, looking back after half a century in the legislative trenches; and, most importantly, instructive reading for serious young people contemplating careers in law, politics, or public service. It's up to them to figure out how we can do better."

Andrew Tobias, author of *Invisible Bankers: Everything the Insurance Industry Never Wanted You to Know* and *The Only Investment Guide You'll Ever Need*

HIGHWAY ROBBERY

STUDIES IN GOVERNMENT AND PUBLIC POLICY

HIGHWAY ROBBERY

The Two-Decade Battle to Reform America's Automobile Insurance System

Peter Kinzler

University Press of Kansas

© 2021 by the University Press of Kansas
All rights reserved

Published by the University Press of Kansas (Lawrence, Kansas 66045), which was organized by the Kansas Board of Regents and is operated and funded by Emporia State University, Fort Hays State University, Kansas State University, Pittsburg State University, the University of Kansas, and Wichita State University.

Library of Congress Cataloging-in-Publication Data

Names: Kinzler, Peter, author.
Title: Highway robbery : the two-decade battle to reform America's automobile insurance system / Peter Kinzler.
Description: Lawrence : University Press of Kansas, 2021. | Series: Studies in government and public policy | Includes bibliographical references and index.
Identifiers: LCCN 2020048506
ISBN 9780700632299 (cloth)
ISBN 9780700632305 (epub)
Subjects: LCSH: Automobile insurance—Law and legislation—United States. | Automobile insurance—Government policy—United States. | Law reform—United States.
Classification: LCC KF1218 .K56 2021 | DDC 368/.0920973—dc23
LC record available at https://lccn.loc.gov/2020048506.

British Library Cataloguing-in-Publication Data is available.

Printed in the United States of America

10 9 8 7 6 5 4 3 2 1

The paper used in this publication is acid free and meets the minimum requirements of the American National Standard for Permanence of Paper for Printed Library Materials Z39.48–1992.

For my family and friends who listened patiently (suffered in silence?)
through all the years as I extolled the virtues of no-fault and
excoriated the vices of its trial lawyer opponents.
This is the whole story.

Figure 0.1. A 1976 Herblock Cartoon, © The Herb Block Foundation. Prints & Photographs Division, Library of Congress.

CONTENTS

ACKNOWLEDGMENTS

All major legislative initiatives involve a wide group of advocates from across the political spectrum and from inside and outside the Congress. When I use the word "we" in this book, I really mean all the people I mention here, albeit not all at once in every situation. Each of them contributed significantly during these two legislative battles to secure markedly, though different, better auto insurance for the motoring public.

In twenty-five years working for the Congress and another fifteen lobbying it, never did I work on legislation that would have benefited more people, and never did I work with brighter, more committed people. The following is a list of all the excellent people I can remember. As this effort occurred over about a thirty-seven-year period—from the 1967 publication of the Keeton-O'Connell book that first brought public attention to no-fault insurance to the end of federal Auto Choice efforts in 2004—naturally, many of the key players are deceased. The ones who left an indelible imprint on the effort are as follows:

- Harvard Law School Professor and US District Court Judge Robert Keeton, the cocreator of no-fault insurance; University of Virginia Law School Professor Jeffrey O'Connell, the other cocreator of no-fault and also the cocreator of Auto Choice, a tireless advocate with whom I worked for years and had the privilege of writing several academic articles; Dick Walsh, the project director for the 1971 twenty-six-volume Department of Transportation study of the tort system that called for replacing it with no-fault; and Stanford Law School Professor William Cohen, the coreporter and drafter of UMVARA, the model state no-fault law. All of them were also very generous with their time in helping members of Congress and staff to understand no-fault.
- Bob Joost, who risked and lost his job to testify in favor of no-fault, taught me the details of no-fault and how to draft bills, and spent

countless hours noodling with me about ways to move no-fault legislation between 1975 and 2008, wrote two powerful Department of Transportation (DOT) reports on the benefits of no-fault, and cocreated the Auto Choice concept.

- Dan Miller wrote remarkably lucid and incisive reports for the congressional Joint Economic Committee on the impact of Auto Choice on various segments of society and estimated the cost savings. Dan and I shared information regularly during the Auto Choice effort, discussing the historical context and the reasons for different provisions, what research needed to be done, and how best to present the results. Dan then applied his brilliant conceptualization skills and technical wizardry to develop models and graphs to present the results. I had the privilege of collaborating with Jeff O'Connell and Dan on an article before Jeff's death in 2013 and before Dan's way-too-early death in 2017 from complications associated with hemophilia.
- Democratic Sens. Phil Hart, Warren Magnuson, and Frank Moss and Republican Sens. Ted Stevens and James Pearson played key roles in the 1970s no-fault fight, while Democratic Sen. Daniel Patrick Moynihan and Republican Sen. John McCain were similarly key in the Auto Choice fight twenty years later.
- My first subcommittee chairman, Lionel Van Deerlin, gave me the time and space to study no-fault so I could provide him with my best judgment and then was supportive throughout the process.
- My third subcommittee chairman, Bob Eckhardt, was perhaps the most brilliant member of Congress at the time. Despite his initial reservations about no-fault, he set out to answer two fundamental questions and tolerated my efforts to convince him of the efficacy of no-fault, both in and outside the hearings. Despite our early differences, he never failed to call on me to ask questions during the hearings, even when my goal was to counter his questions. When he became convinced that no-fault would be much better for injured people, he worked diligently to advance the bill, even though it was not in his political interest. He paid a heavy price in 1980 when a primary challenge by a trial lawyer weakened him badly before the general election he lost.
- Evy Dubrow, the chief lobbyist for the International Ladies' Garment Workers Union, was one of the leading labor lobbyists. Standing four

foot eleven with bright red hair and known as the dean of female lobbyists, she was a fiery, knowledgeable, and effective advocate.

- Robert Quinn of Nationwide Insurance Company was a brilliant advocate in the 1970s who helped educate me on no-fault, worked hard for its adoption, and joined the Coalition for Auto-Insurance Reform (CAR) in the 1990s. In the 1970s, Bob wrote a book about no-fault, which he titled *The Lemon Tree*. He prophetically based the title on the lyrics of the Peter, Paul and Mary song "Lemon Tree": "Lemon tree very pretty, and the lemon flower is sweet, but the fruit of the poor lemon is impossible to eat."

Now for the living! Guido Calabresi, former dean of Yale Law School and now a senior federal appellate court judge on the Second Circuit, wrote extensively and brilliantly about no-fault and was a great help whenever I called him with questions. Steve Carroll of the RAND Institute for Civil Justice produced multiple excellent reports on Auto Choice and was always available to answer my questions.

The work of committee staffs of members of Congress is little known to the public, but without it, no legislation would pass. Foremost among the staff was Senate Commerce Committee General Counsel S. Lynn Sutcliffe. At thirty-two when we started working on no-fault together, he was the best congressional staffer I had ever worked with. Thirty-five years later, when I retired and long after Lynn had moved on, he still was. Other outstanding Senate staffers were Mike Mullen, who staffed no-fault for both the Senate Judiciary and Commerce Committees, and Sallie Adams, Mary Schuman, and Sharon Nelson, who all worked for the Senate Commerce Committee. Mary later coordinated the Carter administration process on no-fault and wrote the decision memorandum for President Jimmy Carter. Cindy Douglass of Sen. Pearson's staff was a friendly, smart, and effective face across the aisle.

On the House side, I worked closely with Mark Raabe, full Committee Chairman Staggers's counsel assigned to cover the subcommittee's issues. Most significantly, Mark helped convince Staggers to bring the bill up for a vote in the full committee (and vote for it) despite the pressure not to do so from Speaker O'Neill. On the subcommittee, my assistant Dale Bechtel and summer law school intern Susan Fry also did invaluable work. I will never forget the help of another of Chairman Staggers's staffers, Jeff Schwartz, who, while assigned to work with the Health Subcommittee, made a strong pitch to Subcommittee Chairman Paul Rogers to vote for no-fault. Among the members' staff, Elaine Fultz of Rep. William Brodhead's staff and Coleman Conroy of Rep. Ralph Metcalfe's staff were particularly helpful.

I owe Mike Lemov, who staffed the issue before me (for then subcommittee chairman John Moss), a great debt of gratitude. We became good friends outside work, as a result of which he helped me get the subcommittee job. He also included a discussion of no-fault, much of which was drawn from our discussions, in his book about Rep. Moss, *People's Warrior.* Mike was one of two people who encouraged me to write this book and offered suggestions as to its form, for which he will receive either significant credit or blame!

Among outside groups, Kathleen O'Reilly of the Consumer Federation of America (CFA), Sandra Willett of the National Consumers League, and Mike Gildea of the AFL-CIO were extremely effective, forceful, and tireless advocates during the 1970s.

Among insurance industry lobbyists, I could always count on Herm Brandau of State Farm and Les Cheek of the American Insurance Association and later Crum and Forster Insurance Group for expert advice on no-fault that they never shaded to further their companies' interests. Mick McCabe, who lobbied for Allstate and later became its general counsel, was also knowledgeable and forthcoming, even though Allstate opposed the federal no-fault bill. Laurie McCarty of Prudential and Steve Lesnik of Kemper were also helpful advocates for no-fault.

After Lynn Sutcliffe left the Commerce Committee in 1976, he took leadership of the outside lobbying effort, the Committee for Consumers No-Fault. There he hired Ted Johnson to lead the publicity effort. Ted identified and lobbied many newspapers and other publications and secured a lot of editorial and columnist support for no-fault. Ted and I became lifelong friends through no-fault, as was the case with many of the others I worked with on it.

Dave Snyder of the American Insurance Association offered many useful suggestions on Auto Choice and served as a good sounding board for different ideas to advance legislation. He also provided useful information as to where specific insurers and trade associations stood.

There were more Republican supporters during the Auto Choice effort than the no-fault effort, and they, too, were very bright and effective. Senator McConnell took the lead in introducing bills and never sought to make the issue partisan. His chief staff person, Hunter Bates, became an enormously knowledge and effective guide to where Republican offices stood and joined Jeff O'Connell and me in writing a detailed section-by-section analysis of the bill that was published in the *Connecticut Law Journal*. Lance Bultena, Commerce Committee Chairman John McCain's committee staff person, was brilliant, collaborative, and highly effective.

Michael Horowitz of the Hudson Institute was a tireless advocate, if not the easiest person to get along with. He opened many doors in Republican offices and charged through every one of them.

On the House side, the bill's sponsor was Majority Leader Dick Armey. Like McConnell, despite his reputation, he sought out Democratic support and never tried to make the issue a partisan one. His staff person Gayland Barksdale also dug into the details and worked collaboratively with Democratic staff and me. They were all very easy to work with.

In addition to the excellent analytical work done by Dan Miller for the Joint Economic Committee and by Steve Carroll for RAND, former President George H. W. Bush staffer Charlie Kolb initiated the publication of a superb study, *Breaking the Litigation Habit: Economic Incentives for Legal Reform*, by the mainstream business group he headed, the Committee for Economic Development (January 24, 2000). Bob Detlefsen wrote an excellent article for the conservative organization Citizens for a Sound Economy. When Detlefsen moved to the National Association of Mutual Insurance Companies (NAMIC), he served as the editor of two no-fault papers, one by me alone and one with Jeff O'Connell and Dan Miller that NAMIC published.

Jim Brown of the Auto Accident Compensation Project of the University of Wisconsin, Milwaukee, with able assistance from Guila Parker, held two very informative conferences in Washington, D.C., that included speakers from across the political spectrum, from Andrew Tobias on the left to Grover Norquist of the conservative group Americans for Tax Reform. The conferences helped generate interest on Capitol Hill.

On the Democratic side, Sen. Joseph Lieberman, who had been the author of Connecticut's no-fault law, took flak from his own party for supporting what it viewed as a Republican bill that would strike at the livelihood of its trial lawyer supporters (and their willingness to contribute to Democrats). He never backed down. His staff Laurie Rubenstein and Bill Bonvillian were also very bright and worked the issue very hard. Bonvillian was familiar with it from his work at DOT during the Carter administration. Rep. Jim Moran (VA) also stepped forward to be the lead House Democratic cosponsor, a politically courageous move in a highly partisan House where Democrats viewed Representative Armey as one of the most partisan Republicans.

Massachusetts governor and 1988 Democratic presidential candidate Michael Dukakis, the author of the Massachusetts no-fault law, the first in the country in 1971, testified before the Senate, joined CAR and set up and participated in a meeting of Auto Choice supporters with the Clinton White House.

In the private sector, Kara Brown and Regina Dillard of State Farm worked extremely hard and effectively in Washington, DC, while Herm Brandau continued to provide deep insurance knowledge for State Farm from his office in Bloomington, Illinois. State Farm General Counsels Kim Brunner and Steve McManus were also very supportive, and Dale Nelson, its chief actuary, provided both brilliant and intelligible actuarial information as the only English-speaking actuary I ever encountered. State Farm provided further assistance through the law firm of Arnold & Porter, with Jim Fitzpatrick, Jack Quinn, and Si Lazarus lending highly skilled assistance during the 1970s and Nancy Perkins doing the same during the 1990s and 2000s. For the United Services Automobile Association (USAA), Susan Callanan worked effectively in Washington, DC, while Jon Palmquist added significant intellectual and insurance assistance, primarily from the home office in San Antonio, Texas.

Unbeknownst to her, Sarah Havens was a big help. As a summer intern for Representative Eckhardt in 1978, she wrote a history of no-fault for a course at Hampshire College. The history helped me fill in some important details I had forgotten or didn't know.

I want to thank Bob Kuttner, a friend since kindergarten, for encouraging me to write the book and Tom Krattenmaker, a friend since law school, for supporting my writing. David Nexon, a neighbor and friend who served as Senator Kennedy's senior health policy adviser and directed Kennedy's HELP Committee health staff from 1983 to 2005, helped me understand the impact that auto primacy would have on health care expenditures.

I also want to thank several people who were kind and patient enough to read early drafts. Bob Litan, longtime Brookings Institution scholar, who worked in the same vineyards of banking and liability issues as I did for twenty years, offered suggestions for how to organize and focus the book for a university press. His encouragement and guidance were invaluable, as was his support in identifying a publisher. Bill Mattea, a friend from my Senate Banking Committee days who worked for Sen. Adlai Stevenson III in the 1970s, confirmed the accuracy of my discussion of Senate Commerce Committee consideration. Others who read early drafts were Janie Kinney, Mike Lemov, and Mark Raabe from the House Commerce subcommittee and full committee staff in the 1970s; Herm Brandau and Les Cheek, my two key insurance industry gurus; Stanford Law School Professor Nora Engstrom, who continues to write thoughtfully about auto insurance; and Peter Markwith, a friend with publishing experience. They confirmed my memories of the time, reminded me of some of the subtle technicalities of automobile insurance, challenged me to consider other ways of looking at the loss of popularity of no-fault, and, in Peter's case, gave me feedback from a nonexpert in the field on my ability to keep the reader's interest. The final product is far better for their input.

I want to thank the editors at University Press of Kansas who guided me substantively and stylistically on this journey. David Congdon, my acquisitions editor, believed in the project and, gently but firmly, helped this novice author identify the core of the story. His two readers who commented on the manuscript also helped me tighten the focus on no-fault without sacrificing the background stories that are an essential part of the tale. Once David was finished, Connie Oehring, my copy editor, introduced me to the rigors of *The Chicago Manual of Style*, 17th ed., which helped me improve the clarity of the manuscript and the consistency of grammatical usage, among other important edits. Finally, I want to thank Kelly Chrisman Jacques, managing editor, for shepherding the book through production.

For technical assistance, I want to thank Jordan Vonderharr. When I was struggling to figure out how to save a scanned photograph in TIF format instead of JPEG format and how to convert a color photograph to black-and-white, I quickly gave up and wisely turned to my twenty-year-old granddaughter. She rapidly recited a series of words and concepts I did not understand and then solved all the issues.

Finally, Andrew Tobias was a witty and brilliant advocate for Auto Choice. His sense of humor helped both sell Auto Choice and keep me from losing perspective.

ABBREVIATIONS

AA	Administrative Assistant. The person in a congressional office responsible for running the office and doing the political work necessary to help his or her boss get reelected. The position is now commonly called chief of staff.
AARP	The American Association of Retired Persons. An active supporter of no-fault legislation in the 1970s, the organization refused to get involved in the Auto Choice effort despite the huge cost savings projected for seniors.
ATLA	American Trial Lawyers Association. After the name acquired a negative connotation, ATLA changed its name to the American Association for Justice.
ABA	American Bar Association. The trade association for lawyers. Its position on no-fault was established by a subcommittee that consisted largely of trial lawyers.
BI	Bodily injury liability. Auto insurance that protects yours assets in case you are found liable for injuring another person.
CAR	Coalition for Auto-Insurance Reform. Outside coalition composed largely of public figures, with some insurers, who worked for passage of the Auto Choice legislation. The author was the president of CAR.
CFA	Consumer Federation of America. National consumer organization that lobbied for no-fault legislation in the 1970s but against Auto Choice in the 1990s.
CU	Consumers' Union. Another consumer group that did the same about-face CFA did.
DOT	US Department of Transportation
HELP	US Senate Health, Education, Labor and Pensions Committee
JEC	US Joint Economic Committee

MED PAY — Auto insurance coverage that you buy to pay for medical losses without regard to fault, just as your health insurance would.

NAII — National Association of Independent Insurers. An insurance trade association that opposed federal no-fault and Auto Choice legislation.

PIP — Personal Injury Protection. The name for first-party or no-fault benefits in the Auto Choice legislation. Also the name for the no-fault option.

RAND — The RAND Institute for Civil Justice. It is a think tank whose membership includes insurers, trial lawyers, and consumer groups. RAND did a series of studies in the 1990s and 2000s identifying compensation and cost issues for fault and no-fault auto insurance.

TMC — Tort Maintenance Coverage. The name for auto insurance coverage for those who choose to remain under the fault and liability insurance system under Auto Choice.

UMVARA — Uniform Motor Vehicle Accident Reparations Act. The model state no-fault law developed by the commission that drafts model laws for states to consider enacting. The acronym for the organization and the name of the organization are even worse: NCCUSL, the National Conference of Commissioners on Uniform State Laws.

UIM — Underinsured Motorist. Auto insurance coverage that pays for your losses when the other driver's liability coverage is insufficient to pay for *all* your loss. It is similar to UM in that it pays only when the other driver is at fault. It provides an extra layer of protection on top of the limits of UM.

UM — Uninsured Motorist. Auto insurance coverage you buy to protect yourself against being injured by an uninsured motorist who lacks the resources to pay for your injury. It is fault-based coverage; i.e., it covers your losses only if the uninsured motorist who injures you was at fault.

HIGHWAY ROBBERY

INTRODUCTION

The concept underlying the no-fault automobile insurance reform was simple: replace the fault-based liability insurance system for resolving auto accidents with a system akin to health insurance. There would be no questions as to whether you were eligible for medical care if you were injured in an auto accident. You would simply submit a claim for payment for the cost of your injuries to your own auto insurer. Unlike the liability system, there would be no need for you to hire a lawyer to prove the other driver was at fault and for the other driver's insurer to hire a lawyer to argue that you were the one at fault. Also, the amount of your recovery would not be dependent on the limits of insurance the other driver happened to purchase. Under no-fault, you would pick the level of protection you and your family needed. Not only would you get faster and more complete compensation this way, you would also see lower premiums because no-fault would eliminate the incentives for excess and fraudulent claims and there would be little need for either plaintiff or defense lawyers and their associated costs.[1] As it turned out, therein lay the rub. The lawyers and insurers who stood to lose money—a lot of it—cried foul and then used their political strength to undermine state no-fault laws and defeat two federal efforts. The simple but elegant pro-consumer solution of no-fault insurance turned into a forty-year battle royal to enact legislation at the federal level.

From shortly after the introduction of the first cars into the United States in the late 1800s until the early 1970s, all states maintained the "fault and liability insurance system," under which a driver was responsible for paying for the injuries he or she caused others as a result of his or her negligence. Historically, negligence, or tort, law was intended to serve three purposes: compensation, deterrence, and punishment. Of course, the single greatest deterrent to reckless driving has always been the risk of doing serious injury to oneself. To the extent that having to pay the losses for injuring someone else might further discourage or deter reckless driving, it was undermined by auto insurance. The reason is that your auto insurer, not you as an at-fault driver, was responsible for paying for the injuries you caused others. As for punishment for bad driving, it consisted simply of a surcharge, or relatively small increase, on your premium. With the fault and liability insurance system offering little or no deterrent impact on bad driving, early criticism focused on the compensation purpose of negligence and found it grossly wanting.

Resolving disputes over fault was a slow process that in many cases left injured people without recoveries as lawyers representing the injured person and the insurance company haggled over the amount of recompense. It was a system that most commentators found did not serve injured people nearly as well as it served the lawyers and insurers. This is a firsthand account of the battle to create a better system against the opposition of the special interests determined to protect their economic stake in the existing insurance system.

This book focuses primarily on the two failed federal efforts, twenty years apart, to enact no-fault automobile insurance reform legislation to apply to all states. It first details the critique of the fault system, how no-fault proposed to remedy those defects, and how the battles in the states influenced the outcome of the federal legislative efforts. Then, it describes both congressional fights. The first took place in the 1970s between the then supporters of no-fault reform, primarily consumer groups and unions, and the opponents, lawyers and insurers with a vested interest in maintaining the present system. The second took place in the 1990s–2000s between the then supporters, primarily individual consumer advocates and conservative organizations, and the same special interest opponents, with surprising help from some consumer groups.

It discusses the roles of members of Congress and committee staffs and their interaction with outside groups as well as interest groups' use of money to hire lobbyists, organize nonspontaneous grassroots efforts, and make campaign contributions to members to influence the outcome. But it does not stop there. It reviews the recent experience in no-fault states, arguing that the weaknesses of those laws attributable to trial lawyer–inserted provisions create an ongoing consumer political demand for reforms to reduce premiums. The book considers four possible scenarios under which the Congress might revisit federal no-fault legislation for a third time: (1) an alliance between Republicans who favor choice and tax cuts (their view of lower premiums) and progressive Democrats who value the importance of significantly lower premiums for low- and moderate-income drivers, using crowdfunding to offset the influence of trial lawyer contributions to Democrats; (2) consumer-driven demand for federal legislation if reforms of state no-fault laws prove that properly constructed laws can save consumers billions of dollars; (3) a Republican-driven effort for the same reasons that they supported Auto Choice, with the political goal of defunding the trial bar, at a time when the Republicans control the presidency and both houses of Congress; and (4) A Democrat-led effort to encourage no-fault to reduce the costs of federal legislation to expand health insurance coverage at a time when Democrats control the presidency and both houses of Congress. Significant savings would arise from having auto insurance be the first source of payment for medical losses in auto accidents.

Much of the story is told through my firsthand experience in both efforts as a congressional staffer in the 1970s and then as the head of a private nonprofit organized solely to help secure passage of a federal bill in the 1990s–2000s. But the story begins long before I was born. In 1896, there were four cars in the United States. The two that were in St. Louis, Missouri, were involved in an accident, seriously injuring one person.[2] Shortly thereafter, auto insurance came into existence. Unlike most insurance coverages, the primary coverage for personal injury, bodily injury liability (BI), is fault-based. If you are involved in an accident, your BI pays you nothing. You can recover only from the other driver's BI coverage and only if that person was at fault. Determining fault is a complicated, slow, and costly process that usually involves lawyers and leaves many injured people with no or inadequate recovery.

Robert Keeton and Jeffrey O'Connell proposed a different model in 1967 that would pay all injured persons without regard to fault, doing away with most lawsuits and the incentives they offer to build up costs to recover a bigger settlement.[3]

If the concept sounds familiar, it is because it is essentially how your health insurance and most other forms of insurance operate. For that matter, it is also how the collision and comprehensive parts of your auto insurance policy that pay for damage to your vehicle operate. In both situations, you just submit proof of the damage and your insurer pays for the loss—no lawyers, no debate over who hit whom, and no long wait.

While the concept of no-fault insurance is simple, the details are complicated. The efforts to adopt no-fault took a two-track approach from the beginning—one at the state level and one at the federal. Massachusetts was the first state to adopt a no-fault law, and sixteen others followed in quick succession between 1971 and 1975.[4] Unfortunately, apart from Michigan, no state law closely resembles the Keeton-O'Connell proposal. Trial lawyers undermined most of these state laws by securing the inclusion of provisions that permitted so many lawsuits that, in effect, most states with nominally no-fault laws wound up operating both no-fault and fault systems. Of course, operating two systems is more expensive than operating just one. Then, the same lawyers who had undermined the state laws used the failure of those laws to successfully oppose the enactment of strong federal no-fault legislation in the 1970s. They also defeated a second federal effort in the 1990s–2000s that not only would have permitted drivers to choose no-fault coverage that would have made it easier to recover in an accident but promised to reduce the cost of auto insurance for personal injury by 60 percent, or as much as $40 billion a year for all drivers.

As a result of the trial bar's success in stopping or undermining good no-fault laws, thirty-six states retain the "fault and liability insurance system." Because it is fault-based, it does not protect you if you are injured; it only protects your assets in case you are found at fault and have to pay for injuries you caused another person.[5] If you are injured, you have to file a claim, and usually a lawsuit, against the other driver alleging his or her negligence was responsible for your injuries. If you prevail, your recovery is limited by the amount of coverage the other driver has purchased.

The requirements to prove fault and freedom from fault on your part make the fault and liability insurance system very inefficient and greatly limit how many people can recover for their injuries and how much. The costs of attorneys and the incentives for fraud also make the system unnecessarily costly. The system remains in place primarily because insurers and trial lawyers make tens of billions of dollars a year from it and use their influence with legislators to resist change to a better system. As the states and the Congress considered no-fault legislation in the 1970s, they had to understand how both the fault and liability insurance system and the no-fault system operated. The hearing process addressed both these issues. Let's start with the fault system. The following two cases from Illinois illustrate in human terms some of its many faults:

At the age of five, Tommy stepped off a curb in front of our home and was hit by a car. At that time, he was taken to the hospital with severe brain damage. Tom had undergone three major brain operations in a matter of 2 weeks at that particular time.

The medical bills and the expensive nursing care and things that he had to have at that particular time, our health insurance that my husband had through where he had worked paid for about 60 percent of it. Tom needed private nursing, which was 24 hours, for a matter of about 3 months with the first surgery.

Our settlement wasn't claimed until about 6 years later. Within this period, Tommy had to have another surgery, which involved removing a rib from his rib cage and enclosing the opening that was in his head, because he had no bone to protect the brain. This also, our insurance paid for part of, but over a series of maybe 5 years, we went into large debt because of the fact our insurance didn't cover most of it, and we paid the doctors and medical bills a little at a time.

I have six other children besides Tom that we were trying to put through school and raise at the same time. Thank goodness, the doctors and the hospitals were very understanding and, over a period of time, we have paid a little at a time out of my husband's salary.

As a result, I ended up going to a trade school myself so that this way, I could go to work and help pay for some of these medical bills and help raise our other children as normal human beings.

The case was settled about 6 years later and, because of the fact that the man had died a year after Tom's accident, we could only sue for the amount of money that his insurance company stated that he had had at that particular time, which was $20,000. He had, I guess, 20/20, which left us with a settlement of about $40,000.

At that particular time, our medical bills went up to about $32,000. By the time the lawyer had taken his top third of what they normally do out of a settlement and the bills that we hadn't paid as of yet, Tom ended up with about $20,000 that we had put in a trust fund for him.

Over the period of years since then, Tom has had to go under another surgery . . . because of scar tissue that had built up on the brain. Tom is an epileptic. He does not have the use of the right arm and the right leg. He wears a brace on the right leg.

. . . We don't know what the future will hold, whether there will be more surgery, whether Tom will be able to get married, have a family and support

> them or not, so we really don't know what is going to come with the future, but we take it day by day. (Testimony of Karen Tuzzolino before the Consumer Protection Subcommittee, US House of Representatives)[6]

This story of a "successful lawsuit" in the early 1970s in the fault and liability automobile insurance state of Illinois was one of several stories described in a 1976 *Chicago Tribune* story responding to consumer complaints about auto insurance. One of the reporters, William Gaines, testified before the House subcommittee with Karen Tuzzolino. He drew attention to the fact that the law that determined the ability to recover in a fault state (the legal term of art for fault is "tort") required the injured party to "prove that he was totally blameless for the accident and that the other driver's negligence was solely responsible."[7] In researching the story, the reporters "learned that more than half of the people who sued for bodily injury damages from auto accidents in Illinois lost their suits and got nothing."[8]

The other reporter, John McCarron, at the same hearing, described the experience of the Krakowski family:

> The Krakowskis', of Illinois, ordeal began in July of 1972, when they were on a vacation trip. Dickie Krakowski, the 6-year-old son, walked onto a road while his family was taking photos at a scenic overlook in a national park. He was hit by a car driven by an elderly woman whose auto insurance contained a $20,000 liability limit. Dickie Krakowski suffered multiple fractures, internal injuries, and permanent brain damage.
>
> Since the accident, the Krakowski family has received more than $100,000 in medical bills. The father's group health insurance paid for 80 percent of most of those medical bills, but not a penny for the many rehabilitative expenses like speech lessons and physical therapy.
>
> Because the accident was not their fault, the Krakowskis' own Illinois auto insurance policy paid only a one-time $1,000 medical payment. So the family hired a lawyer, as is the custom under the fault system, and sued the other driver.
>
> Four years later, an out-of-court settlement was reached for $20,000. Their lawyer told the Krakowskis it would be useless to ask for more than the elderly woman's $20,000 liability coverage, since she was a retired pensioner with no savings. After the lawyer's fee and other expenses were paid, the Krakowskis' settlement shrank to $11,000.

> Dickie's mother, Janice Krakowski, told me that even with that settlement, . . . the family has spent more than $25,000 out-of-pocket since Dickie was hit by the car.
>
> The family has no savings, they drive a used car, and they have not taken a vacation since the accident five years ago.[9]

In both these cases, the families had to hire a lawyer, wait years to recover an amount that was insufficient to cover the losses (with no interim payments from auto insurance), and then saw even that grossly inadequate sum reduced by about one-third to pay their attorneys' fees. As bad as the system was for the Tuzzolino and Krakowski families, it was worse for others. As Gaines reported, at the time of these accidents, in the early 1970s, roughly 50 percent of all people injured in auto accidents in the fault state of Illinois recovered nothing for their loss. This happened primarily for two reasons: first, many of the accidents involved only a single car, where no one else was at fault, and second, the then applicable legal doctrine of contributory negligence denied any recovery if the injured person was partly to blame.

It is important to note that the families got nothing[10] from their own auto insurance. Because their children were injured in a fault state, their coverage was worthless to them. As I described previously, that was because fault-based insurance does not protect the person who purchases it (the insured); it protects only the insured's assets should he or she be found to be at fault and required to pay for the other person's injuries. As the Tuzzolino and Krakowski families were helpless to protect themselves, their recoveries were determined by the amount of insurance the other, at-fault driver carried.

In both cases, the only insurance they could purchase and rely on to help pay the medical bills was not their auto insurance but their health insurance. That is because, unlike their auto insurance, their health insurer was obligated to pay for their children's medical bills without regard to fault. It also paid as losses occurred and without the delays associated with the need to hire a lawyer and go to court.

At the time Keeton and O'Connell were examining the tort system, its rules were so restrictive that only roughly half the people injured in auto accidents recovered anything. In proposing replacing it with a system in which all people were paid regardless of fault, Keeton and O'Connell realized that they had to find a way to pay for nearly twice the number of injured people who would be able to recover under their proposal. For political reasons, they also had to be able to assure that the new insurance would not cost more than the old one. Their proposed solution was to limit lawsuits for noneconomic damages (commonly called pain and suffering) to a narrow class of very serious injuries. The limitation would not affect the ability of any injured person to sue, on a fault basis, for any economic loss not covered by the amount of coverage they had chosen. Keeton and O'Connell did not believe this restriction would take much, if anything, away from injured motorists because the average amount of insurance carried by most drivers was insufficient to pay for the economic losses of a seriously injured person, much less for any noneconomic loss. With these restrictions, they believed the new insurance could pay for the losses of most catastrophically injured persons without increasing premiums.

As I mentioned above, the trial bar used its substantial resources to convince legislators to include poison pills in the legislation that undermined the laws' effectiveness in reducing costs. Only the state of Michigan adopted a law that resembled the Keeton-O'Connell proposal (with unlimited medical and rehabilitation benefits and a tight restriction on suits for noneconomic damages). That proved fortuitous for reporters Gaines and McCarron. In the same series of articles they wrote for the *Chicago Tribune*, they were able to compare the difficulties of recovering damages in auto accident cases in the fault state of Illinois with the ease of recovering much more compensation in the adjacent no-fault state of Michigan. One of the people they wrote about was Rosemary Pryor, who was seriously injured in a case where she would have had no recovery in Illinois. Pryor described her experience in Michigan at the same 1977 Consumer Protection Subcommittee hearing:

> I am here to give an example of what no-fault in Michigan has done for me. Three years ago in April, I was in the back end of a pickup truck, and the girl driving lost control and hit a tree. I broke two vertebrae in my back, four broken ribs, two head lacerations, pretty well messed myself up, and was sent to a hospital.
>
> In the process of the examination, I was told I would never walk again. I

> am paralyzed from the waist down, which, of course, means expensive medical care and rehabilitation.
>
> Right from the beginning, my parents did not know exactly what was going to happen. As soon as they informed the insurance company of what had happened, they said, do not worry about it, you fall under no-fault, and we will take care of everything.
>
> I was in a medical hospital for only 1 month, was in rehabilitation, in and out, from May until November, so a total of probably about 4 months of rehabilitation. From there on, they have still been paying for any medical or rehabilitation needs I have had.
>
> Basically, what I would like to break down for you right now is, as of today, the total that State Farm has paid for me on my accident is $52,000. I have not, nor my parents, have not had to pay 1 cent for any medical or rehabilitation. (Testimony of Rosemary Pryor before the Consumer Protection Subcommittee, US House of Representatives)[11]

Rosemary Pryor's experience is what Keeton and O'Connell envisioned when they first developed the no-fault concept. One of the key reasons that Michigan was able to resist special interest pressure was because there was much less of it than in most states. This was due in no small part to the fact that the Michigan Bar Association was the only state bar association to support no-fault. At the June 13, 1975, hearing, Ivan E. Barris, secretary of the State Bar of Michigan, testified as to why the bar association supported enactment of the Michigan law.[12] In prepared remarks, he said:

> We recognized the problems which had arisen under the traditional tort system, we undertook a careful study of the situation and ultimately came to the same conclusions, we came to some conclusions about how a fair and effective no-fault auto insurance system should be structured and we were active participants in the public debate out of which Michigan's present no-fault insurance system evolved.
>
> We said, then [1971] and now, that any sound auto accident reparations system should have one primary objective: To properly compensate the victim of an auto accident for the damage that the accident inflicts. To do so, we said, the system should accomplish two things:
>
> 1. It should provide prompt compensation to every accident victim for

medical expenses, lost earnings and other direct out-of-pocket costs, without having to wait for determination of who may have been at fault.

2. Having done that, the system should preserve the right to persons who suffer losses beyond such compensation, through no fault of their own, to be fully compensated (through lawsuits).[13]

Another key, not unrelated, factor in Michigan's success in passing its no-fault law was bipartisan support. Republican Governor George W. Romney worked with a Democratic House and an evenly divided Senate to pass the legislation. This is a good lesson for any legislature or the Congress if it wants to pass strong, effective legislation that will last over time.

Unfortunately for no-fault, most of the other sixteen state no-fault laws did not have the same experience, as they were sabotaged by the trial bar to enable trial lawyers to continue to bring lawsuits. The effect was to gut the basic trade-off required to make no-fault less expensive than fault insurance. The trial bar then had the chutzpah to turn around and use the mixed cost experience of the laws they had undermined as grounds for opposing federal no-fault legislation.

While seventeen states[14] were adopting no-fault laws, the Congress was considering no-fault legislation that would have resulted in a Keeton-O'Connell-like plan being implemented in all fifty states. With billions of dollars at stake, the trial bar and much of the insurance industry fought back in the traditional political way, with campaign contributions and well-connected lobbyists. But they were slow to get their efforts off the ground, and the Senate passed a no-fault bill in 1974. Because of its preoccupation with the impeachment of President Richard Nixon, the House did not act on the bill. That inaction gave the opponents enough time to organize, and ultimately, a combination of special interest money, partisan politicians, and plain bad luck succeeded in delivering a fatal blow to federal no-fault legislation in 1978.

Because many of the problems with the fault system could not be fixed by the very terms of the system, despite some improvements in compensation over the years, in the early 1990s, no-fault came back as an option in the so-called Auto Choice legislation. The basic concept was to give consumers a choice between the fault and no-fault systems. The other major changes from the earlier bills were to lower the level of no-fault benefits motorists were required to purchase and to tighten the restrictions on lawsuits. The congressional Joint Economic Committee (JEC) estimated that with these changes, the average motorist would save approximately 60 percent on his or her personal injury premium. The JEC estimated that if all motorists selected the no-fault option, they could save approximately $40 billion a year. At that rate, had Auto Choice been enacted in 1998, the potential savings available to consumers by 2020 would have amounted to $1.4 trillion in today's dollars. This time the trial bar was left with an even weaker substantive case, arguing mainly that good drivers would pay for bad drivers and insurers would not pass along the savings to consumers. However, a weak case, buttressed by huge campaign contributions and bad timing, once again stopped no-fault legislation.

I was thrust into the no-fault fight when I was hired in 1975 as a counsel by the House of Representatives subcommittee with jurisdiction over no-fault legislation. The legislation was supported primarily by liberal groups. Some twenty years later, I joined the fight for no-fault under the banner of Auto Choice from the private sector as president of CAR, only to find that the primary supporters had become conservative groups. When Auto Choice also failed, I was left with the dubious distinction of having been a key player in losing efforts from both the left and the right.

When I started working on the issue in 1975, I had no preconceived notions one way or the other as to the merits of no-fault. In fact, I had no knowledge of the subject matter at all. Tasked by my House boss, US Rep. Lionel Van Deerlin, to dig into the details, I spent two months reading all the literature and listening to all the interested parties. I concluded that no-fault would be a far better system for motorists than the fault and liability insurance system. I spent much of the next thirty years working to enact well-crafted federal no-fault legislation, so it will come as no surprise that I find the data and arguments in favor far outweigh those in opposition. Nevertheless, I have described in detail, I hope fairly, the con arguments as well. Whichever side of the line you fall on, I hope you will find this story of the interaction of substance and politics on an issue of importance to most Americans to be an interesting one.

Like any political/policy story worth telling, the no-fault effort involves a cause worth fighting for, colorful personalities, grand strategies, the influence of money and politics, and dramatic, unpredictable events.

With Democrats being the chief supporters of the first effort and then the chief opponents of the second effort and Republicans doing the exact opposite, the experience does not reflect well on the members of either political party or the role of special interest money in politics. From my positions in the public and private sectors between 1975 and 2004, I had a front-row seat to see and help shape the interplay of these dynamics during most of both efforts to enact no-fault legislation. It is this perspective of time and experience that enables me to share an insider's account of the fascinating story of these unsuccessful ventures.

Was the demise of Auto Choice legislation in the early 2000s the end of federal consideration of no-fault legislation? It would certainly seem so in light of the mixed, at best, cost experience in the twelve states that still have no-fault laws, the continuing influence of the trial bar on the Democratic Party, and the increasing polarization of the Congress. Perhaps not. In the final chapter, I consider four scenarios in which the issue might once again draw the attention of the Congress and the president.

1. Fifty Ways to Lose Your Recovery

So You Think Your Auto Insurance Will Protect You

To appreciate what is at stake in this fight, on both the cost and compensation sides, it is first necessary to understand in some detail the "fault and liability insurance" system that no-fault was designed to replace. Most people believe that they will not be involved in an accident but that if they are, the other driver will be at fault and will pay for their injuries.

Let me use myself as an example. From the time I started driving, I have always thought of myself as a good driver, but I had my first accident when I was seventeen. In the winter of my senior year in high school, I decided to test how well my father's new Lancia Flaminia, an expensive Italian car, would operate in the snow. My friend Lew and I set off in a driving snowstorm to see a movie at a local theater. Unfortunately, the only two ways out of the neighborhood involved steep hills, a Hobson's choice. As we started down a long hill, I realized I couldn't control the car, and we started to skid. We wound up going off the main road, with the car stopping across one lane of the intersecting road, up against a curb two feet in front of a stone wall. As the car was not drivable, I got out and walked the short distance home to call for help. When I returned, my friend Lew was sitting on the hood of the car talking with two passersby, an older woman and a man walking a small dog. Soon thereafter, we all turned to see a car barreling down the hill way too fast for the conditions. We could see what was going to happen next. It seemed to occur in slow motion. The driver jammed on his brakes and skidded off the road—right into the back of the Lancia. Lew flew off the hood but was unhurt. The man walking his dog was not so lucky. When the other car hit the Lancia, it drove the Lancia up on the curb, hitting the man and breaking his ankle. Fortunately, no one else was injured. Not too long afterward, I was served with a complaint alleging that I had been negligent and my negligence was responsible, not only for the broken ankle of the passerby but also for injuries suffered by the driver who hit the Lancia. These were phantom injuries, as he had left the scene of the accident completely healthy, if a bit tipsy. It wasn't until more than three years later that the case went to court. The other driver's lawyer made a compelling case for something that hadn't happened. By then I was in law school and thought I made a pretty good witness, but I think I might well have been found at fault but for the testimony of the other passerby, the older woman, who spoke nervously but sincerely and would not back down under tough questioning. Meanwhile, during all this time wasted with lawyers trying to determine fault, the injured man received not a dime to compensate him from either my insurer or the other driver's insurer. I do not know whether he was adequately compensated in the end.

This example demonstrates some of the problems with the fault system that this book will describe, starting with the belief that you will not be involved in an auto accident and that if you are, the other driver will be at fault and pay. The facts are far different:

- Auto accidents are a common occurrence that most people are likely to experience one or more times over a lifetime of driving, no matter how good a driver they are. In 2017, for example, there were 6,452,000 motor vehicle crashes in the United States, which resulted in 37,133 fatalities and 2,746,000 injuries.[1]
- You are not alone in your belief that the other driver would be at fault. The RAND Institute for Civil Justice (RAND) has found that 90 percent of all drivers believe the other driver was at fault. With all due respect to your driving skill, it's impossible for 90 percent of the people to be right on this question.
- RAND found that if you are involved in an accident, you have a 30 percent chance of recovering nothing for your medical bills and lost wages—not a dime, no matter how seriously injured you are. Most of those situations involve single-car crashes where no one is at fault.[2]
- If you are among the "lucky" 70 percent who recover (such as the Tuzzolinos and the Krakowskis), legal doctrines covering the degree of fault of the parties, the amount of the at-fault motorist's auto insurance coverage, and your own attorney's fee (typically, one-third of your recovery) limit the amount you can recover.
- These limitations are usually not an issue if your injuries are minor. However, they are a big problem if you suffer a serious injury. In a

1991 study, RAND found that the average recovery for people with economic losses over $100,000 was 9 percent.[3]

- Even if you do secure some recovery in a serious injury case, it can take months or even years to get paid this grossly inadequate amount.

Moreover, the fault and liability insurance system is overly costly, does not deter bad driving, and contains inadequate incentives to purchase safer cars:

- Much of your insurance premium is spent on lawyers[4] and the fraud the system encourages in cases of minor injury.[5] Historically, there have been three incentives for fraud. First, minor injury claims have had a "nuisance value" that led insurers not to challenge them, even if they knew the claims to be fraudulent, because it would cost them more to fight the claim (in adjuster and their own attorney fees) than to just pay the inflated claim.[6] Second. the collateral source doctrine prohibits an insurer from introducing into evidence the fact that the victim has received compensation for the same injury from another source; most typically, his or her health insurer. The premise is that the at-fault driver should not benefit from the injured motorist's foresight. The effect is to create yet another incentive to run up one's medical bills to get double recovery for economic loss. Third, there was a convention that pain and suffering awards were typically calculated as a multiple of the amount paid for medical bills and lost wages (often three times the economic loss). Thus, the more medical bills individuals could produce, the higher the payment for pain and suffering. Of course, motorists pay the price for these multiple recoveries through higher premiums.
- The system does not deter "bad" drivers. The main deterrent, of course, is the risk of injuring oneself. In addition, most accidents are caused by matters out of the driver's control (such as youthful inexperience, as was the case in my accident, or environmental conditions) or are not deterrable (such as drunk driving). To the extent that the tort system could have had any deterrent effect, it disappeared with the sale of automobile bodily injury liability (BI) insurance. With BI coverage, the at-fault driver does not pay for your losses; his or her insurer does. The at-fault driver's insurer then imposes a premium surcharge on him or her, but it is far less than the full cost of the injury.

- The system does not provide incentives to drive safer cars because who you are and what car you drive are irrelevant to your insurer. The reason is that under the tort system, your insurance does not pay for your losses. Instead, it protects your assets and provides coverage for them only if you are at fault and must pay for some other unknown driver's injuries and repair of his or her car. Under these circumstances, your insurer cannot reward you for driving a safer car even though it will reduce your chances of injury.

Lastly, the sheer volume of auto accident cases clogs the courts, resulting in long delays not only for recoveries in auto cases but also for handling more important cases:

- For example, in 2001, auto cases represented 35 percent of civil trials in the nation's seventy-five largest counties,[7] by far the largest category of cases.

How did the fault system come into being? It was a "gift" from the British. Don't worry, we won't be here long. The colonial states and then the free states of the United States of America inherited the British "common law" system, based on judicial precedents. The branch of common law that applies to "accidents" is called tort law. When the automobile was introduced into the United States in the late nineteenth century, it was apparent from the beginning that there would be a need for a body of law to govern injuries resulting from crashes. Professor Jeffrey O'Connell, one of the fathers of the no-fault concept, described what happened at the dawn of the automotive age: "In 1896, when there were four motor vehicles in the United States, two were in St. Louis. They managed to collide with such impact as to injure both drivers, one seriously."[8]

State courts and legislatures, without any apparent consideration of alternatives, simply fitted these crashes into the category of accidents and applied the same principles of fault they applied to other accidents. That did not have to be the case. Had Daniel Patrick Moynihan been alive at the time, he would have pointed them toward a more efficient and equitable way to handle these crashes. In "Next: A New Auto Insurance Policy," an article published in the August 27, 1967, magazine section of the *New York Times*, Moynihan pointed out that the automobile transportation system inevitably results in crashes. Writing against the tort system and in favor of no-fault insurance, he described motor vehicle crashes as not accidents but "the perfectly predictable outcomes of a particular transportation system utilizing a specific technology." In simple terms, a lot of high-powered vehicles going at high speeds will inevitably run into one another and injure people. Moynihan's answer was to reject the tort system as expensive, wasteful, and a burden on the courts and instead to endorse the no-fault insurance plan developed by Professors Robert Keeton and O'Connell as a more efficient, lower-cost system of redress for injuries. He called Keeton and O'Connell's 1965 no-fault proposal in the book *Basic Protection for the Traffic Victim: A Blueprint for Reforming Automobile Insurance*, "the one incontestably successful reform [proposed in] . . . the 1960s."

But Moynihan wasn't alive at the turn of the twentieth century, and even if he had been, it was likely that, given their backgrounds, the lawyers and judges who shaped the legal system then and now would have ignored him. The decision to treat motor vehicle crashes as accidents threw injured people into the fault system, which many scholars argue was intentionally restrictive, designed to make recovery very difficult so that the cost of inevitable injuries would not cripple the industrial revolution.[9]

Every state created its own law, but they were broadly the same. To recover damages for medical and work losses, the injured person had to identify the driver who caused the injury and prove that the other driver was at fault. But that wasn't all. In this harsh regime, pursuant to the doctrine of contributory negligence, the injured person also had to prove that he or she was not partially at fault. In most states, if the court found that the injured person was even 10 percent at fault, then he or she was not entitled to any recovery. There were also a host of other restrictions that made it even more difficult for injured people to recover.[10]

Even with all these restrictions, there remained cases where an at-fault driver could be held liable. In those circumstances—where there was no contributory negligence and no other restriction applied—if a person was seriously injured, the at-fault driver could face financial ruin if forced to pay the losses from his or her own pocket. Such an outcome would surely have inhibited the development of the automobile. Thus, it is not surprising that the first automobile insurance policy was sold in the United States in 1897, one year after the accident in St. Louis. Now, in

2021, forty-eight states and the District of Columbia require all motorists to buy auto insurance to exercise the privilege of driving.[11]

Auto insurance largely eliminated any threat to the development of the automobile by providing motorists with protection against financial ruin if they were involved in the small category of accidents for which drivers could be held liable under the tort system. Insurance, in turn, later freed the states to ease what many thought were unfair requirements for recovery, spreading the additional costs among many so as not to raise costs so much that they would limit the demand for cars.

As indicated above, unlike most forms of insurance you carry—such as homeowners and health—your auto insurance does not pay for damage to you if you are involved in an accident. Instead, if you "negligently" injure another person (the legal standard) while you are driving, your auto insurance pays for the losses of that person. The law defines negligence as what "a reasonable person" would have done in the circumstances. This combination of fault law and insurance is called the "fault and liability insurance system." It is the prevailing law in thirty-eight states—and the target for replacement by the no-fault insurance reform.

When I was in law school in the 1960s, most professors taught by the Socratic method. This involved the use of hypotheticals for the stated purpose of helping students understand legal principles and their limitations. A professor would ask a student to stand. The professor would then ask the student to recite the facts of a case from the required reading, and then the "fun" would begin. The professor would pose a series of hypothetical scenarios that were somewhat different than the original case, and the student would have to decide whether the principles in the original case would apply to the hypothetical.

The concept was logical—to help students understand the limits of the original decision. The practice, not so much. It often seemed like a scene out of the movie *The Paper Chase*, with professors more interested in intimidating the students than educating them. I think the fault lay with the professors rather than the method. You can be your own judge of the efficacy of the Socratic method, as the rest of this chapter uses a limited number of examples designed to help you understand how the rules governing recovery under the tort and the insurance system for auto accidents and attorneys' fees left so many injured people with little or no compensation while motorists overpaid for the privilege. The hypotheticals establish the rationale for the rise of no-fault auto insurance.

With apologies to the Paul Simon song, "50 Ways to Leave Your Lover," there are nearly as many ways to lose your recovery in an auto accident case in a fault state. The concept of negligence that prevailed from the onset of the automobile until the late 1960s made it very difficult for persons injured in motor vehicle crashes to recover damages. At the time, over half of all injured motorists recovered nothing at all from the tort system, and people with serious injuries recovered only a fraction of their loss. To understand why, let's examine two accident situations as the law would have treated them in 1965, at the beginning of the no-fault movement.

Assume, first, a situation where Jack suffered $80,000 worth of injuries. He would have recovered nothing if

1. He was injured when he lost control of his car while skidding on a patch of ice and hit a tree. *No at-fault driver (tortfeasor), no recovery.*
2. He was injured when he fell asleep while driving home after working at the office for two days in a row with no sleep. *Jack was at fault.*

Now, let's make it a little more complicated. Assume a second scenario involving Jack and Jill of nursery-rhyme days. Having survived the perilous adventures of their youth climbing hills and falling down and breaking crowns, Jack and Jill were all grown up and were driving up that famous hill in separate cars in a rush to get home from work for dinner. Sally, an intern at Jill's company, was riding with Jill. Jill, tired after a long day's work, didn't see Jack jam on his brakes just over the crest of the hill to avoid hitting a deer until it was too late. Jill plowed into the back of Jack's car, breaking two of Jack's ribs, his left leg, and his left arm. The crash also resulted in minor injuries to Jill and Sally. Jack's medical bills and work loss totaled $80,000, Jill's medical bills $12,000 and Sally's $3,000.

Jack made four phone calls: (1) to the police to document how the accident occurred, (2) to an ambulance to take him to the hospital, (3) to his insurer to report the accident and file a claim, and (4) to a lawyer to handle his lawsuit against Jill. This seems like an open-and-shut case for Jack and Sally both to recover from Jill, but was it in the 1960s?

You would think so, but Jack would have recovered nothing if

3. Jill fled the scene before Jack could get her license number.
4. Jill was an uninsured motorist.
5. Jack couldn't prove Jill was at fault. *No witnesses and circumstantial evidence unclear.*
6. Jack was 10 percent at fault. *The contributory negligence doctrine.*
7. Jack saw Jill in time to take action to avoid the accident but didn't. *The last clear chance doctrine.*

Even if Jack met all the criteria to recover, he would have recovered less than the full amount of his loss, most likely a lot less, if

8. Jill had insufficient insurance to cover all his losses. *The average driver carried far less than necessary to pay for Jack's $80,000 loss.*
9. Jack paid his attorney his fee, usually one-third of his total recovery, even though the recovery was far less than his loss. If he did not pay, his attorney would sue him. This is not an "if"; it is the standard trial lawyer fee, regardless of how much time a case actually takes (the attorneys' downside in this arrangement comes if they lose the case because then they get no fee. In practical terms, this rarely happens because most trial lawyers will not take cases unless they are sure they will win. Good for them; not so good for clients). The standard contingency fee continues to be about one-third today.

And what about Sally, who was simply a passenger? In the late 1960s, she would have recovered nothing if

10. She was Jill's daughter, under the family immunity doctrine that barred family members from suing other family members for their negligence.
11. She was in the car, regardless of the nature of her relationship with Jill, because the suit would have been barred by the host/guest doctrine.

Well, that isn't fifty ways; it took just eleven to show why, through the late 1960s, so many injured people were either denied any recovery or recovered an amount insufficient to cover all their losses.

The lack of payment and inadequacy of recovery were only two of the flaws of the tort system. In 1932, a Columbia University study was the first to take a comprehensive look at the flaws of the tort system. It was not until 1965, however, that Professors Robert Keeton and Jeffrey O'Connell published their book that not only excoriated the tort system but detailed a far better system of compensation. It came to be known as no-fault insurance, a title pinned on it not by its creators but by its trial lawyer opponents in an attempt to label it negatively. We don't call health insurance "no-fault insurance," even though it pays for medical losses the same way that what came to be known as no-fault auto insurance pays for medical losses incurred in an auto accident. It was an early—and quite successful—effort by the trial bar at the kind of negative branding that has become so commonplace in 2020. Finally, in 1971, the US DOT, by Act of Congress, produced a twenty-six-volume study that documented the many flaws of the tort system and endorsed enactment of no-fault legislation.

The following chapter details the findings of these three seminal works.

2. "Las Vegas Has Better Odds Than That"

Studies Detail the Shortcomings of the Fault System, and Support Builds for No-Fault Auto Insurance

The Jack and Jill scenarios explain why injured people fare poorly under the fault and liability insurance system but not why nothing was being done to help them in situations where most people would believe they should recover damages. As is normal in such circumstances, nothing happens until someone identifies the negative impact of these doctrinal obstacles. In this case, the first major study to declare the system fatally flawed and to take the next step and recommend an alternative system was done by Columbia University in 1932. It concluded,

> The generally prevailing system of providing damages for motor vehicle accidents is inadequate to meet existing conditions. It is based on the principle of liability for fault which is difficult to apply and often socially undesirable in its application; its administration through the courts is costly and slow, and it makes no provision to ensure the financial responsibility of those who are found to be liable.
>
> . . . No system based on liability for fault is adequate to meet existing conditions.[1]

The Columbia study did not stop with criticism of the tort system. It went on to recommend a reform—adoption of a no-fault solution:

> The Committee favors the plan of compensation with limited liability and without regard to fault, analogous to that of the workmen's compensation laws. Such a plan would eliminate the use of the principle of negligence, would place the burden of economic loss on the owner or operator to whose activity the loss is chiefly due, would provide for an equitable distribution of the insurance fund according to the extent of the economic loss, and would provide a prompt remedy at small cost to the injured person or his family.[2]

Nothing came of the Columbia study initially, but it did attract the interest of scholars. Thirty-three years later, in 1965, Professors Robert E. Keeton and Jeffrey O'Connell authored a new, powerful major critique of the tort system in a book entitled *Basic Protection for the Traffic Victim: A Blueprint for Reforming Automobile Insurance.*[3] The book quantified in detail the compensation gaps and the money wasted on attorneys' fees under the fault and liability insurance system. They found that only forty-four cents of every premium dollar was spent to compensate the losses of people injured in motor vehicle crashes, a far lower percentage than in other major insurance systems, such as health and workers' compensation, and far lower than the portion of the auto insurance dollar that paid for collision and comprehensive coverage. Then, they provided detailed recommendations for replacing the tort system with a system where auto insurance for bodily injury would become primarily health and work loss insurance. As with other enumerated "first-party" insurances (including the collision and comprehensive coverages in an auto policy), all injured persons would be compensated by their own insurer, without regard to fault, with little or no need for lawyers. The proposal came to be known as "no-fault automobile insurance."

In contrast to the response to the Columbia study, this time the world took notice. The book put no-fault insurance on the political map. After its strong indictment of the tort system and a proposal to remedy its failures through adoption of no-fault insurance, the next step was to translate the Keeton-O'Connell ideas into legislation. Along with the comprehensive twenty-six-volume 1971 study (described later) by the DOT, the Keeton-O'Connell book laid the foundation for seventeen states[4] and the Commonwealth of Puerto Rico to adopt no-fault laws during the early to mid-1970s and for fifteen years of consideration, separated by nearly two decades, of no-fault legislation at the federal level.

The states took the initiative quickly, while the US House and Senate chose to strengthen the foundation before seeking adoption of a nationwide law. The first state to adopt a no-fault law was Massachusetts. It happened almost by accident. Michael Dukakis, a junior state representative in the Massachusetts legislature and graduate of Harvard Law School, where Keeton taught, introduced the Keeton-O'Connell draft proposal from their book as a bill in 1967. Much to Dukakis's surprise, the bill passed in 1970 and went into effect in 1971.

Meanwhile, Sens. Phil Hart of Michigan and Warren Magnuson of Washington were vying for ownership of federal legislation while their staffs were building the foundation. Senator Hart took the initial lead from his position on the Judiciary Committee, only to see Senator Magnuson use his influence as chairman of the Senate Commerce Committee to take control.

While Senator Hart was holding hearings in the Judiciary Committee, Senator Magnuson and his staff were maneuvering to have the Commerce Committee take the lead. Magnuson, who was to be the longest-serving chairman of the Senate Commerce Committee,[5] had started to focus on consumer issues after nearly losing reelection in 1962. That was the product of good staff work. Jerry Grinstein, who was to become Magnuson's administrative assistant (AA) (the head of his personal office), came up with the idea to revitalize Magnuson's career by repositioning him as a consumer champion. Grinstein got Magnuson's buy-in and started stacking the Commerce Committee staff with young consumer activists.

One of them, Mike Pertschuk, who would go on to become Magnuson's chief of staff on the Commerce Committee, got Magnuson to author and secure adoption of legislation to require a federal study of the tort system. On May 22, 1968, Pres. Lyndon Johnson signed into law Public Law 90-313, a Joint Resolution of the Congress[6] authorizing the secretary of transportation "to conduct a comprehensive study and investigation of the existing compensation system for motor vehicle accidents losses." The resolution strengthened the Commerce Committee's claim over the Judiciary Committee to jurisdiction[7] over no-fault and laid the predicate to federal legislative efforts.

Supervised by Dick Walsh at DOT, the report took three years to complete and was released on March 26, 1971. It consisted of twenty-five volumes with experts examining all aspects of the existing fault and liability insurance system. Walsh, a short, stout man with a military bearing and a mind for detail, took it upon himself to write the summary twenty-sixth volume. In it, he succinctly summed up the case against the tort system:

> The existing system ill serves the accident victim, the insuring public and society. It is inefficient, overly costly, incomplete and slow. It allocates benefits

> poorly, discourages rehabilitation and overburdens the courts and the legal system. Both on the record of its performance and the logic of its operation, it does little if anything to minimize crash losses.[8]

The report provided iron-clad documentation of the failures of the tort system to compensate injured persons fairly and offered strong support for replacing it with no-fault. The sections below are a short summary of its main findings.

THE SYSTEM IS INEFFICIENT AND OVERLY COSTLY

Any system that requires attorneys, for both plaintiffs and defendants, to adjudicate fault before compensating accident victims will be a less efficient compensation system than one that pays injured people regardless of fault, without the involvement of lawyers.

Most striking was how little of the premium dollar went to compensate injured people. The study cited the Keeton-O'Connell work that found that only 44 cents of each premium dollar was used to compensate injured persons. As low as that figure was, it grossly overstated the benefit to injured persons. Of the 44 cents, 8 cents was duplicative of payments from other sources (primarily health insurance) and 21 cents went to pain and suffering (almost exclusively to people with the least economic loss). The bottom line—*only 14.5 cents of each premium dollar was paid to victims for their economic losses.*

By contrast, plaintiffs' attorneys (one-third of any recovery), insurance company attorneys, and, to a much lesser extent, insurance investigators consumed 23 cents (with the majority of that amount for plaintiff attorneys' fees) of each premium dollar, or nearly 60 percent more than the 14.5 cents injured persons recovered for economic losses that were not already compensated by some other source. General insurance company overhead accounted for the remaining 33 cents.[9]

THE SYSTEM IS INCOMPLETE AND SLOW

As Table 2.1 shows, *54 percent of all injured persons recovered nothing whatsoever.*[10] This is easy to understand when one-third of all motor vehicle crashes were single-car crashes. If, for example, your car skids on the ice and hits a tree, there is no one to sue, so there is no recovery. Even where there was a recovery, it was long delayed. *The average seriously injured auto accident victim had to wait sixteen months for compensation,*[11] *with no payments in the interim.* Much of the delay was due to significant court backlogs.

Table 2.1 DOT Gross Reparations Table

Total Economic Loss ($)	Percent with Tort Recovery (%)	Ratio of Net Recovery to Loss	
		With Tort	Without Tort
1–499	54	4.5	0.8
500–999	63	2.6	0.5
1,000–1,499	49	2.4	0.7
1,500–2,499	47	2.0	1.0
2,500–4,999	44	1.6	0.6
5,000–9,999	44	1.1	0.6
10,000–24,999	52	0.7	0.4
25,000 & over	42	0.3	0.3
TOTAL	48%	0.6	0.4

The table shows a comparison of reparations received by fatally or seriously injured persons with and without tort recovery by size of loss. Source: US Department of Transportation, "Motor Vehicle Crash Losses and Their Compensation in the United States: A Report to the Congress and the President" (Washington, DC: US Government Printing Office, 1971), 36.

THE SYSTEM ALLOCATES BENEFITS POORLY

As Table 2.1 shows, *the average recovery for people with losses of less than $500 was 450 percent, while those with over $25,000 in losses recovered only 30 percent.* And these figures were for the lucky 46 percent who recovered anything at all. The main reason for the excess recoveries for minor injuries was the "nuisance value" of these claims to insurers. It was cheaper for a company to overpay on a legitimate or even a questionable small claim than to go to court to contest it. It is also often difficult to determine the difference between necessary and unnecessary diagnostic exams and chiropractor visits. From the perspective of the plaintiff and his or her attorney, if the defendant is insured, they know there is a guaranteed pot of money, the mandatory BI limits, from which to recover.

Those limits provide ample room for the payment of noneconomic damages (pain and suffering) in minor injury cases.

On the other hand, the leverage switches to the insurer's side as economic losses mount, and the average driver carries insufficient insurance to cover even a small portion of a large economic loss, let alone to pay anything for pain and suffering. For every person "lucky" enough to be seriously injured by Bill Gates, there are millions hit by the average driver with insufficient insurance to cover a large loss. Also, at the time of the DOT study, only the affluent could afford to pay their medical bills and cover lost wages while waiting sixteen months or more to recover.[12]

THE SYSTEM DOES LITTLE IF ANYTHING TO MITIGATE CRASH LOSSES

As discussed before, the tort system is designed to accomplish two purposes—compensation and deterrence. The compensation inadequacies might somehow be tolerable if the system deterred reckless driving, thereby reducing the number of accidents and the associated losses compared to what they otherwise would have been.

To understand why DOT found that most crashes are not deterrable, "return with us now to those thrilling days of yesteryear," in the famous words of *The Lone Ranger*, and examine how the threat of paying damages to Jack might have deterred Jill from hitting him in the first place.

Let's posit two possibilities for Jill's negligence. First, Jill was tired and slow to react or, second, a sudden thunderstorm made driving conditions hazardous. Does anyone believe that the statistically minuscule possibility of Jill hitting Jack that day and seriously injuring him would have encouraged her to drive more cautiously? The same lack of deterrent effect would occur if Jill were an inexperienced teenager or, for that matter, was driving too close because she thought Jack was driving too slowly.

DOT reached the same conclusion that the tort system had little or no deterrent effect, finding that most accidents were caused by environmental or personal factors, such as a sudden rainstorm or youthful inexperience, which are external to individuals' conscious control and thus cannot be deterred by punishment. On the other end of the spectrum, DOT found that drivers who willfully violate the law (such as those with road rage) are not deterred by the possibility of having to pay damages.

DOT also considered the impact of insurance on deterrence, concluding that even if the liability system acted as a deterrent, liability insurance, by being the actual payer of damages, would surely dilute any deterrent effect.[13] That is because the at-fault motorist (Jill) does not pay for the "innocent" motorist (Jack's) losses. Her insurer pays, and the only impact on her is a surcharge (small increase) in her insurance premium. After all, the purpose of insurance is to spread the risk.

Members of Congress have the rare ability to summarize a lot of information in just a few words. Responding to the Keeton-O'Connell finding that injured persons received only forty-four cents back for compensation of their injuries on a dollar of premium, the Commerce Committee chairman would frequently say, "Las Vegas has better odds than that."

After exhaustively (and exhaustingly) documenting the faults of the tort system, the DOT study endorsed no-fault insurance to remedy the compensation deficiencies of the fault system. Up to that point, Magnuson was delighted with the DOT study, but he did not get the one thing he wanted and needed most politically—an endorsement by the Nixon administration of federal legislation. This came as a bit of a surprise because Pres. Richard Nixon himself had criticized the tort system, just four years after the Columbia study, while a student at Duke Law School:

> But with high-powered cars and concrete highways, the probability that an accident—often the consequence of a fractional mistake in management—can and will be described accurately in court has become increasingly remote, especially where court congestion has delayed the time of trial. . . .
>
> It is doubtless true that in accident cases, the judgment of a jury as to the proportion of the loss for which each party was responsible is at best extremely uncertain and inaccurate.[14]

But politics always trumped principle for Nixon. In this case, the major political drama took place before the report was released. Walsh's final draft endorsed federal no-fault until top insurance executives prevailed on President Nixon to change the recommendation to one that would give the states time to enact their own laws first.[15] Their special interest pleadings won out, and Walsh's recommendation was replaced in the final report with a recommendation that the states be given time to replace their tort laws with no-fault.[16] Only if they failed to do so would the Nixon administration support federal legislation ("As to the length of the time schedule, a period of perhaps five years seems reasonable").[17] This would prove to be the first of several times that no-fault came close to enactment, as Nixon's support would almost assuredly have led to enough Republican support to pass the bill.

3. Early Congressional Action

A Consumer Icon Goes Missing in Action (1968–1974)

In the 1970s, most of the real legislative power resided in the committees and the subcommittees and, more particularly, in their chairmen (I use the term because almost of them were men). Because this was where the members could have the most impact on legislation, most of them became quite familiar with the goals of the legislation and the key details. This was truer in the House than in the Senate because there were fewer demands on the time of 435 members doing the work that only 100 senators were available to do. Serving on fewer committees and subcommittees, they could devote more time to details.

Even so, major legislation was often long and complicated, with many technical but important decision points. It was not unusual for it to run seventy pages or more, as did the no-fault bills of the 1970s. The political side, identifying and helping unite political support for major legislation inside and outside the Congress, was also frequently quite complicated and time-consuming. As a result, most chairmen delegated much of the detailed orchestration of these tasks to staff, subject to member supervision.

In a job where the devil truly is in the details, the ability to hire top-notch staff is an important quality for members. Magnuson understood this well and stocked his personal office and committee with bright, aggressive staff. As previously mentioned, Senator Magnuson hired Jerry Grinstein to head his personal office and then took Grinstein's advice in repositioning himself as a consumer champion in the 1960s. Grinstein, in turn, supported Mike Pertschuk in his efforts to prioritize consumer legislation in the Commerce Committee.

It was Pertschuk who orchestrated the legislation of DOT's study of compensation of motor vehicle accidents. Then, Pertschuk had the good sense to turn no-fault over to Lynn Sutcliffe, whom he had hired in 1968. Sutcliffe became the staff maestro, a role he performed brilliantly. Despite his youth—twenty-five when he was hired in 1968—Sutcliffe possessed a brilliant substantive mind and an innate sense of strategy and tactics. It didn't hurt that he had the same good looks as tennis star Stan Smith (only Sutcliffe was about five inches shorter) and a preternatural calm in tense situations that belied his age.[1] He was to need all those skills to move no-fault in the face of powerful opposition from the interest groups that had close allies in both parties.

Sutcliffe grew up in the Seattle suburb of Bellevue. He attended Princeton, where he excelled not only in academics but also as a defensive back on the undefeated 1964 Tiger football team. He was awarded the Charles W. Caldwell Memorial Trophy, which goes to the senior who has shown the greatest improvement in football during his years at Princeton. His intelligence and competitive spirit were to serve him well in the Senate.

After graduating from Princeton, Sutcliffe returned home for law school at the University of Washington School of Law, where he was editor in chief of *Washington Law Review*. Upon graduation, he was selected by Senator Magnuson for the senator's Washington Scholar program, which brought the brightest Washington law school graduates to work on Magnuson's Commerce Committee. His hiring was to prove good for both the committee and Magnuson's home-state politics. Sutcliffe joined the most progressive and aggressive proconsumer committee in the Congress under the leadership of Magnuson as chairman and Pertschuk as staff director.

Sutcliffe's timing could not have been better, as he joined the staff shortly after the DOT study resolution became law. He quickly realized that the study would provide the fuel necessary for federal no-fault, as a thorough federal study would be more powerful than the excellent but more limited work of Keeton and O'Connell.

Just as Sutcliffe was coming to work for the committee, Senator Hart, in his position as chairman of the Judiciary Subcommittee on Antitrust and Monopoly, in 1969 initiated a series of hearings on automobile insurance costs. Thereafter, in 1970, he introduced a series of reform bills, including bills to permit the sale of group auto insurance and to reduce auto damage. Those bills never advanced, but the third one was the first no-fault bill. He then reintroduced his no-fault bill early in the Ninety-Third Congress, on February 25, 1971, as S. 945, the Uniform Motor Vehicle Insurance Act, with Senator Magnuson as the lead cosponsor. These early bills extended well beyond no-fault. They would have involved the federal government in insurance regulation, including rate setting.

The House and Senate coordinated submissions of no-fault bills early in the Ninety-Third Congress and then started hearings in April. Rep. John Moss (D-CA) conducted eight hearings (on April 20, 21, 22, 26, 27, 28, 29 and 30) through his position as chairman of the Commerce and Finance Subcommittee. Senator Hart, deservedly known as "the conscience of the Senate,"[2] conducted twelve hearings (on March 10 and 18; May 4, 5, 6, 7, 10, 11, 12, 13, 14, and 28; and June 16) through his position on the Commerce Committee.

As the hearings moved along, Hart knew he needed a star witness to dramatize the subject, and he found one in Bob Joost. More specifically, Dean Sharp, a key staffer for Hart, discovered Joost. Sharp had heard that Joost, a law school friend of Dukakis, had become a no-fault supporter, contrary to the views of his employer. Sharp invited him to Washington to testify at a hearing on Hart's no-fault bill. Joost refused at least twice to testify on S. 945, but Sharp persisted until Joost finally agreed to testify.

On May 6, 1971, Joost boarded a plane and flew from Boston to Washington, DC, to testify in favor of federal no-fault. He opened his testimony directly: "I am submitting this statement in support of the Hart-Magnuson bill as an act of conscience, as an attorney, and as a citizen."[3] He testified that the American Trial Lawyers Association (ATLA) had developed a national strategy to defeat federal or state no-fault insurance plans. It involved fundraising and "key men" in multiple states who represented the power to control their state legislatures. He described one ATLA meeting and the impact of the ATLA strategy on his decision to support no-fault at the federal level:

> In Chicago on April 24th, I heard the ATL key men from Ohio and Illinois make such smug associations [*sic*] of control of their State legislatures, in whole or in part, that I was absolutely and totally disabused of my States-first leaning.
>
> . . .
>
> As I mentioned, until recently I leaned toward the position that [the decision to adopt no-fault should be left to the states]. I no longer do. I now believe firmly that a decision to leave it to the States is, in fact, a decision to

> retain the automobile negligence system with all its waste, all its excessive administrative costs, all its duplication, all its slow pace of operation.
>
> . . .
>
> To summarize and reiterate, it is my considered judgment that the trial lawyers will probably prevent any meaningful no-fault legislation from being enacted in any of the State legislatures, with a few possible exceptions. It is naïve to argue that there is a choice between Federal legislation and legislation in the other 49 State capitals. The only choice is between Federal no-fault legislation or maintenance of the present negligence system, the system which the Department of Transportation's $2 million study so carefully and painstakingly criticized.[4]

After Joost completed his testimony, Senator Hart made these remarks before asking questions:

> On the very first page you describe your professional qualifications. I have met a magna cum laude man from Harvard Law, and I have known Harvard Law Review editors. I am not sure if I ever met a magna cum laude graduate from Yale. I have met Phi Beta Kappas. But this is the first time I have met all of them at once. Do you understand my reluctance to ask you questions?[5]

Joost paid a heavy price for his act of conscience. Once he mailed his testimony to the committee, the ATLA executive committee ended his nine years with the organization, eliminating his position and firing him.[6] Sutcliffe shrewdly hired Joost. Soon thereafter, Sutcliffe discovered that Joost not only knew no-fault cold but could draft legislation brilliantly.[7] In fact, he was such a good draftsman that the Commerce Committee stopped using the legislative counsel assigned to them by the office of legislative counsel.

In contrast to Joost's statement of conscience, at the May 10, 1971, hearing, Ralph Nader refused to take a position on no-fault, saying he hadn't studied the bill. Under questioning by Sutcliffe, Nader made general statements about favoring the right to sue for pain and suffering and an alternative option if the plaintiff didn't want to go into the no-fault system (when confronted with legislation that would have provided such an option in 1996, Nader testified against it). Given Nader's concerns about auto safety, Sutcliffe asked him about other testimony that no-fault would provide incentives for people to purchase safer cars or additional safety features. The logic was that in a first-party system where the insurer knows the person and the car he or she will be driving in a crash, insurers can provide discounts for safer cars because their insured is less likely to be injured. This cannot happen in the tort system because there, the insurer is obligated to pay an unknown motorist driving an unknown car. Nader refused to express an opinion.[8]

The DOT study provided ironclad documentation of the flaws of the tort system. It eliminated any argument that the tort system provided good compensation of injuries efficiently. While it recommended replacement of the system with a no-fault system, it left open the question of exactly what no-fault legislation should look like at either the federal or state level. Of course, more importantly, it left open how to put together a broad enough coalition to make it safe for members of Congress to support no-fault.

The starting point for legislation was the proposal included in the Keeton-O'Connell book. Keeton and O'Connell could have proposed a no-fault system in which all lawsuits were eliminated. That would have been clean and simple and, most importantly, not subject to abuse. Instead, they called for a "threshold" level of injury after which the injured person could sue for pain and suffering. They did recognize the need for limiting such suits to very narrow categories of cases, calling for a threshold of serious and permanent injuries that also involved substantial economic loss.

A tight threshold was the key to keeping costs down when nearly double the number of people who could recover in tort were going to be eligible to recover under no-fault. Trial lawyers, desperate to maintain their livelihood, knew that if they could weaken these thresholds to permit more suits, they would not only continue to make money bringing suits but could also make no-fault less popular by increasing its costs.

All states considered no-fault legislation in the early 1970s, but only seventeen enacted no-fault laws. It quickly became apparent that Joost was correct in stating that the trial bar had the political clout in the states to either stop or undermine real reform. The trial bar's most common device was to secure the inclusion of "dollar" thresholds, whereby one could sue if one's losses exceeded a specific dollar amount. As a result, most states initially adopted laws with dollar thresholds ranging from \$200 to \$2,000. The lowest of these represented barely a speed bump on the way to filing a lawsuit, not even requiring falsely increasing medical costs to breach the threshold. The higher ones were, in some ways, worse because they represented a target for fraud. Contemporaneous studies found that it was easy to find unscrupulous, friendly doctors to submit phony bills to inflate losses to reach a \$2,000 threshold. Doctors won because they got paid for doing nothing, and lawyers and clients won because they could sue for pain and suffering. Of course, the costs of this fraud—which increased both the cost of no-fault benefits and the cost of lawsuits—was passed along to all consumers in the form of higher premiums.

The trial bar then cited these flawed state laws as an argument against other no-fault legislation, at both the federal and state level, on the grounds that it was too costly. As the trial lawyers were the ones undermining state no-fault laws, their actions were akin to those of the boy who kills his parents and then pleads for mercy in court on the grounds that he's an orphan.

The state experience reinforced Sutcliffe's view that more substantive and political work needed to be done to pass a federal bill. He knew that the ticking-time-bomb thresholds in the weak state laws would undermine support for both state and federal legislation and that the pace of state action would falter in the absence of federal legislation. But what should the details of the bill be?

To get the answer, Sutcliffe followed up the DOT study with a second step, the development of a model law. To accomplish this, he encouraged Chairman Magnuson to request that DOT fund the creation of a model state law. In 1971, DOT joined with the Ford Foundation to finance the drafting of a model state no-fault law by the National Conference of Commissioners on Uniform State Laws. The commissioners, with work done primarily by academics, including Professor Keeton, drafted a model law that was issued in August 1972, the Uniform Motor Vehicle Accident Reparations Act (UMVARA). The model law called for "payment of all reasonable medical and rehabilitative expenses without limit" to injured persons. To keep premiums from being higher than existing premiums, UMVARA called for a tight restriction on lawsuits for noneconomic damages ("if there is permanent significant loss of body function or death or permanent serious disfigurement or more than six months of total disability").[9]

While the commissioners were developing UMVARA, Sutcliffe had already worked with the Hart staff to draft a no-fault bill based on his knowledge of what UMVARA would look like. That bill, S. 945, which contained high benefits and a tight threshold but dropped the earlier rate regulation provisions, was referred to the Commerce Committee. The committee held hearings on it and reported the bill on a bipartisan basis in late 1971. Then, with the UMVARA language, which was very close to that of S. 945, in hand in 1972, Sutcliffe had a bill that Chairman Magnuson could say represented what the states would do if they were free of pressure from the trial bar and insurers. It was both a substantive and a political win for no-fault. However, the opponents were able to derail it on August 8, 1972, by voting on the Senate floor to refer the bill to the Judiciary Committee for further consideration, effectively killing the bill for the rest of the Ninety-Second Congress. Some Senate staff blamed the loss on Nader: "Three liberal, usually pro-consumer, Democrats [Thomas Eagleton, Frank Church, and Joseph Montoya] killed no-fault automobile insurance in the Senate last month, and some disgruntled staff aides are blaming Ralph Nader for the death."[10]

The House also held hearings on its no-fault bill, H.R. 10, during the Ninety-Second Congress. However, Representative Moss was unable to move his bill through his subcommittee because of the inability to obtain a quorum to mark it up, a problem that would recur in future subcommittee deliberations.[11]

Sutcliffe was undeterred by the defeat. In the fall of 1972, he encouraged Magnuson to request a study of the state-by-state cost impact of adoption of the model no-fault law and S. 945. DOT, again in conjunction with the Ford Foundation, financed a project of the National Association of Insurance Commissioners (NAIC) to develop a computer model and database to explore the cost and price implications of different no-fault approaches, including that of UMVARA. The NAIC subcontracted the development of the model to the actuarial firm of Milliman and Robertson. The firm's analysis came back in the spring of 1973 and concluded that S. 945 would save drivers money in almost all states.

I said this was a two-pronged effort, although UMVARA and the cost study were really both substantive and political. More narrowly political, Sutcliffe used the time to help create an outside umbrella coalition of supporters. The National Committee for Effective No-Fault, headed by Gary Frink (who was handpicked by Sutcliffe), included many labor unions, consumer groups, and some insurers, most prominently those represented by the American Insurance Association (a trade group that represented stock insurance companies, which sold 30 percent of all auto insurance) and State Farm, the largest auto insurer in the country (a mutual company owned by its policyholders).

Thanks to Sutcliffe, at the beginning of the Ninety-Third Congress in 1973, Chairman Magnuson was armed with the strong DOT report documenting the faults of the fault system, a bill based on the model state law, and a cost study that showed nationwide savings. Magnuson quickly pushed no-fault through the Commerce Committee by a vote of 15–3. On the Senate floor in September, the Judiciary Committee again secured a referral of the new bill (S. 354) to the Judiciary Committee. This time, however, Magnuson got the Judiciary Committee chairman, James Eastland of Mississippi, to agree to report or discharge the bill from the committee by February 1, 1974, freeing the bill for Senate action.

With all these necessary legislative predicates in hand and clever utilization of Senate procedures, the Senate passed a no-fault bill by a bipartisan vote of 53–42, with 15 Republicans joining 38 Democrats, on May 1, 1974 (obviously, this was before the divisions in the Senate meant that all bills of consequence had to meet a 60-vote test to break a filibuster).

Even in victory, there were concerning signs of the influence of the trial bar on Democrats. In one such case in 1974, Mike Gildea of the AFL-CIO, Kathleen O'Reilly of CFA, Les Cheek of the American Insurance Association and other no-fault supporters met with Sen. Gaylord Nelson (WI), a true-blue liberal Democrat with a strong proconsumer record. Senator Nelson told them that he agreed with everything they said about the virtues of no-fault. He added that he should be an easy yes for no-fault but noted that he was up for reelection and then walked them through his campaign reelection structure: "The chairman of my reelection committee is a trial lawyer; my finance chairman is a trial lawyer and so are the chairmen of my local committees. I can't afford to vote for it."[12]

Unfortunately, the glow of victory was short-lived, as progress on a House counterpart came to a halt when the House stopped considering most "nonessential" legislation to focus on proceedings to impeach President Nixon. This was the second bad break for no-fault (the first being Nixon's insistence on the DOT study supporting longer consideration by the states before any federal action), and one can withstand bad breaks only so many times when facing powerful political opponents.

Still, entering 1975, no-fault had gained great momentum and, along with legislation to create a Consumer Protection Agency, had become the top Democratic consumer priority for the Ninety-Fourth Congress.

4. How to Get a Committee Counsel Position on Capitol Hill

My involvement with the no-fault effort started on April 1, 1975, when I was hired as a counsel to the Consumer Protection and Finance Subcommittee of the House Interstate and Foreign Commerce Committee. The path to securing a counsel's job today is similar to what it was in 1975, although the role of a committee counsel is far different. I would argue that the skill set described below would be the same if the committees were to reassert their role in the legislative process.

The previous chapter focused on action in the Senate because several Senate no-fault bills had been reported from committee and considered (and, in one case, passed) on the Senate floor. By contrast, in the House, no bill had even been reported from the relevant subcommittee of the House Interstate and Foreign Commerce Committee despite strong support from the highly effective Rep. John Moss, the subcommittee chairman.

That was about to change in 1975. Chairman Moss switched subcommittee chairs, and his position as chairman of the Consumer Protection Subcommittee was filled by Rep. Lionel Van Deerlin (D-CA), the next most senior Democrat on the committee. Van Deerlin did not have any substantive experience with the two major bills before the subcommittee, no-fault and one that would establish a regulatory scheme for toxic substances, and he had no staff with expertise on either subject. To fill the gap, he hired two people. One was Janie Kinney, a lawyer who had been a legislative assistant (LA) to Rep. Bob Eckhardt (D-TX), and the other was me. I, too, had been a LA to another member of Congress, Rep. Lud Ashley (D-OH), but he was not a member of the Commerce Committee. Van Deerlin hired me at the recommendation of Mike Lemov, who had been chief counsel to former Subcommittee Chairman John Moss. I will explain my connection to Lemov shortly. My involvement in no-fault was not foreordained, as I had no expertise in that area of law. It occurred by accident, by a metaphorical flip of a coin. There were two major bills before the subcommittee—one dealing with regulation of toxic substances and one dealing with no-fault auto insurance. Fortunately, there was no argument over who was assigned to do the staff work on which bill, as Janie was interested in the toxic substances one and I in no-fault. As it turned out, the Toxic Substances Control Act was enacted in 1976, while my work on no-fault was to continue for thirty years.

What happened not by accident—or at least only partially by accident—was my getting the counsel's job. My journey to the Hill, and the reasons I chose it, provide a snapshot of a common path to committee counsel positions in the 1970s. The path has not changed much since my time on the Hill ended in 1995, although the reasons people choose to seek employment on the Hill have. Importantly, also, most staff serve far fewer years than the twenty-five I served and rarely spend substantial time in both the House and Senate, as I did.

The 1960s were the formative political years for young Americans, including me, growing up at the time. They started with the hope and idealism of the Kennedy presidency. Many were stirred by Pres. John F. Kennedy's call to public service in his inaugural address: "Ask not what your country can do for you; ask what you can do for your country." Much of the rest of the decade was filled with traumatic events that raised questions about the nature and values of America—with the assassinations of President Kennedy, Sen. Robert Kennedy, and the Reverend Martin Luther King and the Vietnam War. As a result, many of us who went to the Hill at this time arrived with an idealism that was tempered by deep cynicism about the future of the country.

Nevertheless, young people flocked to Washington, DC, to try to make the country a better place. I got the counsel position through a combination of heredity, academic performance, relevant work experience, and accidents (several of them) or luck regarding where I worked and lived. My parents not only gave me my DNA but also gave me the opportunity to attend one of the top public schools in the nation by moving from New York City to the suburb of Scarsdale after World War II.

I took advantage of the opportunity, graduating near the top of my class from Scarsdale High School in 1961 and then again, in three years, from Trinity College, an elite private school. With the Vietnam War looming, I entered Columbia Law School, another excellent school, despite lacking any real interest in law. What little interest I had did not last long, as I found the classwork boring, the competition more rigorous than at previous levels, and the professors intimidating. It was much like the experience portrayed in the movie *The Paper Chase*, as the professors bullied and abused the students. By the end of my second year, I was ready to quit. Fortunately, a friend talked me out of it, using the most effective argument—that the alternative was an all-expenses-paid trip to Vietnam, courtesy of the US Army. He also pointed out that a law degree could turn out to be an effective credential for work. I was dubious, but he proved to be correct.

I didn't quit, but I steadfastly avoided courses that had anything to do with business law, such as insurance and banking, because I was interested in a career that would help people. Little did I know that I would have benefited from taking those courses, as I wound up having to become an expert in those subject areas of law. My career path dictated that I understand them in order to draft consumer legislation in those areas.

In my last year at Columbia, I finally found a course I loved and did well in: labor law. The major reason I liked it was because of the professor, Mike Sovern. He was an excellent teacher with a terrific sense of humor. He endeared himself to me forever in one exchange with another student. After Professor Sovern had asked a series of questions, the student realized that he was hopelessly lost and heading in the opposite direction from which he had started. The student finally said, "Professor Sovern, I think you're leading me down the primrose path." Professor Sovern replied, "Well, you found me out." That simple phrase had special meaning to me. It was Mel Brooks's retort to Carl Reiner in the "Peruvian Coffee Maker" routine from the *2000 Year Old Man* album. The line was the culmination of a series of answers that led Reiner to guess that Brooks was not a Peruvian at all but a German (Nazi). Being the mature twenty-one-year-old that I was, I decided on the spot that labor law was for me. It was this serendipitous experience that led me to Washington, DC, and my career in politics and public policy.

The accidental part of my journey started when I failed to obtain a labor law job in New York. Then, with the help of a friend of my father's, I got a job at the National Labor Relations Board (NLRB) in Washington, DC. My starting salary in the fall of 1967 was $7,696, less than half that of my classmates who went to work for Wall Street firms. It was a sacrifice I was willing to make to work for what I believed to be the public good.

Unfortunately, the experience was not nearly as interesting as Professor Sovern's class, and I quickly became bored. At the same time, I became extremely interested in trying to stop the Vietnam War.

After only a year and a half at the NLRB, in 1969, I secured a job as an LA to a very liberal member of the House of Representatives, Rep. Thomas Ludlow (Lud) Ashley (D-OH). As the sole LA in Ashley's office, I was responsible for helping him develop policy statements and drafting legislation on domestic and international issues. I wrote statements that Representative Ashley placed in the *Congressional Record* as his views on everything from the detrimental effects of the pesticide DDT on the environment to opposition to the Vietnam War. I also drafted legislation, including a resolution to impeach President Nixon.

I stayed in my job with Ashley for five years. While he was gruff, he was also honest and forthcoming. His constituents' responses to this direct man led me to believe that honesty was also good politics and that it was better to tell people what your positions were than to shade them in the hope of leaving a misleading impression. One example occurred when Ashley responded to a letter critical of his views on a number of subjects with a clear statement that he disagreed with every point the constituent made. The appreciative letter he got back led me to believe it was possible that Ashley's constituent might have considered voting for him just because he was honest. However, there is (or at least used to be) such a thing as being too direct. During the time I worked for Ashley, one of the senators from Ohio was Stephen Young. I saw more than one letter he wrote to constituents with whom he disagreed that started, "Dear Sir or Madam, You are an ignoramus, or the North end of a horse heading South."

My work in Ashley's office served me well when I moved to committee staff and worked on bills that had a far better chance of becoming law because bills must first be considered by the committees of jurisdiction before they can go to the floor of the House or Senate. My education in how the House operated was furthered by attending a series of seminars on House procedure and by listening to the daily House floor proceedings. I say "listening" because they were not televised in the early 1970s. Listening to the proceedings and reading the *Congressional Record* helped me learn which members were showhorses, those who talked a good game and constantly sought press attention but didn't sway other

Figure 4.1. US Rep. Thomas Ludlow Ashley, Democrat, Ninth Congressional District, Toledo, Ohio, 1955–1980.

members, and which were workhorses, those who did the heavy lifting of developing legislation and whom other members followed.

By 1974, I had checked off several of the boxes—a good education, a law degree, and experience on the Hill—that would prepare me for the challenging substantive and political no-fault battle. The next one was substantive knowledge in an area of jurisdiction of the subcommittee. I fulfilled that requirement in 1974 when I left Ashley's office to work at the Federal Trade Commission (FTC). I got a job at the FTC despite the fact that a Republican, Nixon, was president and even though Ashley had introduced a resolution to impeach him!

The fourth piece of the equation for getting the committee job was accident, or luck. This was important because in 1975, there was no congressional employment office that helped people find committee jobs. Luck, in this case, meant getting to know a well-placed Commerce Committee staffer. This happened entirely accidentally. In 1970, three years after moving to DC, my wife and I moved to River Park, a cooperative development in southwest DC that attracted many socially conscious government workers.

Among other friends I made were several who worked on the Hill, including Mike Lemov, who worked for the Commerce Committee. Unbeknownst to me, Lemov was part of a bit of a feeder system from River Park to jobs on the Hill. Before I moved to River Park, Mike Pertschuk, the staff director of the Senate Commerce Committee, had got to know his neighbor Mike Lemov at River Park. When the Senate Commerce Committee secured a study of the safety of consumer products, Pertschuk recommended Lemov to be the general counsel for the project. After the study was complete, Lemov, logically, wound up as special counsel to Representative Moss, the chairman of the Commerce and Finance Subcommittee of the House Commerce Committee, which had jurisdiction over consumer products.

I met Lemov when we moved into River Park, and we became friends through playing tennis and a mutual interest in politics. Then, in 1974, the Nixon impeachment proceedings and his resignation led to the election of a huge number of Democrats in the House, who were dubbed the "Watergate Class." The new members were not content to sit back and learn but insisted on changes to the seniority system whereby the most senior members had dominated committee chairmanships.[1] Representative Moss led the rebellion in the Commerce Committee, which resulted in full Committee Chairman Harley Staggers (D-WVA) ceding his chairmanship of the Oversight and Investigations Subcommittee to Moss. That meant that the newly named Consumer Protection and Finance Subcommittee needed both a new chairman and staff.

5. "I'm Just a Bill on Capitol Hill"

A Primer on How to Move Legislation in the 1970s

For those who skipped or skimmed the last chapter, here's the condensed thirty-second version of how I got the job working on no-fault. After World War II, my parents moved to the suburbs of New York City so my sister and I could get the best possible education. I performed well academically in high school, which enabled me to go to a good college, where I also performed well, which enabled me to go to a very good law school. I hated law school and avoided business classes to focus on courses that might enable me to help others. I started out in labor law because I liked the professor and accidentally moved to Washington, DC, because that's where I got a job. I then secured a job on the Hill to help end the Vietnam War. That job gave me the opportunity to learn how the Congress operated. I went from there to work for the FTC and became friends with a key Hill committee staffer through living in a socially active community. The sum of all those experiences and relationships gave me the necessary credentials and put me in the perfect political position when a job opened on the House Consumer Protection and Finance Subcommittee, the subcommittee with jurisdiction over no-fault automobile insurance.

With the organization of the Commerce Committee in January 1975, Rep. Lionel Van Deerlin (D-CA) assumed the chairmanship of the Consumer Protection Subcommittee, which, among other things, had jurisdiction over the FTC, where I was working. Lemov, who had been the subcommittee's chief counsel in the previous Congress, recommended me to Van Deerlin to be a counsel. Thus, in April 1975, because of the entirety of events and experiences I described, I became a newly minted counsel for the Consumer Protection Subcommittee. In the following six years, I would serve as counsel to four vastly different chairmen of the same subcommittee, a rare experience on the Hill. Shortly after I started work on April 1, 1975, I was assigned to staff the no-fault bill for the subcommittee.

Everyone knows how a bill becomes law; many from the song "I'm Just a Bill" from a 1976 *Schoolhouse Rock* segment. A member of the House or Senate introduces a bill, it is referred to a committee for hearings, the committee reports it, and it is considered on the floor. The other body does the same thing. Any differences between the two bills are worked out in a House-Senate conference, and then the president signs the bill into law.

To understand the story of no-fault, you have to ignore the reality of legislating in 2020, where, on major legislation, the House and Senate leadership agree with the president and the bills then go pretty much straight to the floors of the two bodies for approval. This part of the tale is about legislating in the 1970s, when the process involved many members from both bodies as well as the president and staff from both the legislative and executive branches.

The simple "How to Make a Law" described above probably never existed. It was to the real legislative process as a stick figure is to a human being. It's worth several paragraphs to explain in more detail some of the key elements in developing and moving legislation. It has always been true in both the House and Senate that whatever party was in the majority held most of the cards. The majority party chose all the committee chairmen and subcommittee chairmen, had a majority of the members on every committee and subcommittee, and controlled what legislation was considered by the committees and the full House or Senate (while the majority party retains control of the process today, much of the power to legislate that resided in the committees has fallen to the leadership, I would argue to the detriment of both the quality of the legislation and the power of the House and Senate). While any member of Congress could always introduce legislation, for all practical purposes, whether that legislation moved in the 1970s was largely within the control of the subcommittee and full committee chairmen.

It is important to note that the Congress was not divided so clearly along partisan lines during the 94th and 95th Congresses, the time period of this portion of the story, as it is today. While Democrats had a large majority in each body, the dominant voting bloc consisted of Republicans and conservative Southern Democrats. This did not affect the ability of Democrats to choose the leaders of the House and Senate and committee chairmen and to set the agenda, but a simple count of Democrats and Republicans grossly overstated the power of liberal and moderate Democrats to advance their desired legislation. This reality played out during the no-fault debate as it did in all others.

The majority party also had far more staff than the minority. In the Senate, staffing ratios traditionally have been two to one in favor of the majority, while House ratios have varied over time (during the no-fault fight in the House, the relevant subcommittee had about a four-to-one staffing ratio).

Then, the staff played a much larger role in the development of legislation because the members gave them a great deal of leeway. As a result, the staff tended to be entrepreneurial. The best staff recognized that good ideas for legislation come from both the majority and the minority as well as from both the private sector and the public. The goal was to come up with the best, most workable, politically doable ideas to improve Americans' lives from one's political perspective. Thus, it was vital to be open to others' ideas and, most important, to be able to tell the difference between a good idea and a bad one.[1] It was also important to give credit to others when they provided valuable input. It was not only intellectually honest but also gave others an investment in the final product. As one of my bosses, Sen. Christopher Dodd of Connecticut, used to say, "You can accomplish a lot when you are willing to give others credit."

In the days when committees dominated the development of legislation, once a chairman decided to tackle an idea, there was an intimate interaction between the member and the staff to determine whether to proceed from a concept to legislation and, if so, what elements should go into a bill. When dealing with a complex subject matter, this placed a lot of responsibility on the staff. It often meant reading thousands of pages of material, both pro and con, and talking with all interested parties.

Understanding the nuances of an issue was a necessary, but not sufficient, requisite for staff. In addition, the staffer had to have both strong written and verbal skills. He or she needed to convert the knowledge gained into a form that fit the chair's limited time and ability to digest materials. This usually meant short memos, no more than three or four pages in most cases, and in-person discussions of both the substance and politics. While staff had great freedom and power to perform these duties, they were walking a high wire. There were no civil service protections on the Hill (and there still aren't). If staff failed/fell, most members were not there to catch them. That left the staffer on the street, fired. Many of today's committee staff lack these skills because the members seem less willing to delegate broad authority to them and because most major legislation, while it may go through committees first, is negotiated by the leadership and included in omnibus bills.

In the case of no-fault, the issue came to Sen. Phil Hart's attention through a combination of the senator's reading and the work of Dean Sharp, a staffer on the Senate Antitrust and Monopolies Subcommittee of the Judiciary Committee, a subcommittee that Senator Hart chaired. He owed his position to the seniority system, through which members were rewarded for their length of service.

Both Hart and Sharp had read the Keeton-O'Connell book. The book had been well publicized, in part because of the ability of Professor O'Connell to describe the issues in simple but colorful terms. At a time when the Congress was passing major consumer and regulatory legislation—such as the creation of the Environmental Protection Agency (EPA), the National Highway Traffic Safety Administration (NHTSA), the Occupational Safety and Health Administration, the Consumer Product Safety Commission and the Pension Benefit Guaranty Corporation and the revitalization of the FTC—no-fault was ripe for federal legislation. But that begged the question of which committee would have jurisdiction to consider it and what form it would take.

As described earlier, Senator Hart decided to include the issue in broader hearings he was holding on many automobile issues, including safety and ratings. As with any hearings, it was Sharp's job to identify witnesses who could explain the issue in a manner that would attract both member and press interest. The witnesses often also needed the skill to counter arguments from other witnesses who disagreed with their views. As in most other areas of the legislative process, the majority always had the advantage. When committees dominated, that meant that they got to determine when the hearings would be held and to choose more witnesses than the minority. Most hearings had one or two panels of four witnesses apiece, with the majority choosing three of the four witnesses on each panel. Having the right witnesses was critical, whether they were sympathetic victims, academic experts, or interested businesses—or all of the above. It was also important whom the chair and staff chose to put on each panel, another matter within the control of the majority, as they wanted to make sure the supporters weren't outshone by the opponents. This meant finding witnesses who were not only knowledgeable but articulate, capable of speaking in language members understand.

Senator Hart's subcommittee started with hearings on the topic rather than on a specific piece of legislation. Once Senator Hart decided to proceed with legislation, it was up to Dean Sharp to work with the Office of Legislative Counsel (the technical drafters for the House and Senate) to write legislation. Good staff, as Sharp was, also had to be deeply involved in the actual drafting. Legislation had to be written precisely to carry out its purpose and be workable for those in the private sector who must implement it in order to be successful. Too many staff simply present a legislative counsel with a general idea and then leave it up to the counsel to draft the actual language. The best legislation is the product of staff and legislative counsel working together. In the case of the no-fault bill that I drafted later in 1975, it took three of us six weeks and eight drafts to get it right. Had the bill become law, the work product would have been clear enough to withstand judicial misinterpretation and easy to implement. The workability part was the by-product of spending countless hours with insurance industry experts until we knew how their business worked, both on paper and in practice, and with consumer and labor groups until we understood the problems of injured people and the best way to address them.

Committee staff also had to work with member press staff in outreach to the media to explain the legislation and why it was needed. In addition, they needed to be able to explain the legislation to the staffs of other members of Congress and to people who would be affected by it in the hope of generating outside support for the legislation.

There was another key component that was more feel or "art" than knowledge. It involved an almost innate sense of when the time was right for action, whether it be to hold hearings or to move a bill to markup (committee consideration of the bill and amendments) and when and how to compromise. In my experience, this sense of timing was almost instinctual; it could not be taught. Acting too early or too late could be disastrous, as could failing to compromise when necessary to move a bill forward—or giving away too much by compromising when you didn't need to.

The members needed to believe there was a need for legislation, both on substantive grounds and because the public was demanding it. Getting to that point often involved careful orchestration, with staff identifying interested parties and educating them as to the benefits of a bill for them and their need to organize on behalf of legislation, and outreach to opinion leaders, in all the different media. In the case of no-fault, the staff (including me) spoke to innumerable interested parties and consumer and labor organizations and reached out to editorial boards and writers. Without all this advance work, the members would not have been as receptive to the witnesses or to the bill.

It was also staff's job to know not only where the members stood on an issue but how to influence them to support the chair's legislation. That could take many forms, including understanding the member's political philosophy, constituents, and politics of reelection as well as what the chairman could do to help—or harm—the member. The staff needed to be diplomatic, developing and using arguments that were most likely to move members toward the chair's goal and doing so without members believing they were being manipulated.

After hearings were completed, the chair, again in consultation with staff, had to decide when the time was ripe for markup. If a bill was reported from committee for floor consideration, then the staff had to draft a committee report. The report described the purpose of the bill and contained a section-by-section analysis of its provisions. As with drafting legislation, writing reports required detailed knowledge of the subject matter and precision in writing because being 99 percent correct wasn't good enough. The best committee reports told a story in a clear and convincing narrative. At the same time, inasmuch as[2] any incorrect statement of fact could be used by the opposition to bring into question all the accurate statements, I chose to use footnotes to the simple narrative to address technical issues. In this way, the technical points did not get in the way for people interested in the basic rationale but were there for those interested in more detail and acted as a defense against those looking to discredit the report by finding an inaccuracy. I also found it valuable to include in the bill a summary of the need for the legislation and how the bill would meet that need for members who might read only the first few pages.

As it says in all the civics books, after legislation is reported from committee, it moves to the floor of the House or Senate for amendments and a vote on final passage (this was true in the 1970s and is still true for the more limited number of bills that go through the committee process today). In the days when the committees were the main source of legislation, once a bill was on the floor of either body, it was vital to know the rules and to work with the leadership's floor staff to try to orchestrate what amendments were offered and to identify where members stood on the bill and what needed to be done to secure their support. This work was often quite technical and subtle, but it was very important. For example, during consideration of FTC legislation in 1981, we knew we were going to lose badly on an amendment by Rep. Elliott Levitas (D-GA)[3] to strike a provision in the bill limiting congressional review of FTC actions. The goal was to avoid a recorded vote so the bill wouldn't go into conference with a clear showing of House support for a provision the chairman opposed. That would have afforded him more leeway to negotiate a compromise. Since only a member on the losing side of a voice vote can request a recorded vote, we asked Speaker Tip O'Neill's staff to have him rule that the Levitas amendment had won on the voice vote (which we knew it would). Of course, things don't always go as planned, and in that situation, the speaker ruled that the Levitas amendment had failed on the voice vote, which it clearly hadn't. His ruling enabled Levitas to secure a recorded vote, which he won handily, the outcome we had tried to avoid. That vote, in turn, limited the House's ability to try to weaken the Levitas amendment in conference more than would have been the case if the speaker had ruled that the amendment had prevailed on the voice vote.

Finally, a good staffer had to help his or her boss prevail on important issues in the House-Senate conferences that resolved differences between House- and Senate-passed bills. Conferences were primarily an inside game involving the key members (conferees) and staff and, in the early 1970s, were often conducted behind closed doors (in the words of Lin Manuel Miranda, "in the room where it happens").

In sum, to be a good Hill committee staffer in the 1970s, one had to be able to (1) identify issues that were important to people's lives; (2) research each issue thoroughly; (3) incorporate the knowledge of public and private interested parties and other Hill staff, majority and minority, to devise a detailed idea; (4) distinguish good ideas from bad ideas; (5) plan hearings to learn more about an issue and to increase support for an idea from both members of Congress and the public; (6) participate fully in the drafting process to produce legislation that would work as intended in the real world; (7) identify outside interested parties and work with them to generate public support; (8) work with members and staff to secure the necessary votes; (9) write committee and conference reports that clearly explained the bill's rationale and how, in detail, the legislation was intended to work; and (10) be an expert in committee and floor procedure. Finally, as I mentioned, the best staff also had to have intuition, a sense of when the time was right to move a bill forward and when to compromise. This was the art part of legislation, which few staff had.

While the same qualities are required of good staff today, the diminution in importance of the committee role in major legislation and the increase in partisanship have made work on the Hill less attractive. As a result, staff tend to stay for shorter periods of time. The Bipartisan Select Committee on the Modernization of Congress in the House in 2019 addressed this loss of staff expertise and its implications: "The median tenure for every staff position in Congress is three years or less, decreasing expertise and eroding what few bipartisan bonds exist among staff, [Rep. Derek Kilmer (D-WA)] said. 'The capacity of the institution erodes and what fills that space is the executive branch and lobbyists.'"[4] The commentary is right on the mark. If Congress wants to become an effective legislative body again, one of the things it will have to address is what it will take to make staff want to stay long enough to develop the skills needed to be effective.

6. “Van Deerlin’s a Really Nice Guy, but that Kinzler’s a Son of a Bitch”

Early House Hearings and Chairman-Staff Relationships (1975)

I enthusiastically started work on the subcommittee on April 1, 1975. Van Deerlin was an extremely nice, laid-back Californian. As Van Deerlin had been a television broadcaster before being elected to the House, he spoke in perfect sentences. That was a great boon for all who worked for him, as one of the jobs of a congressional staffer is to correct members’ grammar for the official record of hearing and floor proceedings, a second chance that most people do not get in their daily pursuits.

What Van Deerlin had not been was a lawyer or a member of the Consumer Subcommittee, so he had limited knowledge of no-fault. Like many members of the Commerce Committee, he had cosponsored a no-fault bill, H.R. 1272, the National No-Fault Motor Vehicle Insurance Act. Like most of those who had cosponsored the bill, he had done so out of respect for its author, Rep. Bob Eckhardt, one of the leading consumer legislators in the House. However, H.R. 1272 was unlike the no-fault bill the Senate had passed and the House companion bill authored by Rep. John Moss, Van Deerlin’s predecessor as subcommittee chairman, all of which meant that Van Deerlin was interested in no-fault as a consumer issue but not knowledgeable about the details of the different proposals.

To become better informed, he tasked me to study the issue and then make a recommendation as to whether to proceed with legislation and, if so, what approach to take. I undertook this assignment at a considerable remove from the main House office buildings. With large new subcommittee staffs[1] because of the Watergate Class, space was at a premium. The House took over the old Federal Bureau of Investigation (FBI) fingerprinting building, located three blocks and one major road from the foot of the Rayburn House Office Building. It was to become the Ford House Office Building, but when the subcommittee staff moved in, it

Figure 6.1. Subcommittee Chairman Lionel Van Deerlin. The inscription reflects his sardonic wit.

was just House Office Building #2, a rundown building with window air conditioners and leaking PCBs in the basement.

Its remove by a four-lane road from the main House office buildings and committee hearing rooms had one significant advantage over greater proximity. It meant that lobbyists couldn't just drop in. If they wanted to see any subcommittee staffer, they had to make a conscious effort. The greater quiet facilitated the ability to concentrate.

I was starting my no-fault research at a disadvantage because I had avoided taking an insurance law course in law school, and there was no way to understand the subject or draft legislation that would carry out its consumer goals without intimate knowledge of how auto insurance works. I also needed to understand the negative implications of the existing fault and liability insurance system for people injured in automobile accidents.

To make this mammoth task manageable, I decided to ask each interested party represented in Washington, DC—from trial lawyers and insurance defense lawyers to insurers, labor unions, consumer groups, and DOT—to provide me with their best one hundred pages on the subject. In addition, I agreed to have lunch with each of them so they could make an in-person pitch. After that, I told them that unless I had questions, I did not want to hear from them again until I had worked my way through the materials.

My first task was to sort out the substantive arguments. To do so, it was important, but not dispositive, to know each organization's economic interest in the outcome. It was easy to understand why lawyers for both plaintiffs and defendants would oppose the legislation, but they had serious arguments that I needed to assess. Insurers, who had a direct economic interest, were divided, and I needed to understand why.

Meeting with these groups with a wide array of views and interests proved a fascinating experience. Among lobbyists for insurers that supported no-fault, Les Cheek of the American Insurance Association, Herm Brandau of State Farm, and Bob Quinn[2] of Nationwide were deeply knowledgeable. Cheek and Brandau had encyclopedic knowledge of both no-fault policy and the everyday workings of the insurance industry. They couldn't have been more different in background and appearance. Cheek, a prematurely gray-haired WASP patrician whose given name was Leslie Cheek III, had been educated at elite East Coast schools—Harvard University, Columbia School of Journalism, and Georgetown Law School—and was always well tailored. Brandau was Jewish, shorter, had been educated at Midwestern schools—University of Illinois and Loyola University Chicago School of Law—and wore loud suits (I was not really one to talk about loud clothes, as I favored homemade suits with highly unusual patterns and handmade ties made from drapery materials). The only difference was availability. Cheek was headquartered in DC, a local phone call or short cab ride away. Brandau, on the other hand, was headquartered in Bloomington, Illinois, a long-distance paid phone call away (there were such things in 1975), although he came to town frequently. Brandau did have one significant advantage over Cheek—access to State Farm's wondrous chief actuary, Dale Nelson. While quite different in style and appearance, Cheek and Brandau were whip-smart and equally conversant with insurance issues and no-fault. They were great resources to answer my endless questions.

Dick Walsh, described in a previous chapter, was the key player for DOT. He had overseen the writing of twenty-five-volumes of the DOT study of the tort system and motor vehicle crashes and written the summary twenty-sixth volume that recommended adoption of a no-fault system.

The interests of consumer groups, labor, and the AARP were less obvious. As much as anything, they were part of the political landscape of the time. The late 1960s and 1970s were a time when the consumer movement was at its peak, and the federal government had responded by taking actions it believed would provide consumers with the information they needed to make more informed buying decisions, to protect themselves against unreasonable risks of injury and to secure more competitive lower prices. As noted in a previous chapter, among the successes were the revitalization of the FTC, with both consumer protection and antitrust bureaus, and the creation of the NHTSA, the Occupational Safety and Health Administration, the EPA, the Pension Benefit Guaranty Corporation, and the Consumer Product Safety Commission.

By the mid-1970s, the two major pieces of legislation that remained on the consumer agenda were bills to create a Consumer Protection Agency and to establish standards for no-fault insurance. The efforts to enact them lasted through much of the 1970s until the point where the consumer movement waned. With the notable exception of Ralph Nader and Public Citizen, the organization he founded, all the major consumer groups supported no-fault. They had no economic interest, just the public interest of better compensation for injuries and lower premiums. The good news was that I didn't have to identify an economic interest; the bad news was that they didn't have members who were willing to go the extra mile to protect their livelihood. Kathleen O'Reilly, legislative director of

CFA, was the most knowledgeable and effective of the consumer group supporters.

The AARP and the unions each had an economic interest in the legislation, but it was not as direct as that of the trial bar. The AARP's interest stemmed from the fact that seniors stood to see much lower premiums for personal injury if the Congress passed no-fault legislation. This was the case because premiums would have been based primarily on the potential loss of the insured. Because many seniors were retired, they had little or no work loss and were less likely to have long-term medical issues because of shorter life expectancies. They also had Medicare to pay much of their medical bills, which would also have reduced their auto insurers' obligations. Overall, this meant seniors would use fewer no-fault benefits and cost insurers less, a fact that could be reflected in lower premiums.

The unions also had an economic interest, albeit more speculative than that of the AARP. They hoped to use no-fault in collective bargaining with employers to secure group auto insurance as a benefit to their members. The most active, effective lobbyist for the AFL-CIO was Mike Gildea. The United Auto Workers (UAW), the United Steelworkers and the Communications Workers of America (CWA) were individual unions that were active supporters.

Among the opponents, the most effective—if not the most knowledgeable—was Thomas (Tom) Hale Boggs, Jr., the son of the former majority leader of the House who had died in a plane crash in the Alaskan wilderness. Stout and jovial with a flushed face, Boggs, in another time, could have been a stereotypical lobbyist in a Thomas Nast cartoon. He represented ATLA, whose members stood to lose more than $1 billion a year if the tort system were replaced by a no-fault insurance system of compensation. That would occur because most auto cases would be away from the courts and handled the way health insurance cases are, with insurers paying all injured parties without regard to fault and without the involvement of lawyers.

Boggs showed up one day at my office and made ATLA's pitch against the bill, emphasizing the arguments that injured individuals were entitled to their day in court (the right to sue) and that good drivers would be forced to pay for bad drivers' negligence. I asked him if there were any amendments that ATLA would like to see in a House bill. Boggs pulled out a thick black binder and said, "I have seventy-five amendments. If you adopted all of them, it would gut your bill—and my client would still oppose it!" Well, there's something to be said for honesty.

Given the DOT's comprehensive documentation of the inadequacies of compensation under the tort system and the generous benefits in the no-fault bills, I was convinced that the guaranteed benefits in the no-fault bills were far more valuable to injured persons than a right to sue under the tort system that the DOT study found resulted in recoveries for only half the victims and paid them only 30 percent in serious injury cases. As for the argument that good drivers would pay for bad drivers, the bill excluded drunken drivers and intentional injuries from the limitations on the right to sue. Moreover, drivers who caused accidents would be treated exactly the same way under no-fault as they were under the tort system—with a surcharge on their premium.

I also heard from insurers who opposed the legislation. Darrell Coover, who represented the National Association of Independent Insurers (NAII), the largest insurer trade association, was tall, thin, balding, a member of Mensa (a fact he shared with all, whether anyone asked him or not), and oily. I disliked him the minute I met him, and that didn't change over time. It's possible that my descriptions of the key players could be colored by my view of the positions they held, but I leave that up to the reader.

Coover's main argument was one of federalism: that auto insurance was traditionally a matter handled at the state level and was best left there. He argued that the states should be given more time to consider reforms before the Congress considered federal legislation.[3] He said that his trade association wasn't anti-no-fault, pointing to the fact that its largest member, Allstate, was working for the adoption of no-fault in the states. While the federalism argument was a perfectly reasonable one, I discovered that most NAII members were small insurers, and they had three more practical concerns. The first was that they were afraid that a standardized no-fault system would enable large insurers to use their economies of scale to drive smaller insurers out of business. The second was that if auto insurance were transformed into a primarily health insurance system, health insurers would enter the business, providing yet another competitive threat to the existence of NAII's smaller insurers. The third was that if the federal government mandated no-fault insurance, it would be the first step towards either a federal takeover of the business or regulation of insurance. In the latter, more realistic scenario, what insurers feared most was rate regulation. The industry's fears were not unfounded, as earlier no-fault bills had contained federal rate regulation provisions, and there was still significant support for rate regulation within the consumer community and in the Congress.

I had two problems with Coover's arguments, however: (1) by 1975, it had already become clear that most states would not enact no-fault laws, so if no-fault were to become law universally, it would have to be through the enactment of federal legislation, and (2) the same NAII companies that opposed federal no-fault on states' rights grounds had, only a few years before, supported the federal legislation that had created the National Flood Insurance Program, the Federal Crime Insurance Program, and the Federal Riot Reinsurance Program. This hypocrisy undercut much of my sympathy for their opposition to federal no-fault. The fourth and final concern was that the lower costs no-fault promised would have an impact on the stock price of NAII companies that operated as stock companies. Lower revenues, even with the same markup, would result in lower profits; thus, they feared lower stock prices.

While I believed that the NAII's federalism argument was largely a smokescreen to protect the economic interest of its members in maintaining the tort system, I was to find out just how powerful the argument could be when presented by more respected and well-placed opponents. The same month I was starting my investigation of no-fault, Attorney General Edward Levi was arguing that the Ford administration should oppose federal legislation on the grounds of federalism. As the next chapter shows, Levi's opposition proved to be the key reason that the Ford administration decided to oppose the bill. Its opposition, coupled with significant opposition within the auto insurer community, led to near-universal opposition from Republicans in the House and to six Republican senators changing their votes.

As the subcommittee counsel working on no-fault, I had access to some of the most brilliant law professors. It was in their interest, as advocates for no-fault, to help me understand insurance law and its policy implications for motor vehicle crash victims and to understand the limitations of the general principles of tort law. This knowledge enabled me to draft defensible and workable legislation. Drafting legislation in a way that works for those who must live by its terms is critical to its success.

A good idea without a practical, workable form of implementation disserves both the idea and the people who must follow the law. For no-fault, that was to mean a lot of time drafting.

The first academics I consulted were the creators of no-fault, Professors Keeton and O'Connell. They were a bit of a Mutt and Jeff couple, with O'Connell serving as Mutt. Keeton was tall and balding and answered questions in a professorial manner. O'Connell was shorter, much more aggressive, and very colorful, much in the manner of a trial lawyer. They were the most helpful to me initially, along with two others. The first was Yale Law School Prof. Guido Calabresi, an Italian immigrant who was voted one of the top ten law professors under age forty in the United States. He was soon to become the school's dean and later a federal judge on the Second Circuit Court of Appeals. Calabresi's no-fault work was brilliant but harder to understand. He, too, made time to answer my questions. The fourth helpful professor was William Cohen of Stanford Law School, who was the coreporter and drafter of UMVARA (the model state law). He was the rare law professor who specialized in both tort and constitutional law and was a great help in addressing the constitutional issue raised by Pres. Gerald Ford's Department of Justice (DOJ). During the two months I was learning the subject, I spent countless hours talking with all of them. As with Cheek and Brandau, I never had to worry that any of them would mislead me.

Among all the wonderful sources of information I had access to, my greatest source of knowledge came from the Senate Commerce Committee. Less than twenty-four hours after I was assigned no-fault, I got a call from Bob Joost, the Senate Commerce Committee's legislative counsel who had drafted the Senate bill and had testified before the Hart subcommittee. Joost, at the request of Lynn Sutcliffe, the general counsel of the Senate Commerce Committee, "volunteered" to help educate me. Joost was a handsome, if somewhat disheveled, individual, but what stood out were his brilliance, perseverance, and commitment to no-fault (and revision of the US criminal code). As he represented the public interest, with no private stake in the outcome, I took him up on his offer. As I waded through the mounds of materials, I regularly sought out Joost's help. The good news was that Joost had either an answer to every question or a creative solution to every problem. The bad news was that Joost spoke at great length, sometimes eating up hours at a clip.

I quickly discovered Joost's background and connection to no-fault. A magna cum laude graduate of Yale, Joost was in his second year at Harvard Law School when he lost emotional control. He found himself in a mental institution, from which he was not released until the doctors discovered, with Joost's help, that lithium offered a successful treatment for bipolar disorder. Joost returned to Harvard, where he was an editor of the *Harvard Law Review* and again graduated magna cum laude. While there, he became friends with both Michael Dukakis and Elizabeth (Liddy) Hanford. Dukakis went on to become the governor of Massachusetts and the unsuccessful Democratic candidate for president in 1988, while Hanford went on to marry Sen. Robert Dole and to become a US senator and secretary of labor, among several high-profile jobs. Joost also became friends through the law review with future Supreme Court Justice Antonin Scalia. Joost even introduced Scalia to his future wife.

As described earlier, Joost's initial involvement with no-fault was notable—hopping a plane to testify in favor of no-fault before Senator Hart's subcommittee in 1971 despite the fact that he was employed by the trial bar, the most significant opponent of no-fault. Then, after he was fired by ATLA and hired by the Senate Commerce Committee, he worked tirelessly to advance no-fault in the Congress.

As I worked to understand the issues behind no-fault, I discovered which lobbyists I could trust to give me the complete picture. Some lobbyists try to cut corners on behalf of their clients, giving members of Congress and staff partial or misleading information to secure a benefit for their clients. While they might win one victory this way, it is shortsighted, as they are likely to be shunned afterward. Staff typically will give lobbyists who provide full information the opportunity to explain any weaknesses in their client's position and, if necessary, the opportunity to work together to address their concerns in a way that would not undermine public policy.

After reviewing all the arguments, I found those in favor of proceeding with legislation to be compelling. As for arguments by interest groups opposed to the legislation, I concluded that the primary reason for opposition was the potential for lost revenue, the billions (1) Insurers stood to lose if no-fault lowered premiums and (2) trial lawyers stood to lose if their services were no longer required. What I did not fully appreciate at the time was that by the mid-1970s, ATLA would have the largest single-issue political action committee, according to Common Cause, and that it gave most of its money to Democrats, the bill's primary congressional supporters.

Finally, on June 12, 1975, I handed Van Deerlin a thirty-four-page memo describing criticisms of the fault system and the arguments for and against replacing it with a no-fault system as well as the politics. He read it, and we talked about it at length. Then he instructed me to develop a House bill along the lines of the Senate bill and the Moss bill for hearings and consideration by the subcommittee.

In retrospect, what stands out about the memo is its length. Later, during twelve years in the Senate, my boss, Senator Christopher J. Dodd (D-CT), wanted short memos, no longer than two pages and preferably just one page. As mentioned before, the primary reason for the difference is that the Senate has only 100 members to do the work that 435 do in the House. Senators serve on far more committees and subcommittees and have to respond to statewide constituencies. As a result, they do not have the time to read such lengthy memos, with a few exceptions (I will discuss later my experience with one such individual, Sen. Jay Rockefeller [D-WVA], on product liability legislation).

I took one uncommon step before planning the hearings. The trial bar and some law professors had argued that the structure of the no-fault bill was unconstitutional in that if a state refused to adopt a state plan that conformed with its provisions, an older version of the bill would have required the state to administer an alternative state no-fault plan (which had been defined in the bill). The trial bar hired Prof. Norman Dorsen of New York University School of Law to write a letter endorsing that position. Responding to the constitutionality concern, the Senate redrafted the provision to eliminate the constitutionality issue by having the secretary of DOT, rather than state officials, administer an alternative state plan. I picked up the phone and called Dorsen. He agreed that the change solved the problem, so Van Deerlin followed up with a letter on July 1, 1975, to lock in Dorsen's position. On August 7, 1975, Dorsen responded with a letter confirming that there no longer was a constitutionality issue. Then Boggs called to complain that we[4] had violated protocol by directly contacting the professor they had hired to support their provision. Like all interest groups, ATLA was interested only in experts who agreed with its position.

With Van Deerlin committed to moving no-fault legislation, he and I discussed how to structure the hearings and whom to invite. Van Deerlin was able to take advantage of the majority's right to choose the lion's share of the witnesses. Typically, at the hearings, there would be four witnesses: three chosen by the majority and one by the minority. Then Van Deerlin circulated a fifteen-page memorandum on June 13, 1975, that described the background of the hearings and the arguments for and against federal legislation and identified the witnesses for the first three hearings.

The subcommittee started holding hearings to build support among the subcommittee members so that the votes would be there to report the bill to the full committee. The subcommittee held nine hearings between June 17 and July 25, 1975, during which it received fifty-two statements from witnesses and other interested parties. Thirty-four organizations were represented, including three national insurance trade associations, six state bar associations and the American Bar Association (ABA), the American Association of Retired Persons (AARP), CFA, the defense bar, and DOT, per Sec. William Coleman.

Secretary Coleman, on behalf of the Ford administration, was the lead (and very unhappy) witness on the first day. Coleman, a dapper dresser and somewhat rotund African American, had played a significant role as a lawyer in the civil rights movement and was a very well-respected lawyer. He was unhappy because he had lost a fight in the new Ford administration to have it endorse federal no-fault legislation. Secretary Coleman, of course, played the good soldier, doing the best he could to defend the administration's position while making the case for no-fault. He grounded his argument in federalism:

> We believe there is much to be gained from allowing the States to continue experimenting with different paths and approaches. At least as important, however, is the fact that President Ford and this administration is [*sic*] strongly committed to the principles of federalism—to keeping the decisions of Government and the administration of Government's functions as close to the people as possible. This philosophy, which as I understand it, is the basis of the Federal Constitution, results in political decisions to take away from the States only those functions which are . . . matters in which the State's failure to resolve the problem is clear, undisputable, and beyond

> doubt delayed too long after there is recognition that the basic change must be made.
>
> Some have argued and will continue to argue that the State actions in accepting no-fault have been too slow or misdirected.
>
> Progress is being made and experience gained, but I for one—and I am pretty sure I can speak for Secretary Brinegar and also Secretary Volpe [his immediate predecessors at DOT] would have hoped for more State action. This, however, is really not the point. Either we believe in a Federal system or we don't. We will not have a Federal system if the Federal Government interferes with the State activity every time we in the Federal sector disagree either with the pace or direction of the State activity.
>
> Having said that, I want to underscore that we do agree with much of the substantive reform processes contained in these various pieces of legislation. It is very wrong to categorize the administration's position in any way as opposition to no-fault. We support the principle but we seek the adoption through actions of the individual states.[5]

Van Deerlin and other Democrats peppered him with questions as to why the subcommittee should wait any longer to see if the states would act when it was clear they wouldn't. Secretary Coleman parried that enough time had not elapsed to justify federal actions. Finally, under questioning from Rep. Ralph Metcalfe (D-IL) about how much time the administration believed would have to pass before federal action was justified, Secretary Coleman opined that the states should have another two to five years before congressional action.[6]

Secretary Coleman's time frame was a frustrating one for subcommittee members who supported no-fault, as then DOT Secretary John Volpe had told the Senate Commerce Committee at a March 18, 1971, hearing that the Nixon administration supported the concept of no-fault insurance but preferred that the states be given an opportunity to enact their own no-fault laws before the federal government intruded. Volpe recommended that Congress enact a resolution urging the states to adopt their own laws: "We believe that the change should take place at the State level but that there should be general national goals or principles [comprehensive no-fault benefits and a tight restriction on the right to sue] towards which the States will be moving."[7] At the end of 25 months, the secretary would report back to Congress on progress in the States, "concluding with the Secretary's views regarding the feasibility of attaining a satisfactory and compatible motor vehicle accident reparations system without further Federal legislation."[8]

As the last member was finishing his questioning, two bells rang on the committee hearing-room clock, signifying a recorded vote on the House floor. Van Deerlin, aware that my mother was in the audience, leaned over and asked if I'd like to have Coleman stay so I could ask him questions. While I had nothing brilliant in mind, I agreed for the same reason. After making Coleman wait for some twenty-five minutes while the members voted, Van Deerlin resumed the hearing, and I asked my own questions for the first time. After I finished, Van leaned over and chided me, saying, "I made the secretary of transportation wait twenty-five minutes for that?"

Having counsel ask questions after the members had completed theirs was a fairly common practice on some committees. Given that the witnesses often had deeper knowledge of the details of the legislation and, of course, of their own businesses or professions, they sometimes were able to provide misleading answers to members. As staff were more steeped in the details, their ability to ask questions helped ensure more accurate information for the members.

The second witness, Tom Downs, testified about the model state law as chairman of the Committee of the National Conference of Commissioners on Uniform State Laws. Downs was a wonderful witness, presenting clear, cogent arguments for a federal bill in colorful fashion. He used a cloth board with different-colored pieces to demonstrate where an insurance dollar went under the tort system. He used white cloth to show the injured person's limited recovery and then commented on yet another risk (not previously mentioned): "I did make one presentation in which this whole white part fell down, and I told the committee that that was to show the committee that the individual lost the appeal that he had in his original claim."[9]

On June 19, 1975, the second day of hearings, the first witness was Craig Spangenberg, the chairman of the Auto Reparations Committee for ATLA and its lead spokesman on no-fault. It quickly became apparent why he was such a successful trial lawyer, as he put on a dazzling performance. He started by discussing the history of accident law, tracing it back to pre-1600 England and the doctrine of absolute liability, under which a person was liable for the consequences of his or her actions regardless of any other considerations.[10] He followed by describing, in detail, the changes in accident law from 1600 to 1975. Then he moved to his main thesis, that the twenty-six-volume DOT study was either wrong in its critique of the tort system or was being misinterpreted. With most members' eyes glazing over, Spangenberg tried to use insurance industry jargon to undermine one of the key findings of the DOT report and a key rationale for no-fault, that too little of the bodily injury liability premium wound up in the pockets of injured persons, as opposed to insurers and trial lawyers. To do so, he cited the statistic that the "insurance company payout" to injured people from a dollar of auto liability premium was 64.1 percent, He contrasted that with the fact that only 59.2 percent was paid out under collision insurance, a no-fault coverage. He concluded, "So they pay out more for fault liability insurance than they pay out in no-fault collision."[11]

Spangenberg was attempting to undermine one of the key rationales for the no-fault legislation, and it was important to set the record straight for the members. It presented the first opportunity for Van Deerlin and me to work as a team during a hearing to make sure the members understood the facts. First, Van Deerlin brought Spangenberg up short by asking, "Is this take-home money for the beneficiary?" Spangenberg tried to dance around the answer by asking Van Deerlin to tell him such things as who the claimant was and whether he had hired a lawyer and by challenging the methodology of the DOT study.[12]

After the other members had completed their questions, it was my job to drive home the point the chairman had made with more details to make sure the members saw through the witness's attempted deception:

> Mr. Kinzler: Those figures [the 64.1 percent insurance company liability payout] also, however, included approximately 8 percent for such things as defense attorneys' fees [and 16 cents for plaintiffs' attorneys' fees, as well as other monies not paid to the injured person]. When you add all these figures up, they come to about 30 percent; 30 percent of those benefits are not dollar bills going to the claimant. So, they are insurance company pay-out, but not consumer paid-in.
>
> Mr. Spangenberg [conceding the point but trying to change the sub-

ject]: They are not consumer retention. My only argument was that if the consumer didn't have the attorney he would not get the benefits.[13]

Spangenberg was followed by Prof. William Cohen, the coreporter and draftsman for the Commissioners on Uniform State Laws that had drafted the model state law, UMVARA. Cohen used his professorial skills and detailed knowledge of tort and liability insurance to lay out the case for no-fault.[14] As both Spangenberg and Cohen were far more knowledgeable than the members about the intricacies of the issue, the members asked whether the subcommittee could hold another hearing with a debate between proponents and opponents.

Expectations for fireworks were high for the July 23, 1975, hearing that featured a debate between one of the cocreators of no-fault and Craig Spangenberg, the lead spokesman for the trial bar. The choice for the pro-no-fault position was between Prof. Robert Keeton of Harvard Law School and Prof. Jeffrey O'Connell of the University of Illinois College of Law at Urbana-Champaign. Having had many conversations with both, I preferred O'Connell because he was by far the more aggressive debater of the two. Then-Professor Calabresi described O'Connell as follows: "He was, without doubt, Bob Keeton's bulldog. He was the explainer, the developer and the broadest and most effective proponent of 1st party."[15]

The timing was not good for O'Connell to testify, as he was very frustrated that the federal bill had not become law in 1974 after it had passed the Senate. He told me, rather brusquely, that he would not testify before the subcommittee unless I could assure him no-fault would move through the committee. As I could provide no such assurance, O'Connell declined the invitation, and the subcommittee invited Keeton instead.

While I was a little concerned about how Keeton, the tall, thin, urbane Texan, would fare against the slightly disheveled, experienced Cleveland trial lawyer, nevertheless, we were expecting a dynamic, educational confrontation.

Unfortunately, my fears were realized. First, Keeton laid out the case against the tort system and in favor of no-fault in a calm, professorial way. After his formal testimony, he answered members' questions in the same manner. While Keeton was speaking, Spangenberg was loudly shuffling papers, tapping his pencil against the witness table, and frantically scribbling on his yellow legal pad, as one might expect a lawyer to do in court to distract attention from his opponent's argument.

Then Spangenberg attacked every one of Keeton's premises and conclusions while gesturing flamboyantly. Instead of enacting no-fault, he proposed the alternative favored by the trial bar, so-called add-on no-fault. The idea was to require insurers to offer no-fault benefits but place no restrictions on lawsuits. Spangenberg argued that the add-on approach would not increase insurance costs because injured persons would be satisfied if their insurer treated them fairly by giving them no-fault benefits and not sue afterward. He went further than most in the trial bar by calling for an "add-on/take-off" approach whereby, if a person sued and prevailed, the recovery would be reduced by the amount the person had received in no-fault benefits.

In fact, the predictable result was that, with a little help from their lawyers, injured people would do both—take the no-fault benefits and then sue. They used the no-fault benefits to undermine insurers' most effective tool to force settlements—the fact that it took more than a year to resolve most contested cases because of overcrowded court dockets. This reality often forced the injured person in the tort system to settle for less than the available amount because he or she could not afford to wait that long without any compensation in the interim. The system was unfair to seriously injured people, but it did keep costs down. Add-on no-fault took away this cost control tool and "financed" the suit by giving the injured person benefits for his or her losses as they accrued so that he or she could afford to wait longer for a larger settlement. Absent the threshold in the no-fault bills that limited suits to cases involving serious and permanent injuries, the cost of add-on laws would be much higher.[16]

After the witnesses concluded their testimony, the debate occurred as members asked their questions and Keeton and Spangenberg gave their answers. However, there were no sparks, because of the different styles of the witnesses. Keeton gave short, concise answers, while Spangenberg gave long, complicated answers that confused the members. Furthermore, Spangenberg continued to fiddle with his pen and pad whenever Keeton spoke, often keeping the members' attention on him and distracting them from Keeton's response. Frustrated, when it came my turn to ask questions, I challenged most of what Spangenberg had said, turning the hearing into a debate between Spangenberg and me. Of course, that was not nearly as effective with the members as if Keeton had taken the challenge or one of them had questioned Spangenberg aggressively.

The most memorable hearing was a field hearing that took place on July 14, 1975, in Daytona Beach, Florida. Many in the public think congressional field hearings are wild affairs. Far more field hearings are held in places such as Newark, New Jersey, than in nice climes, and most are calm affairs. This one was at a beautiful site and lived up to the public stereotype. Van Deerlin chose Florida to examine its experience as the second state to adopt a no-fault law, in 1971. The night we arrived in Daytona Beach, our ranking minority member, Rep. John Y. McCollister (R-NE), kept asking where his counsel, Nancy Nord, was. By the time Nord arrived back at the hotel around midnight, she had seven phone messages from McCollister, who threatened to send her home before the hearing. She had been out with Rep. Matt Rinaldo, a Republican member from New Jersey. Both were single; McCollister was not. Others at the hotel included Van Deerlin and his wife, Mary Jo, and Rep. Jim Scheuer (D-NY). Scheuer was also married, but his female companion, his AA, who stayed with him, was not.

The day after the hearing, another subcommittee member, Rep. Bill Stuckey (D-GA), arranged for everyone to fly to NASA's Kennedy Space Center near Cape Canaveral, Florida, on a private plane to see the last Apollo spacecraft liftoff. The plane was owned by a friend of Representative Stuckey and was decorated with a drawing of a Georgia bulldog on the tail, "tastefully" lifting its leg by a fire hydrant! As we boarded the plane, Scheuer asked me who the woman with Van Deerlin was. That was amusing, as Mrs. Van Deerlin was a former airplane stewardess, with the emphasis on former, as this was some thirty-five years later, and the years had taken their normal toll. Obviously concerned about the implications for him, Scheuer left his AA sitting in the back of the plane and moved forward to sit next to Mrs. Van Deerlin. He spent the trip telling her about his wonderful family and showing her pictures.

I had my own troubles on the way over. The plane was a DC-3 prop, one of the first planes used for commercial aviation in the 1930s and 1940s. It was a rocky flight, and I had not brought any Dramamine with me. When we deplaned, I was an unusual shade of green (about the same color I was while dressing in scrubs for my daughter's birth). Noticing my coloring, Van Deerlin asked how I was feeling before embracing me in a bear hug (wisely from behind). We had a spectacular view of the liftoff, which generated a lot of heat, and then headed back to DC for the hard work of moving a no-fault bill through a closely divided subcommittee.

By the end of July, the subcommittee had completed its hearings. Most had gone as anticipated, with state officials and attorney groups opposing federal legislation in order to protect either their regulatory roles or their pocketbooks. On July 22, 1975, William Huff, the insurance commissioner of Iowa, testified as president of the NAIC. When it was my turn to ask questions, I pointed out to him that Iowans experienced the same lack of compensation in many situations as the residents of more urban states, Huff responded, "In the rural areas they are compensated like this. If you have a disability situation in most of the rural areas, what happens is the neighbors come over and have a picnic, plow the field or plant the corn or run the combine, or feed the cows—whatever it is."[17] Initially stunned, I pointed to the limits of neighbors for the seriously injured person: "Let's say that you became a quadriplegic so your neighbors could only do so much and certainly couldn't help [with] your medical costs—you would have whatever the limitations were of your own insurance on medical."[18]

Huff then pointed to health and disability insurance, another red herring, as few people living anywhere had the high levels of such insurance included in the no-fault bill that would protect them against a catastrophic injury. Huff wandered back into the cornfields of Iowa and never admitted to the advantages of no-fault for seriously injured persons.

At the next-to-last hearing, on July 24, 1975, John Martin testified on behalf of the National Retired Teachers Association and AARP. Martin was in his eighties at the time. He was fond of saying bluntly, in private, that "the elderly need no-fault because they could be dead by the time it takes to get paid under the tort system." At the hearing, Martin made the point less bluntly by saying, "Naturally, when a retired person is injured and must await settlement of claims for injuries sustained in an accident, any long delay is a great burden for the elderly person."[19] In a later hearing on July 22, 1977, he testified explicitly about the importance of prompt payment: "Older people, especially the old older people, don't have time to wait, they don't have 5 years to wait [for recovery in more serious injury cases under the tort system]."[20] He went on to explain that

> it is the serious cases that are involved in the maximum delay because it is the serious cases that make it worthwhile for insurance companies and for insurance lawyers to carry on a case at greater length until a settlement can be finally reached so that there is really no question but what the older person is the beneficiary in the situation and that prompt and adequate payment (under no-fault) are the real answer.[21]

The other hearing of note was the last one, on July 25, 1975, when representatives of the ABA and the state bar associations of Texas, Illinois, Missouri, and New Mexico testified. Some knew what they were talking about; most didn't. All merely parroted ATLA talking points. The ABA's opposition was no surprise, as membership on its Special Committee on Automobile Insurance Legislation was voluntary, and most of the members were trial lawyers trying to protect their vested interest in the tort system. As noted in a Ford administration memorandum, "the ABA, in an action wholly consistent with the economic self-interest of its members and with its past positions on no-fault, formally condemned UMVARA at its winter meeting last year [1974]."[22]

The same was true for the state bar associations. Once again, after the members completed their questions, I wound up asking a lot of the questions because many of the issues were too arcane for the members. Afterward, a friend who had been sitting in the audience told me he had overheard one of the bar association representatives say, "Van Deerlin is a really nice guy, but that Kinzler's a son of a bitch." What he failed to understand was that Van Deerlin or, for that matter, any chairman would not let counsel do anything that he or she didn't approve of. Van Deerlin just sat back and played the good cop, leaving me to be the bad cop.

A similar thing happened during the summer when Van Deerlin asked me to fly to California to meet with the Southern California trial bar. He opened the meeting and stayed for about fifteen minutes, leaving them smiling and me to engage with the trial lawyers for another two hours. Afterward, Van Deerlin invited me to play tennis with him. After I beat him 6–2, 6–0, he said with a smile, "You're not supposed to beat your boss." I replied, "After leaving me alone with the trial bar for two and a quarter hours, you're lucky you won two games!"

The flip side of my California experience occurred on August 11, 1975, when Lynn Sutcliffe asked me to substitute for him as a speaker at the

NAIC meeting in Hilton Head, South Carolina. Giving speeches to interested parties is an important part of the job for both members and staff because it plays a role in building support for legislation. In this instance, it was both a generous and shrewd offer from Sutcliffe. I appreciated the opportunity to spend a few days at a lovely resort. However, it was the first time I had spoken formally since I had argued appellate court cases for the NLRB in 1968, and I was nervous. I wrote an eleven-page speech and read every single word.

After giving a few more speeches, I started to relax and give twenty-minute speeches from notes I wrote on a three-by-five card. While that was far more effective, there were times when it didn't matter how articulate I was. One stands out, a speech I gave to a union group on November 11, 1975. The Pittsburg, Pennsylvania, branch of the United Steelworkers had come to DC to lobby members on consumer issues, specifically no-fault and toxic substances regulatory legislation. The first two speakers were Sens. Ted Kennedy and Hubert Humphrey. Both gave rousing stump speeches, barely, if at all, mentioning the two issues. When Humphrey left the room, almost the entire audience followed him out. I was left with my three-by-five card and a roomful of empty chairs. The person organizing the event asked me to refrain from speaking until the workers could be corralled back into the room. I agreed, as I saw no need to have a conversation with myself. The time also gave me the opportunity to try to figure out some hook to get them to listen to what would be a dry speech in comparison to what they had just heard.

About twenty minutes later, the organizers had rounded up about half the audience. I opened with "First, I'd like to thank my warm-up speakers, Senator Kennedy and Senator Humphrey." That got a good laugh, so I continued, "You see, they have an advantage that I don't; they have speechwriters. If my boss, Lionel Van Deerlin, were here today, I'm sure you would hear a rousing speech filled with witty one-liners because, he, too, has a speechwriter—me. Since I don't have a speechwriter, I'm afraid you're going to have to listen to a serious speech about an important issue." I had captured their attention, and the speech went well. I had relearned the value of using humor to engage people.

7. The House Consumer Protection Subcommittee Reports a No-Fault Bill, Only to See the Senate Bill Falter (1975–1976)

By the time the last hearing ended, on July 25, 1975, Van Deerlin felt comfortable proceeding to a markup. Subcommittee markup is the process where members consider a bill and offer amendments and then, if there is support from a majority, send the bill on to the full committee for consideration. If there is support from a majority at both the subcommittee and full committee levels, then the bill goes to the House floor for action. The same process is followed in the Senate.

With the congressional summer recess, which runs from early August until after Labor Day, rapidly approaching, the question was where to advance no-fault next? The Senate appeared to be in good shape. It had passed a bill in 1974, and the Senate Commerce Committee had reported its revised version of S. 354, the National Standards for No-Fault Insurance Act, on July 15, 1975. However, the trial bar was arguing to senators that they shouldn't take a tough vote because the House would not act, and it was having a negative effect. Magnuson and Van Deerlin decided the best way to disprove this argument and provide momentum for the Senate was to mark up and report a bill from the Consumer Protection Subcommittee for the first time. This left a short window for action, as the House was likely to recess in October, about a month after members returned from the summer recess.

Before starting markup, there was still a lot of political and substantive work to do. The subcommittee members were split pretty evenly. To prevail would require the proponents to secure the votes of three members beyond a core of four supporters: (1) the liberal Eckhardt, whose previous work involved using the courts to help clients and whose fertile mind left supporters uncertain as to how he would vote; (2) the sometimes erratic and difficult Rinaldo;[1] and (3) the flaky Jim Scheuer

(D-NY). It was also important to protect Bill Stuckey, a secret supporter, who would help in critical situations but couldn't vote to report a bill because of political considerations at home.

Having listened to the subcommittee members' questions through nine hearings, Van Deerlin and I recognized that the Senate bill was not a good fit for subcommittee markup. The Senate bill had been drafted to pass the Senate. That meant a bill similar to the model state law, UMVARA, so that Magnuson could argue that all the Senate was doing was adopting the bill the states would have adopted if free of political considerations. Once that argument was generally accepted, it was easy to mark up the bill in the Senate Commerce Committee because the committee markups were generally not rigorous and typically lasted just a day. When a senator raised a concern, Chairman Magnuson simply directed the staff to fix the problem *after* the vote to report the bill.

By contrast, it was clear that the House opponents would use every procedural option to prevent markup or drag it on so long that the members would stop coming. In the previous two Congresses, they had used the absence of a quorum to thwart Chairman Moss's attempts to mark up a bill (a subcommittee or committee cannot act in the absence of a majority of its members). Van Deerlin did not want to suffer the same fate. Also, unlike the loose procedures often followed by the Senate Commerce Committee, the House marked up bills line by line. The supporting members had to be prepared for the opponents to offer scores of amendments in the hope of securing the adoption of a killer amendment (one that so undercut the bill that supporters would abandon it) or of trying the supporters' patience by the sheer volume of amendments. It was clear the opponents would also try again to get enough members to stay away to deny the establishment of a quorum. As members served on several subcommittees and had other demands on their time, if the markup went on for days or even weeks, the members who supported the bill would give up and ask Van Deerlin to abandon it.

In this environment, the Senate bill suffered from multiple defects. The bill language was arcane. for example, using the term "reparation obligor" to mean an insurer. A discussion of these terms alone could take hours, both because of their usage and because the definitions section was located at the beginning of the bill. As a result, they would be the first topic for amendment—and delay.

To reduce obstructionism and increase the chances of passage, it was critical to rewrite the Senate bill to avoid a long markup. Van Deerlin agreed that we needed a bill that was similar in substance to S. 354 but without the arcane, professorial language of that bill and one that moved the key substantive provisions from late in the bill to the beginning to shorten the markup.

To effectuate the necessary changes, I invited Bob Joost to join the House legislative counsel and me. The first decision was to move the definitions to the end of the bill and rewrite them, and all other provisions, in terms in common use—the "English-language" version of no-fault. Next, we decided to include a "Findings of Fact; Purposes" section at the beginning of the bill that detailed the deficiencies of the present system and the benefits of no-fault. The section turned out as follows in H.R. 9650, the "National Standards for No-Fault Benefits Act":

DECLARATION OF POLICY

Sec. 102. (a) FINDINGS.—The Congress finds as follows:

(1) Motor vehicles are the major mode of transportation for individuals within the United States. Such transportation occurs in, or affects, interstate commerce.

(2) Since 1946, the Federal Government has expended $79,276,000,000 to build and improve highways for motor vehicle transportation. Since 1946, 1,246,596 persons have died as a result of motor vehicle accidents in the United States and at least 10,000,000 more have been seriously injured.

(3) The maximum feasible rehabilitation of individuals injured in the course of such transportation, and compensation for the economic losses of such individuals or their survivors, are necessary and proper for the protection and advancement of interstate commerce and a suitable and desirable concomitant to the establishment of post roads and the expenditure of moneys therefor.

(4) The prevailing system for compensating such individuals makes recovery of loss contingent upon—

(A) the victim first identifying and showing that someone else was at fault;

(B) the victim first showing that he was without fault or less at fault;

(C) a lawsuit, whenever those showings or others are in dispute; and

(D) the party at fault having sufficient liability insurance or their financial resources to pay for the victim's losses.

(5) This fault system is inefficient, overly costly, incomplete, and slow; allocates benefits poorly; discourages rehabilitation; overburdens the courts; does little if anything to minimize crash losses; and, accordingly, constitutes an undue burden on commerce.

(6) A motor vehicle accident compensation law that—

(A) eliminates, except in cases involving property damage or very serious injuries, the lengthy and costly process needed to determine fault;

(B) assures victims prompt payment of all their medical and rehabilitation costs, recovery of most of their work loss, and compensation for a reasonable amount of replacement loss and loss due to death;

(C) is funded through the mechanism of insurance; and

(D) provides incentives to improve motor vehicle safety and, thereby, minimize loss due to accidents;

is an efficient, low cost, comprehensive, and fair system. The establishment of such a no-fault system nationwide, in place of the prevailing system, would remove such undue burden on commerce.

(7) The Federal Government is authorized to establish and maintain, directly or indirectly, such a nationwide no-fault system, pursuant to the constitutional powers vested in Congress "To regulate Commerce . . . among the several States" and "To establish . . . post Roads."

(8) Direct Federal Government preemptive action is neither necessary nor desirable for this purpose. The uniformity that is necessary among all the States as to the essential elements of such a system can be achieved by Congress by the establishment of national standards for State no-fault benefit plans and a means for assuring compliance with such standards.

(b) PURPOSES.—The purposes of this Act are—

(1) to establish, at reasonable cost to consumers, a comprehensive and fair system which will provide the maximum feasible restoration for motor vehicle accident victims and compensation for the survivors of such victims;

(2) to establish national standards for State no-fault benefit plans funded through insurance and a means for assuring nationwide compliance with such standards; and

(3) to recognize and maintain the authority of the states to regulate the business of insurance, in States with approved State no-fault benefit plans.

The section was designed, in the first instance, to expedite the markup by enabling Van Deerlin to answer key questions by simply pointing to language in the bill itself. The larger purpose was to explain the reasons for federal no-fault legislation to both outside groups and Members of Congress without the need for any document other than the bill. This could prove particularly advantageous on the floor of the House, where members sometimes come with little knowledge of legislation and start to read the bill. The "Findings" section would be a way of making a complicated subject easy for them to understand. We also drafted it to make it easy to find any provision a person might be interested in by including page numbers for every section and subsection in the table of contents. This was rarely, if ever, done in bills when they were introduced. Everything we did was intended to enable people to better understand why no-fault was needed and how it worked in the belief that understanding would increase support.

The most important tactical decision was to move the key substantive provisions—the level of no-fault benefits and the restrictions on lawsuits—to the beginning of the bill, right after the findings and purposes, so the real battle would be won, or lost, quickly.

Little did we know, though I should have suspected based on past experience with Joost, that it would take the entire six weeks of Congress's summer recess and eight drafts to make the changes and reorder and rewrite the bill in English. All three of us had the ability to look at revised drafts with fresh eyes that permitted us to find any flaws. It made the revision an exhausting process, but the final product was an understandable, workable bill and rationale, with all the key decisions in provisions within the first fourteen pages. It was a bill I thought could withstand the strong opposition we expected. And, importantly, the bill was ready for markup when the members returned from the August recess after Labor Day.

To understand the challenge of reporting any bill, it is necessary to understand the composition of the subcommittee. In this case, the subcommittee chairman, Van Deerlin, had been a television broadcaster by trade before being elected to the Congress to represent San Diego, California, in 1962. Van Deerlin was easygoing, albeit with a sharp, sarcastic wit. Because he was not a lawyer, he had let me do much of the questioning during the hearings to bring out the key points. The other five subcommittee Democrats were Bill Stuckey (GA), Bob Eckhardt (TX), Ralph Metcalfe (IL), William Brodhead (MI), and James Scheuer (NY). The full committee chairman, Harley Staggers (WVA), served as an ex officio member, meaning that he had the right to vote. With the ranking minority member, Sam Devine (OH), also having the right to vote, the effect was to bring the ratio of Democrats to Republicans on the committee to 7–3, the Democrats' idea of how to apportion membership in a body that had one more Democrat than an absolute 2:1 majority.[2] There were no women on the subcommittee, which was not a big surprise since there were only nineteen women in the Ninety-Fourth Congress.

Stuckey was a colorful, sharp-witted Southern businessman whose father had founded Stuckey's chain of gift shops and fast food. He was a conservative Democrat who had become familiar with no-fault through hearings he had held as chairman of a subcommittee of the District of Columbia Committee. He favored no-fault—for the District of Columbia, just not for the nation.

Metcalfe was pretty much the opposite of Stuckey, a slow-talking African American from Chicago. In his youth, he had been quite a fast runner, a four-time Olympic medal winner in the sprints at the 1932 and 1936 Olympics. But by 1975, he had slowed considerably, leading me to the hypothesis that all people had an average lifetime speed. Because Metcalfe had used up so much speed as a youth, he now tended to amble. He looked at no-fault through the prism of how it would improve recoveries for low-income people.

Scheuer was from a wealthy Manhattan family. With all the Manhattan congressional seats filled, Scheuer had used his wealth to win a seat representing the Bronx (later, when the number of seats representing the Bronx was reduced by one, Scheuer used his wealth to win a seat representing a district in Queens). Scheuer suffered from a short attention span.

There were only two Democrats, Eckhardt and Brodhead, who were lawyers, and they played critical roles in the markup. Eckhardt was a brilliant, colorful liberal from Houston. A large, handsome man with a prominent nose, he favored bow ties and, in the summer, seersucker suits, which he tended to wear for multiple days at a time. The poor relative of the very wealthy Texas King Ranch family, Eckhardt had used his legal training to represent unions and poor people. His choice of clients enabled him to help a lot of poor people, but it did not help his bank account. Eckhardt had a healthy skepticism about insurers and restrictions on the right to sue, including those necessary to make no-fault work. He had tried to address his concerns by proposing an even more generous no-fault bill. H.R. 1272, the National No-Fault Motor Vehicle Insurance Act, called for no-fault benefits for unlimited medical losses and limited work loss. Unlike other no-fault bills, it would also have allowed an insured to recover no-fault benefits for noneconomic damages. Many thought he had authored the bill as a ploy for the trial bar as a way to kill no-fault, but it was just typical Eckhardt—not confined by any conventional box. The bill would have provided better compensation but at the cost of a huge jump in premiums. But it also presented a political problem. Such was other Democrats' respect for Eckhardt that his bill had garnered the most cosponsors of any of the House no-fault bills, including the cosponsorship of Chairman Van Deerlin. Most important, it was unclear going into the markup whether Eckhardt would vote for the new bill.

Broadhead was a first-term member from the Detroit area, part of the huge Democratic Watergate Class of 1974 that was set on changing the Congress and the world. He was familiar with no-fault from his service in the Michigan House of Representatives at the time that Michigan passed the country's most comprehensive no-fault law, which closely resembled the federal bill. He and his legislative assistant were strong allies in the effort to advance no-fault through hearings and markup.

While only three of the ten members of the subcommittee were lawyers (Rinaldo was one as well), Van Deerlin warned that the large number of lawyers in the House would represent a bar to passage. He cited a *Congressional Quarterly* study that showed that 220 of the 435 members of the House (157 Democrats and 63 Republicans) in the Ninety-Fourth Congress were lawyers. The study showed that an even higher percentage of lawyers served in the Senate (44 Democrats and 22 Republicans).[3]

More challenging were ATLA's political contributions. Common Cause found that in 1976, the Attorneys Congressional Campaign Trust (ACCT), the congressional "gift-giving" arm of the trial bar, had given $127,500 to Senate candidates and $107,150 to House candidates to oppose no-fault. ACCT had contributed $21,500 to 21 of the 43 members of the Commerce Committee.[4] While that level of contributions would be small potatoes today, even adjusted for inflation, it was real money at the time.

The three Republican members were McCollister, the previously described conservative ranking member, Rinaldo, and Devine. While Rinaldo was a no-fault supporter, he had his own bill. The major difference was one provision that was designed to help a specific insurer. The bill's supporters, including its insurer supporters, agreed that its inclusion would likely kill the bill. Still, going into the markup, Rinaldo refused to commit to voting for the new bill, which was nearly identical to his. With the subcommittee members so narrowly divided, Rinaldo had the ability to kill the bill or, at a minimum, cause a great deal of mischief—and he did.

On September 17, 1975, Van Deerlin introduced the product of the summer's drafting, H.R. 9650, the National Standards for No-Fault Benefits Act. Markup started on September 25, 1975, in a hearing room in the Rayburn House Office Building. There were seats and name placards for the members, who were seated on a dais behind a low wooden wall. As counsel, I sat at a long wooden table below, facing them. It was my job to answer any questions they posed to me. These were typically technical questions about how the bill worked.

On the first scheduled day of markup, Scheuer was absent. With only four Democrats and McCollister present for just enough members to establish a quorum (the ex officio members did not count towards a quorum), Van Deerlin banged the gavel and called the subcommittee to order. But before he could even read the first words of the bill, Representative McCollister got out of his seat and headed for the minority staff room. Just as he exited through the door, McCollister raised a point of order that a quorum was not present and then left the room. Without McCollister's presence, there was no quorum, and Van Deerlin had to acquiesce to a motion to adjourn. Denying a quorum was a repetition of the tactic the Republicans had used (with the cooperation of some conservative Democrats) to prevent markup when Representative Moss had chaired the subcommittee in previous Congresses.

The subcommittee was off to a bad start, with two problems to fix. The first was how to get the markup going. This being Van Deerlin's and my first rodeo, we did not know the technicalities of starting the process.

Off I went to check with Charles Johnson, the assistant House parliamentarian, the rules expert. He informed me that if Van Deerlin succeeded in reading the first few lines of the bill while a quorum was present (in the room), the subcommittee would at least have started the markup. I also asked Johnson about the adequacy of the subcommittee markup notice, which quoted the language from the bill that immediately followed the bill number but did not indicate the bill number, H.R. 9650. Johnson indicated that the notice was sufficient because all that is required is notice of the "subject matter," a message I passed along to Van Deerlin. We knew we had to be prepared for any technical challenge. With a full understanding of these rules, we were hopeful that, at worst, we could show progress by technically starting the markup—if we could solve our second problem, getting and keeping a quorum in case we didn't have five Democrats at the next markup.

We set out to solve the problem the easy way, by making sure five Democrats were there. Given Stuckey's awkward political situation, we focused on making sure Scheuer would be there. The Scheuer problem turned out to be easily fixable, albeit in an unusual fashion. We had been surprised by Scheuer's absence because he was a sponsor of the bill that was being marked up, and he had told outside supporters that he would take a leading role in advocating for it. These same supporters spoke with Scheuer after he failed to show for the markup, reminded him of his support for the bill, and addressed several false representations that the trial bar had made to him, including the argument that the bill would put all trial lawyers out of business. While that steadied him a bit, it was clear they needed to do more. One of the lobbyists found the way to make sure Scheuer didn't flake again. He contacted a good friend of his in Scheuer's district, explained both the benefits of the bill and Scheuer's (mis)conduct, and asked him to talk to Scheuer. The friend happened to be Scheuer's rabbi. The rabbi then urged Scheuer to support the bill, which he did. A little unorthodox—but successful.

Per Johnson's ruling, I advised Van Deerlin that the notice was sufficient and how he should rule if McCollister raised a point of order about it. Van Deerlin was also prepared to rapidly recite the necessary language to get started should McCollister again be able to break a quorum. The last thing we needed to do was to make sure McCollister couldn't break a quorum by leaving the room before Van Deerlin started the markup.

The subcommittee had to show some progress in the markup. The plan was to slow McCollister's ability to leave the room and break a quorum if his presence was the only basis for a quorum, i.e., if Scheuer flaked again. As the meeting began, the subcommittee staff clerk went into the minority office, which was located a few feet from McCollister's seat, and locked the door from the inside. If McCollister tried to break a quorum, he would have to leave by the back door, which was much farther away. To slow even that possibility, Gary Frink, the head of the no-fault coalition and a large man, placed himself in front of the back door of the hearing room. Fortunately, Scheuer showed up, and with five Democrats present, there was no need to activate the "obstruct the obstructor's" obstruction plan.

Van Deerlin called the meeting to order and started the markup. As expected, the Republicans challenged practically every provision, starting with the "Findings of Fact." They questioned the figures for the amount of funds expended under the Highway Trust Fund, even though those were official government figures. They succeeded in amendments to add the words "at least" before both of the dollar figures cited in paragraph (2) and to water down section (5) by replacing the conclusions about the deficiencies of the fault system with the qualifier "in some instances," even though the findings were drawn directly from the twenty-six-volume DOT study.

The chairman's first attempt to offer an amendment didn't fare any better. Van Deerlin offered an amendment to provide a subsidy to low-income people. When Representative McCollister derided the amendment as "counsel's amendment" (calling me out as the source of it), Van Deerlin called for a vote on "counsel's amendment, as offered by the Chairman." Not surprisingly, the amendment failed badly. While embarrassing to both Van Deerlin and me, it neither harmed nor advanced the objective of securing the five votes needed to report the bill to the full committee. Going into markup, there were three sure votes—Van Deerlin, Metcalfe, and Brodhead—and it was reasonably likely that Scheuer would vote for the bill. The uncertainty was where the fifth vote would come from. Supporters thought they had made progress with Eckhardt during the hearings, but he was notorious for drafting amendments during markups, which could upset the best-laid plans. Just when it looked as if there were five votes to report the bill, counting Rinaldo's support, he decided to play both ends against the middle. He announced that he would not vote for the bill without a significant rewrite. The substantive changes he insisted on were minor, but the time commitment to rewrite the bill would be substantial. Rinaldo and the opponents believed his ploy had bought them several weeks and even the end of the markup. They were wrong. Les Cheek, the in-town knowledgeable insurer lobbyist, Bob Joost, and I spent the weekend in Les's office rewriting the bill. The following Tuesday, the next possible time for continuing markup, the revised bill was complete, printed, and on the members' desks, ready for the markup to resume.

The next obstacle was subtler. With Rinaldo's vote still uncertain and Eckhardt's unclear, a fifth vote was needed to make sure the two essential provisions that united the supporters—unlimited medical benefit levels and the tight threshold restrictions on permissible lawsuits—remained intact. A significant change in either could have undermined the bill. Representative Stuckey proved to be the semisurprise fifth vote. When the votes on medical benefit levels occurred, Stuckey got up and left the markup. Without his opposition, the amendment to lower the benefits failed. After the vote, Stuckey returned to the room just as McCollister was offering an amendment to weaken the threshold. When he heard the amendment, Stuckey turned around and left the room a second time, once again assuring that the amendment would fail.

Stuckey's help was not a total surprise because his staff person had indicated that Stuckey had been sold on no-fault in his work as chairman of a subcommittee on the District of Columbia Committee. But his support was far from certain, as he was taking a political risk in his conservative district by voting for the bill. Thus, he, too, tried to have it both ways, being absent to protect the key provisions of the bill but planning to vote against final passage if there were enough other votes to report the bill.

What Stuckey had not counted on was a good reporter being present in the room. Leah Young of the *Journal of Commerce* noticed Stuckey leaving the room on the key votes and wrote about it for the next day's edition.[5] Stuckey took some flak from trial lawyers in Georgia, but the key parts of the bill had survived. Putting the substantive provisions at the beginning of the bill paid off. Once the subcommittee was past the key issues, the Republicans lost their appetite for amendments to the less important provisions and submitted to the inevitable. After five sessions, the House Consumer Protection and Finance Subcommittee, with Eckhardt's and Rinaldo's votes, reported a no-fault bill to the full committee for the first time on October 19, 1975. The final tally: 5–4.[6]

With the subcommittee having taken longer to act than anticipated and the Congress preparing to recess until January, Senate Commerce Committee Chairman Magnuson decided to hold off another Senate vote on S. 354 until 1976 (the Senate bill was numbered S. 354 for the second Congress in a row to provide familiarity for the senators; another excellent idea by Sutcliffe). The delay proved fatal for a combination of reasons: (1) the ongoing ideological opposition of President Ford's attorney general, Edward Levi; (2) an election-year primary challenge to Ford from the right by Ronald Reagan; and, (3) ironically, the failure of William Timmons and Tom Korologos, Ford's former top legislative advisers and two of the best Republican political strategists of their time, to investigate where Reagan stood on no-fault. Timmons and Korologos had left the White House in 1975 to form the lobbying firm of Timmons & Co.

The role of Attorney General Levi was a critical one in the decision the Ford administration made on no-fault. Levi had been the dean of the University of Chicago Law School and then president of the university, playing a key role in establishing the ideologically conservative tone of the university, before being appointed attorney general on February 7, 1975. Almost all law professors who wrote about no-fault at that time wrote favorable articles. The two prominent exceptions were University of Chicago Law School professors—Harry Kalven and Walter Blum—who argued that taking away the tort law obligation to pay when a driver negligently injured another would remove the deterrent effect, thereby resulting in more, not fewer, accidents and higher, not lower, premiums.[7] As mentioned earlier, the problem with the argument was that the greatest deterrent to reckless driving was the risk of maiming oneself. Further, most "accidents" were caused by factors that had nothing to do with safe driving and, to the extent the tort system provided any deterrent to bad driving, it was greatly weakened by the fact that it was the driver's insurer, not the driver, who was obligated to pay any damages. The penalty for bad driving was the same as that paid in the tort system—a premium surcharge, which was far less than the cost of the injury.

The Ford cabinet took up no-fault in April 1975, before Secretary of Transportation William Coleman was scheduled to testify before the

Senate Commerce Committee on April 30. The cabinet was split, with DOT, the Department of Housing and Urban Development (HUD), the Office of Management and Budget (OMB), and the Office of Consumer Affairs in favor and DOJ (Levi) and several key White House staffers opposed.[8] Levi endorsed the Kalven and Blum arguments, questioning whether no-fault was really a success. He also argued that federalism dictated that the issue be addressed state by state and that the federal bill was unconstitutional (an issue that the Senate had already put to bed by making changes in the 1975 legislation). Levi's logical counterweight on the subject should have been the new secretary of transportation, William Coleman, himself a distinguished lawyer. But Coleman had been appointed to his position in March, one month later than Levi, and was not fully prepared when President Ford ordered a meeting to develop a position on no-fault. Sadly for no-fault, Levi prevailed, and the Ford administration continued the position of the Nixon administration, supporting state no-fault laws but not federal action until such time as the states proved incapable of solving the problem. Had the decision gone the other way, no-fault likely would have been enacted.

On September 24, 1975, on the eve of the Consumer Protection Subcommittee markup of H.R. 9650, a better-prepared Secretary Coleman sought reconsideration of the Ford administration's opposition to federal legislation, citing, among other changes, the new provisions that ended any constitutional questions. On October 28, 1975, Attorney General Levi responded in a memorandum to James M. Cannon, assistant to the president for domestic affairs and executive director of the Domestic Council. In it, the attorney general acknowledged that the constitutionality issue had been resolved but then shifted his focus to federalism in shooting down Secretary Coleman once again. His tests for when federal action was appropriate were the same as those Secretary Coleman articulated in his congressional testimony—is federal action necessary to institute the program, and is the cause good enough to warrant overriding state action? Unlike Coleman, Levi did not believe so: "In the case of no-fault insurance, we believe that the answer to each of these questions is negative."[9] It is clear from Levi's memorandum that he agreed with Blum and Kalven, his University of Chicago colleagues, that no-fault was not a good idea. That stood in sharp contrast to the strong public testimony of the Nixon and Ford administrations endorsing no-fault. There are no records that indicate whether the White House took any further action after the attorney general's memorandum, but it did not change its position.

At the end of the day, however, it was not the federalism argument that led to the defeat of no-fault in 1976; it was politics. The federalism issue had not stopped fifteen Republican senators from voting for no-fault in 1974. They approached federalism as most Democrats did—from the opposite end of the telescope in comparison to the attorney general. Rather than focus on the fact that the states had been regulating auto insurance since the Congress in 1945 had ceded its jurisdiction in the McCarran-Ferguson Act, they sought to determine the federal government's role in auto accidents. What they found was extensive: Between 1946 and 1975, the federal government had spent nearly $80 billion to build and improve highways, and in 1973 alone, 74 percent of accident fatalities and 51.3 percent of motor vehicle injuries occurred on federally aided highways.[10] Moreover, Secretary Coleman submitted DOT data that estimated that 22.8% of motor vehicle accidents involved a vehicle that was registered out of state.[11]

The initial level of opposition of the Ford administration probably would not have been an insurmountable obstacle had they not chosen to push their position. What made them do so was their perception of Ford's position in the Republican primaries for the presidency in 1976. When Ford narrowly squeaked out a win in the New Hampshire primary on February 24, 1976, and then was upset by Ronald Reagan in the North Carolina primary on March 23, 1976, Ford and his advisers panicked. He turned to his former top political aides, Timmons and Korologos, for their judgment when S. 354 was scheduled for action in late March. They advised strong opposition, ostensibly to avoid giving Reagan a campaign issue. However, their judgment might have been colored somewhat by the fact that one of their first clients was none other than the trial bar. With Timmons, Korologos, and White House lobbyist Joe Jenckes working the Republicans[12] and Tom Boggs working the Democrats, S. 354 was recommitted to the Commerce Committee by a vote of 49–45 on March 13, 1976. Six moderate Republican senators, including Sen. Robert Taft (OH), a cosponsor of S. 354, switched their votes from the previous Congress as a favor to Ford and with some inducement by the trial bar. Boggs played a key role in getting three Democrats to change their votes as well.

That inducement had been predicted by Bob Joost in his 1971 testimony before the Senate Commerce Committee, when he said that the trial bar had already put in place plans to defeat or undermine state efforts to enact no-fault laws. What the trial bar hadn't anticipated was the rapid federal action that led to Senate passage of no-fault legislation in 1974. To counter congressional support for no-fault, ATLA hired Washington superlobbyist Boggs and then, in 1977, moved its offices from Boston to Washington. But it didn't wait until 1977 to start donating heavily to candidates for federal office. As it was lobbying only one issue, its political action committee (PAC) in short order became the largest single-issue PAC in DC. Its contributions reinforced President Ford's aggressive action to get Republican senators to change their votes in 1976. Such changes on publicly recorded votes are a rarity for members of Congress. It was unprecedented for so many senators to change their votes just two years apart. Common Cause noted the entrepreneurial connection between ATLA PAC contributions and five of the six Republicans and two of the three Democrats who switched their votes (emphasis added):

> Contributions by the campaign fund of the American Trial Lawyers association are a "classic example of how campaign contributions are used to attempt to influence members of Congress," CC's [president] Fred Wertheimer said in February when a CC study of contributions by the Trial Lawyers fund (ATLA) was released.
>
> . . .
>
> Five Senators [Roth (R-DE), Stafford (R-VT), Beall (R-MD), Cannon (D-NV) and Taft (R-OH)][13] who were running for re-election in 1976 and voted for no-fault legislation in 1974 switched their position to oppose it in 1976, and later received substantial contributions from ATLA for their 1976 campaigns.
>
> . . .
>
> Two other Senators [(Hathaway (D-ME) and Packwood (R-OR)] who switched their position from supporting no-fault in 1974 to opposing it in 1976 received ATLA contributions in 1977.
>
> . . .
>
> In all, ATLA contributed nearly a quarter of a million dollars [real money then] to Congressional candidates in the 1976 campaign.
>
> "ATLA blanketed the 1976 Senate races with money," Wertheimer said. "Past votes on no-fault insurance legislation played a key role in determin-

> ing whether an incumbent got money or no. Challengers opposed by ATLA during the campaign suddenly became ATLA favorites after they won in November. *ATLA did not run a campaign fund, it ran an investment fund.*"[14]

In all, six Republicans (the other was Charles "Mac" Mathias of Maryland, who received no ATLA contributions) and three Democrats (the other was James Symington [MO], who received no ATLA contributions) reversed their positions from 1974.

The most dramatic contrast among prior supporters was between the actions of Sen. Edward Brooke (R-MA) and Senator Hart. Senator Brooke, a liberal African American Republican who had voted for the bill in 1974, absented himself during the 1976 vote, giving supporters one less vote than they had counted on. At the same time, Senator Hart, who was dying of cancer, left his sickbed at Bethesda Naval Hospital and came to the Senate floor to vote for the bill he had worked so hard to advance.

The 49–45 vote to recommit the bill was even more dramatic than just described. Senator Moss, the floor manager for the bill, was far less experienced in the role than Senator Magnuson. As the vote was drawing to a close, the tally was 47 in favor of recommittal and 46 against. Fearing that Sen. Claiborne Pell (D-RI), a supporter, would not show up, Senator Moss changed his vote to "no" so that, under Senate rules, he would be in a position to ask for another vote (a motion to reconsider the previous vote). When Moss switched his vote, so did freshman Sen. Wendell Ford (D-KY), a squishy vote for no-fault. That left the tally at 49–44. Then, Senator Pell arrived and voted for no-fault. Before Senators Moss and Ford could unwind their switches, the vote was announced as 49–45 to recommit the bill. Had Moss and Ford changed their votes in time, the vote would have been 47–47, and the motion to recommit would have failed on a tie vote. If you follow all of that, you are well on your way to mastering Senate procedure. If you did not, the bottom line is the same—the Senate voted to return the bill to the Commerce Committee.

For all the importance of trial lawyer money in the 1976 reversal of the 1974 no-fault vote, the drama would likely never have occurred had President Ford not been concerned about Ronald Reagan's challenge to his presidency. But was the concern warranted? It is the job of political operatives to know or find the answer. In this situation, ironically, Timmons and Korologos, two of the most highly skilled professional political operatives of their time, had assumed that Reagan was opposed to federal no-fault. Had they dug deeper, they likely would have discovered that that was not Reagan's position. To retain their influence in the White House, they would have to have told President Ford.

Not long after the vote, Joost came into possession of a March 14, 1974, letter that California governor Reagan had written to Archie Stubbs, secretary of the South Carolina Republican Party. The letter started by stating the normal states' rights position of all governors: "It would be far better if we could obtain legislation at the state level without having to have a federal standards bill." Then, he proceeded to lament the fact that California would not enact a no-fault bill in the absence of a federal standards bill and wrote that "federal legislation may be enacted with or without our input." He noted that "if we oppose federal no-fault standards on principle, we will probably not have the opportunity to work with the sponsors to gain the kind of changes we would like to see." He concluded that, "while we have not given up on the no-fault fight in California," there were areas "where constructive criticism would probably be well received [by Congressmen] if it were offered by supporters in principle." Alas, the supporters' timing in unearthing the letter had been as bad as the failures of Timmons and Korologos (although their error benefited their trial lawyer clients).

With the Senate having failed to pass a bill, it was easy for House opponents to convince House Commerce Committee Chairman Staggers not to mark up the bill with the same argument used to delay the Senate vote—why take a tough vote if there is no chance it can become law? For yet a fourth time, another good opportunity to pass no-fault was lost.

On May 21, 1976, Rep. Torbert (Torby) MacDonald (D-MA) died, leaving the Communications Subcommittee chairmanship open. As Van Deerlin had been a broadcaster before coming to the House and was familiar with the issues, he decided to switch subcommittee chairs. The new subcommittee chairman was Rep. John (Jack) Murphy (D-NY). Murphy was very different than Van Deerlin. He was a West Point graduate who was friendly with two other West Point graduates, world-famous dictators Anastasio Somoza of Panama and Ferdinand Marcos of the Philippines. Murphy was straitlaced, with a military demeanor. He represented one of the strangest congressional districts in the country, staunchly conservative Staten Island and very liberal Greenwich Village.

Murphy was especially headline conscious, taking an approach not dissimilar to that of Donald Trump. Murphy once asked his administrative assistant, Carl Perian (possessor of one of the highest, if not the highest, pompadours among congressional staff), why everyone knew Joe DiMaggio's name. Carl said, "Because he was a great Yankee." Murphy responded, "No, Carl, because he was in the lineup every day." That was Murphy's philosophy; any mention in the press was good, even if it was negative. A couple of years later he was to rue that philosophy.

When Murphy took over the chairmanship, he agreed to let all the staff stay, just adding some of his people. His decision begged the question of whether the staff wanted to stay. Most of us were not particularly comfortable with Murphy. Unlike Van Deerlin, he was very military, having graduated from West Point, and slick. For me, the decision turned on what it always did: issues, not personality. I had become convinced that passage of the no-fault bill would dramatically improve the lives of auto crash victims. Thus, I decided I would stay if Murphy supported continuation of the effort. Murphy decided to support no-fault and even introduced an excellent bill, accompanied by a strong statement of support in the *Congressional Record.*

Much as I appreciated Murphy's support for no-fault, I was so uncomfortable with him that I decided I would leave if he retained the chairmanship in the next Congress. Having reached that conclusion, I started to grow a beard, which I knew Murphy would not like. At the same time, as I wanted to continue to work on no-fault, I set out to find another place for Murphy to land. To get Murphy another position would require one big rule change and one big favor from my former boss Lud Ashley.

The rule change was already in the works as part of a package of reforms supported by the powerful Democratic Study Group designed to further enhance the powers of the younger members. The change, which was adopted by the Democratic Caucus (all the House Democrats) in 1977, prohibited a member from serving simultaneously as chairman of a full committee and chairman of a legislative subcommittee on another committee. It was the key to getting rid of Murphy. Here's why: In 1976, Rep. Leonor Sullivan (D-MO), the chair of the Merchant Marine and Fisheries Committee, retired, opening the job with the organization of the Ninety-Fifth Congress in January 1977, and Murphy wanted the job. With the adoption of the new rule regarding chairmanships, Murphy could not continue to serve as chairman of the Consumer Protection Subcommittee if he took the Merchant Marine chairmanship. It was, I thought, the perfect outcome—Murphy would no longer be the chairman of the subcommittee, but his vote for passage would be secured because he had made a commitment to no-fault by introducing his own no-fault bill.

After the rule change, there was one remaining obstacle—Representative Ashley also was interested in chairing the Merchant Marine Committee, and he was senior to Murphy on the committee. I knew that Ashley's interest was personal. During Pres. Lyndon Johnson's administration, Nicholas Johnson, administrator of the US Maritime Administration, had recommended that the United States reduce the requirements for shipping a certain percentage of US goods on US- registered vessels. All the Democrats on the committee opposed the proposal because of union opposition, except for Ashley. In retaliation, the maritime union contributed to Ashley's opponent in the following election. So in 1977, Ashley was in a position to get even and then some by taking the chairmanship of the Merchant Marine Committee.

I knew that Ashley's real interest was in housing and that he was in a position to chair the Housing Subcommittee on the Banking Committee, but thanks to the new rule, he could do so only if he turned down the Merchant Marine Committee chairmanship. Since Ashley was talking about taking the Merchant Marine post, I didn't want to leave anything to chance. My ace in the hole was the famous actor Robert Redford. Here's the backstory. In the spring of 1976, the House and Senate were about to go to conference on the Resource Conservation and Recovery Act, which was in the jurisdiction of the Senate Commerce Committee but for which jurisdiction was spread among multiple committees in the House. Lynn Sutcliffe was concerned that the various House committees would all insist on appointing conferees, and the situation would be too unwieldy to reach agreement in the limited remaining time. Sutcliffe had become friendly with Redford through his wife, Lola, who was a consumer advocate and served on the CFA board. Sutcliffe knew Robert Redford was a strong supporter of energy conservation, so he asked him to come to Washington to help push the bill across the finish line. Knowing that I had worked for Ashley, Sutcliffe asked if I would shepherd Redford around to encourage Ashley and another key Banking Committee member, William Moorhead (D-PA), to cooperate in limiting the number of House conferees.

Redford arrived on June 11, 1976, shortly after the opening of the Watergate movie *All the President's Men.* When I met him, he had just spent a week promoting the movie and had had little sleep. He was all hepped up, even before he started drinking coffee that morning. I was convinced that the effort was going to be a disaster. On the way over to Ashley's office, Redford asked me what legislation Ashley was most proud of. I told him it was the new towns provision of a housing law. When we got to Ashley's office, he was clearly impressed by Redford's fame. As the meeting droned on, Redford "spontaneously" suggested that the energy conversation measures in the bill could be tried in new towns. He had Ashley. Ashley buzzed his secretary and said, "Sandi, Sandi, please bring Bob a copy of my new towns legislation." Ashley subsequently helped expedite passage of the bill. Shortly thereafter, Ashley named his price—a campaign ad from Redford—and asked me to get it. Redford hated to do campaign ads but was so pleased the bill had passed that he agreed to tape a radio ad.

In early 1977, that left me with an ace to play in my effort to move Murphy out of the subcommittee chairmanship. I spoke with Ashley and told him I couldn't work for Murphy and asked him to please take the Housing Subcommittee instead of the Merchant Marine Committee. I told him if he thought he owed me a favor for Redford's ad, now was the time to repay it. Ashley took the Housing Subcommittee, and Murphy became chairman of the Merchant Marine Committee.

Not long thereafter, in the late 1970s, Murphy was caught in Abscam, an FBI sting of members of Congress taking money in exchange for agreeing to introduce "private immigration bills." He was convicted of receiving an unlawful gratuity and served sixteen months in jail. That was definitely one time that it was not good for Murphy to see his name in the *New York Times.*

8. New Key Players in the Ninety-Fifth Congress

Rep. Bob Eckhardt, Pres. Jimmy Carter, and Sen. Howard Cannon Tackle No-Fault (1977)

Having helped Murphy secure the chairmanship he wanted, and helped myself in the process, I had a decision to make—whether to stay on with the incoming chairman, Rep. Bob Eckhardt (Figure 8.1). Eckhardt was a liberal by any measure. He had been a member of the "Gang of 10," a group of ten liberal Democrats who had taken the early lead in opposing the Vietnam War in the House. Eckhardt, who was from Texas and had a strong drawl (a Northerner's view, of course), commented drily, "They couldn't understand how a person who spoke like I did could think like they did."

Eckhardt had a unique personality. He was very funny. To give two examples: "Trying to organize liberals is like trying to teach quail to hunt bird dogs" and "When driving down US 59 in Houston, should you happen to pass wind, you're better off rolling the windows *up*" (to capture the fact that the highway ran by gas, oil, and chemical plants). He was also a unique dresser (a trait I shared with him, although I had a different style), wearing white linen and seersucker suits (usually for multiple days at a time) with bow ties and often with a white panama hat. Once he came to the House floor with a large leaf attached to his lapel. I asked him how that had come to pass, and he said he was crossing the Capitol grounds and happened upon a beautiful leaf. That was understandable; what was harder to comprehend was why he had stapled it to his lapel! Eckhardt also favored an unusual form of transportation at the time—he traveled by bicycle. Of course, it was an old bicycle that he tended to drive down the middle of the road, unsteadily. Eckhardt once received a note from Pres. Lyndon Baines Johnson saying that Eckhardt had been the first congressman in history to arrive at the White House for a signing ceremony on a bicycle. He was also a brilliant cartoonist and caricaturist,

Figure 8.1. US Rep. Bob Eckhardt, the subcommittee chairman in 1977–1978, crossed his trial bar friends by tackling no-fault. It cost him dearly in his next election.

Figure 8.2. US Rep. Bob Eckhardt on his bicycle, his main mode of transportation, wearing his signature bow tie with one of many hats and, as always, with a piece of legislation nearby.

regularly capturing witnesses during hearings. In the cartoon shown in Figure 8.2, he captured himself on his bicycle with his signature bow tie and one of many interesting hats, and, as always, with legislation under this arm.

Eckhardt often captured legislative phrases of the time, such as "interface," in his cartoons. They also frequently included caricatures of President Johnson, the dominant politician of the time from Texas (Figure 8.3).

Eckhardt was always focused on helping consumers. In the cartoon shown in Figure 8.4, he captured some of the costs that were weighing consumers down in 1978. The list included many costs that are still a challenge for American consumers, including auto insurance and legal fees, excessive hospital costs, and name-brand drugs.

His political philosophy and mine were in accord, and I very much appreciated his sense of humor. My concern was that I was unsure whether Eckhardt would push no-fault, as my loyalty was to issues, not

Figure 8.3. US Rep. Bob Eckhardt "cartoonizes" a common legislative phrase of the time, "interface." In this cartoon, as in many of his others, one of the figures is President Johnson.

to people. That made me a valuable commodity for a member interested in hiring a person who agreed with him on policy and appreciated my skill set of substantive and process knowledge. It is why I was hired by four successive Consumer Protection Subcommittee chairmen,[1] all with different personalities and constituencies. It made me a less valuable commodity when the job was based primarily on loyalty to a person. I suspect that is why Senator Dodd hired me for top legislative positions but not to be his administrative assistant, a job whose key function was to get him reelected.

Eckhardt's worldview, including his view on no-fault, was grounded in his experience as a labor lawyer. Before being elected to the Congress, he had represented unions and poor people and had a strong bias for making sure they had their day in court. I very much appreciated his field of law (which had been my initial area of practice) and choice of clients, but I was concerned that his success in court might prejudice him against a system designed to eliminate the need to go to court to get justice. He had introduced a no-fault bill of his own, but it was one with such generous benefits that its cost would have been astronomical.

Figure 8.4. Eckhardt cartoon about costs burdening consumers in 1978, including auto insurance. *Bob Eckhardt's Quarterly Report*, no. 16 (Summer 1978).

On the other hand, he had voted to report the Van Deerlin no-fault bill, H.R. 9650, in 1975 despite strong opposition from his trial lawyer friends in Texas. One of them, Jim Kronzer, later scribbled in the margins of a letter he wrote to Eckhardt, "No-fault is my Armageddon. I cannot support any person who supports no-fault." Eckhardt's subsequent support of the mainstream no-fault bill was to play a role in his losing his bid for reelection in 1980 (the trial bar weakened him by running a trial lawyer against him in the primary).

Eckhardt told me he wanted to hold a series of field hearings to see how no-fault was working in the states before deciding whether to proceed with federal legislation. That was good enough for me. I knew he would give the idea a fair shot. He expressed concern about two issues: (1) Was more of the insurance dollar going to injured people in no-fault states than in tort states? and (2) How would no-fault treat people in unusual cases, i.e., "horrible hypothetical" cases? Later, during the hearings, he would raise the example of the draftsman injured in an auto accident who recovers physically but because of either pain or some impairment doesn't advance in his job. He articulated this concern in the following ways at two hearings:

> I am not sure what a permanent limitation of use of a function is nor to what extent that would be satisfied by my example of this case of a draftsman. His back is injured and every day he works he is in pain; he does not progress on his job and he never becomes an architect because he only works maybe 5 hours a day. Now, he is definitely injured, but I am not sure that that means that kind of function [the bill permitted suits for noneconomic damages in cases of "the permanent loss of an important bodily function"].[2]
>
> Suppose the victim is a young man whose customary activity is, as I have used in several examples, drafting. He works at a drafting board and he can go back to the drafting board, but his abilities are impaired and his future is impaired. All the time he works at the drafting board, he is in pain, but he can go back and do the job and he will make about the same money when he reaches 56 as when he was 22 except for the injury.[3]

Believing it was possible to answer Eckhardt's questions, I decided to stay on.

The rest of the subcommittee staff also stayed. We added one person from Eckhardt's personal staff, Kathy Seddon, and an economist, Milton Lower, the husband of Eckhardt's administrative assistant, Ann Lower. In addition to Janie Kinney, who had previously worked in Eckhardt's office, already on staff, Kathy gave the staff another voice to help us gain a better understanding of Eckhardt. Perhaps her most revealing story was that one day in the Capitol, Eckhardt had hailed her, saying, "Kathy." Kathy welcomed the salutation as, prior to that moment, she wasn't sure Eckhardt knew her name, even though she'd worked for him for several years.

Figure 8.5. The Consumer Protection Subcommittee staff, minus me, of Chairman Bob Eckhardt, ca. 1978. *From left to right*: Janie Kinney (counsel), Susan Fry (counsel), Corliss Yancey (support staff), Denise (support staff), Milton Lower (economist), Marion Reid (support staff), Judith Quinn (support staff), Dale Bechtel (support staff), Franz Opper (securities counsel who died early of ALS), Mary Foldes (counsel), Kathy Seddon (counsel), and John McLaughlin (counsel).

Despite his quirks, and maybe in part because of them, Eckhardt's staff was devoted to him and what he stood for. Figure 8.5 shows the subcommittee staff in 1978 (minus me, for some reason). Many of the staff stayed on when Eckhardt switched subcommittees in 1979 to become the chairman of the Oversight and Investigations Subcommittee of the Commerce Committee.

Milton Lower was a character. When the subcommittee staff was told that Eckhardt was going to add an economist instead of another lawyer, we were universally opposed. Then Milton showed up. He was ten years older than most of us, overweight and with a gray goatee, and a chain smoker. Milton was an excellent economist, but he endeared himself to us with his knowledge of both high-minded subjects and his quirky, often lowbrow humor. He introduced us to Zeno's paradox, the notion that a person closing the distance between her- or himself and an object in motion by half can never reach the object (that's my summary of it). He also introduced us to the Fibonacci sequence. Often called the Golden ratio, it is a series of numbers whose ratio is frequently found in nature and in architecture. Leonardo da Vinci used the ratio in painting the *Mona Lisa*.

Milton had a unique way of addressing difficult issues. For example, he was the only person I know who had the foresight to enlist in the army to avoid the upcoming Vietnam War—in 1955! Early in his career, Milton was teaching economics at the University of Texas, at a time when it was a conservative school. His department head decided he was too liberal and set out to find a way to fire him. His solution was to make Milton miss teaching too many classes by assigning him an 8 A.M. class. The idea was a clever one, as Milton was a night owl who rarely arose before mid-morning. However, Milton was cleverer. After pondering the issue for a few days, Milton hit on his solution. On the days before his scheduled 8 A.M. classes, he would stay up all night, teach the class, and then go to bed. Milton won and kept his job.

When bored, Milton would xerox his face, and other parts, on the copier. When not bored, Milton wrote the most erudite, but obscene, graffiti on the men's bathroom wall. While others would write standard drivel and draw male and female body parts, Milton would respond with references to Zeno's paradox and clever rhyming verses in the country-and-western genre. The graffiti was so good that one day, the men in the office stood guard while the women went into the men's room to read Milton's work.

Nothing was sacred to Milton, including no-fault. One day I walked into my office and found the following sign and acronym he had come up with for no-fault (Figure 8.6). I chose not to share it with others, as I was afraid the trial bar would use it against us!

The subcommittee membership had changed substantially since H.R. 9650 had been reported in 1975. Representatives Metcalfe and Scheuer, two Democratic supporters, continued on. However, two other key Democratic supporters moved on—Van Deerlin to chair the Commerce Committee's Communications Subcommittee and Brodhead to a more prestigious assignment on the Ways and Means Committee. The on-occasion helpful Stuckey also moved on. They were replaced by one

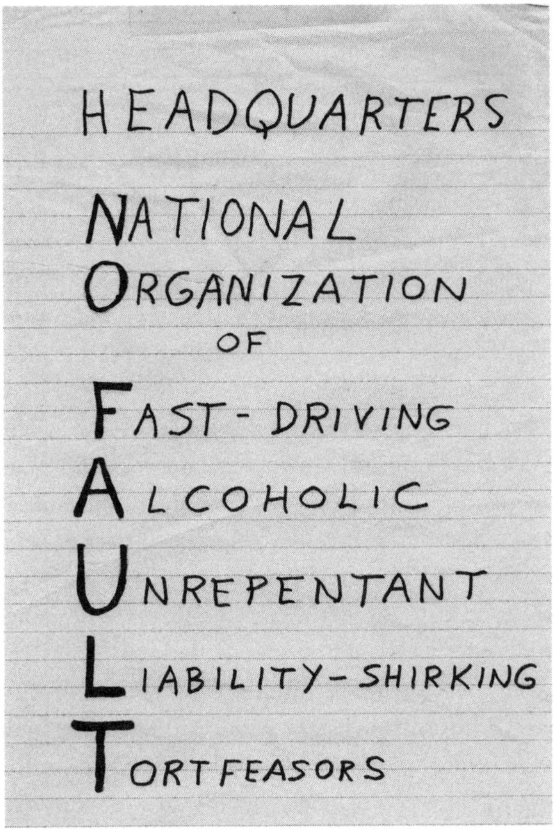

Figure 8.6. Milton Lower's acronym for no-fault. The trial lawyers couldn't have come up with a better one for their viewpoint, and fortunately, they didn't.

supporter and two conservative Democrats. The supporter was Charles Carney of Youngstown, a short man with curly steel-gray hair with the look of a stereotypical Irish descendant who came out of the union movement. The conservative Democrats were Bob Krueger and Tom Luken. Krueger was a highly articulate member from the largest congressional district in Texas who had taught English literature at Duke University. The other conservative Democrat was Tom Luken, a burly ex-marine from Cincinnati, Ohio, who had been elected in a special election in 1974. He wasn't, in fact, conservative on many issues, having marched with Martin Luther King in the South, but he was a pragmatist. He very much wanted to win reelection, and he saw the shortest distance between the two points of his narrow special election win and reelection as the trial bar. He proved to be receptive to the influence of trial bar arguments and, more importantly, trial lawyer contributions. Rep. Jim Broyhill of North Carolina replaced Representative McCollister as the ranking minority member. Once again, it looked as if the subcommittee would be closely divided on no-fault.

On the positive side, three developments boded well. The first was the election of Jimmy Carter, a Democrat, as president, replacing Republican Gerald Ford. The second was Lynn Sutcliffe leaving the Senate Commerce Committee and starting the Committee for Consumers No-Fault. Sutcliffe was able to bring the wide range of supporters under one roof and provide highly skilled political advice. He was able to raise more money than his predecessor, enough to bring on Ted Johnson, a seasoned press person who had worked on the Hill for Sen. Mike Gravel of Alaska. The two of them devised a brochure, the cover of which stated, "No-fault, the way to end auto insurance roulette" and included a picture of a roulette wheel (Figure 8.7). The derivation of the cover, of course, was Senator Magnuson's comments that one could get better odds of recovery at a Las Vegas casino than in an auto accident. However, he was not able to raise nearly enough to counter the trial bar, as it turned out.

The third development was Sutcliffe arranging for a successor before he left the Commerce Committee. It was Mike Mullen, who had handled no-fault the two times it was referred to the Judiciary Committee. Mullen was to prove adept at maneuvering the bill through a much more divided Commerce Committee, including helping to return new Chairman Howard Cannon to the pro-no-fault side. Senator Cannon had previously voted for no-fault in 1974, only to reverse himself and vote against it in 1976. At the start of the Ninety-Fifth Congress in 1977, no one knew what role Chairman Cannon would play on no-fault and whether he would even support it. Mullen, as his counsel, was likely to have a huge impact on Cannon's decision.

Meanwhile, early in 1977, it was encouraging that Representative Broyhill replaced Representative McCollister as the ranking minority member. Broyhill was an honest and thoughtful man who had frequently devised compromises with Eckhardt to move other legislation. He was one of the Southerners who taught me that just because one speaks slowly doesn't mean that one thinks slowly. Broyhill spoke so slowly that I could barely restrain myself from finishing his sentences. It reminded me of the Bob and Ray skit, which involved Ray Goulding interviewing

Figure 8.7. Committee for Consumers No-Fault brochure. The committee organized the outside effort on behalf of no-fault in 1977–1978.

Bob Elliott as the president of the Slow Talkers of America. Bob talks so slowly that Ray keeps trying to finish his sentences. At a performance at the National Theatre in Washington, DC, the curtain ending the first act of the show fell in the middle of the president responding to a question. When the curtain rose for the second act, Ray was sound asleep and snoring, and Bob was just finishing his answer to the question that he had been asked in the first act.

Slow speech aside, it was even more encouraging when Broyhill stopped me in the hall of the Rayburn building to say he was prepared to support a federal bill because he thought no-fault was a good idea, and he knew North Carolina would never enact a law. Broyhill invited me to supply him with a memorandum on the cost implications of no-fault in different states, which I did on October 11, 1977. I continued to be encouraged when I spoke with Tom Green, Broyhill's chief staffer on the committee, on March 21, 1978. In a memorandum to Eckhardt, I reported that Green told me he "felt Broyhill was reasonably sanguine about no-fault."

However, three events changed Broyhill's mind. The first was the influence of Nancy Nord, his staffer on no-fault. She was much less independent-minded than Green and consistently fed Broyhill the opponents' propaganda. Second, soon after my conversation with Green, Broyhill was lobbied against no-fault on a golf course by Rep. Charles Wiggins, a Republican from California. Third, and most effective, the trial bar then threatened to finance a primary opponent against Broyhill. In the face of all that pressure, Broyhill abandoned his support for federal legislation, even though the threat presented no danger to his reelection prospects because the Broyhill family furniture business was the largest employer in the district, and Broyhill was extremely popular. Sadly, this experience was consistent with what I observed throughout my time on the Hill—that members' foremost concern is always their reelection, and they are extremely risk-averse. The best present example of this phenomenon is how rapidly Republicans who opposed Trump in 2016 and early 2017 folded when confronted with the possibility of primary challenges, even when they had built up strong constituent bases. Nevertheless, with Broyhill's defection, the fate of the bill would once again have to rely almost completely on Democratic votes.

While Eckhardt was taking control of the subcommittee and deciding his position on no-fault and Chairman Cannon was deciding what to do, newly elected Pres. Jimmy Carter also had a decision to make. As a former governor, he was hesitant to support a federal bill. With Carter favoring state action and Eckhardt seeking to answer his two key questions, there were two challenges to address if no-fault was to move. Eckhardt decided to hold field hearings to answer his questions, probably in the hope of avoiding the issue. Knowing Eckhardt's intellectual bent, I arranged to have two key law professors testify at the hearings and then have dinner with him afterward so they could kick the subject around.

In an attempt to reinforce Eckhardt's plan to act, or at least hold hearings, I orchestrated the introduction of a new, revised bill, H.R. 6601, the "Standards for No-Fault Motor Vehicle Accident Benefits Act," by the three previous chairmen of the subcommittee—Moss, Van Deerlin, and Murphy. For the first time, the bill permitted insurers to limit the amount of benefits for medical and rehabilitation losses, to $100,000, to calm insurers concerned about providing unlimited benefits. To provide further momentum, the House and Senate sponsors introduced identical bills, S. 1381 and H.R. 6601, on the same day, April 25, 1977. It was the first time the two bodies had introduced identical no-fault bills.

At the first hearing,[4] in Boston on March 18, 1977, Governor Dukakis and Sen. Edward Kennedy (D) testified in favor of federal legislation, as did Professor Keeton of Harvard Law School, the cocreator of no-fault and a fellow Texan. After the hearing, Eckhardt and I joined Keeton for dinner at the Harvard Club. What we hadn't counted on was the early-spring snow that had started falling during the hearing. On the way to dinner, Eckhardt wore a pair of galoshes, Keeton shivered in a raincoat, and I raised my umbrella against the unwelcome elements. Among the three of us, we had enough equipment for one person to ward off the snow. While Eckhardt knew exactly what I was trying to accomplish, he enjoyed talking with Keeton and limited the discussion of no-fault by steering much of the dinner conversation to such colorful Texas characters as Maury Maverick, the person whose escapades resulted in the term "maverick" entering the English language. As the airport was snowed in, Keeton was nice enough to put us up at the Harvard Club for the night.

The second hearing[5] was on April 7, 1977, in the much warmer climate of Fort Lauderdale, Florida. Thankfully, it was less exciting than the 1975 Florida hearing. The original plan had been to hold the hearing in New Jersey because its law was similar to the bill the subcommittee was considering and because it was Representative Rinaldo's home state. To our surprise, Rinaldo did not want to have the hearing in his state. He wanted to have it in Florida because it was still winter in New Jersey, and the weather in Florida was much warmer. What convinced Eckhardt to choose Florida was Rinaldo making an offer he couldn't refuse—to vote for the bill if the subcommittee would hold the hearing there. It wasn't really much of an offer because Rinaldo had already indicated that he would vote for the bill, but we figured it wouldn't hurt to reinforce his support when his vote was needed to report the bill. Florida was also popular with the other subcommittee members because of its weather at that time of the year. Many of the witnesses testified to the abuse of the then $1,000 threshold (which later was revised to a verbal one), particularly in Dade County. The Florida insurance department estimated that as many as 30 percent of the claims paid by companies were "outrightly fraudulent or contain at least an element of fraud through exaggeration of damage and injury" in order to breach the threshold to file a lawsuit for pain and suffering.[6]

The third hearing[7] was at the Waldorf Astoria in New York City on April 23, 1977. One of the witnesses was former subcommittee chairman Jack Murphy, the author of two no-fault bills, who would soon be playing a starring role in the denouement of no-fault. Among the witnesses was Sen. John Dunne, one of the lead sponsors of the New York no-fault law. Dunne was a Republican, as was the administration of Gov. Nelson Rockefeller; both actively supported the New York law. In fact, the impetus for the law was a three-year study by Governor Rockefeller's Committee on Compensating Victims of Automobile Accidents, which issued its report, *Automobile Insurance . . . For Whose Benefit?* on February 12, 1970. It was a common experience for Republicans to take or share the lead in supporting the creation of state no-fault laws. In addition to the key roles played by Republican Governors Rockefeller and Romney in the passage of no-fault laws in their states, the New Jersey law was passed when Republican William Cahill was governor. In most states, there was significant bipartisan support. At the federal level, Democrats took the lead in both houses, but Republicans chose different paths—many supporting the Senate legislation and few supporting the House bill.

Testimony at the hearing showed that no-fault was paying more people for more of their losses more promptly than the tort system had. After the hearing, one of the witnesses, Thomas A. Hartnett, the superintendent of insurance, submitted data that addressed one of Chairman Eckhardt's main concerns: how much of the no-fault premium dollar was returned to victims in compensation. The data revealed that "74.6 percent of an adequate no-fault premium dollar was being returned to victims, while about 53.5 percent of an adequate premium dollar for residual bodily injury—almost entirely for general damages—was available to victims for their own use."[8] As in Florida, the no-fault law was meeting its goals on the no-fault side, but there was considerable fraud designed to breach the threshold to sue for general damages. In both states, consumers were paying nearly as much for the lawsuit portion of the premium as they were for the no-fault portion, contrary to the original design of no-fault.

Once again, the lead witness was a brilliant law school professor who supported no-fault, Guido Calabresi of Yale Law School. Given Eckhardt's interest in the Constitution—he had coauthored a book titled *The Tides of Power: Conversations on the American Constitution* with fellow Texan and renowned Yale Law Professor Charles Black—the hearing was more like an advanced legal seminar on the Constitution than a hearing. Bruce Bliven, Jr., a journalist and occasional *New Yorker* contributor, attended the hearing and dropped a note to Professor O'Connell afterward describing his impression of the exchange between Eckhardt and Calabresi:

> Dropped in on that Subcommittee hearing at the Waldorf, Bob Eckhardt, Chairman, . . . and there was an amazingly erudite exchange—a conversation, really, between Eckhardt and Calabresi. I could tell how witty it was, without quite knowing what they were talking about. I wasn't surprised that Calabresi was brilliant in debate (they were mostly *agreeing* with each other, however) but Eckhardt, up until then, had been playing the role of good ole boy, making polite little jokes, and suddenly still smiling, he was off in the flights of fancy about tort law. I had a feeling he had been saving it up for Calabresi—and I wasn't sure how many others in the room (there were only a handful) knew what the hell they were talking about. It was fun.[9]

After the hearing, Eckhardt and I went to dinner with Professor Calabresi and his wife at a fine Italian restaurant that Calabresi chose. After dinner, Eckhardt picked up the check. The following Monday, I got a call from Ann Lower, Eckhardt's administrative assistant, who told me that my share of the bill was $X and instructed me to call Calabresi and tell him what his share was. While Ann was looking out for Eckhardt, who had limited funds, I was not about to call Calabresi. I told her I would gladly pay my share, but she would have to call Guido if she wanted him to pay.

My efforts to persuade Eckhardt of the merits were not limited to arranging for him to interact with law professors. During the hearings, as under Van Deerlin, I would have the opportunity to ask the witnesses questions after the subcommittee members had completed their questioning. I would use my time to try to get witnesses to address Eckhardt's concerns about the draftsman who doesn't advance after he is injured in a car crash. I was also able to encourage several insurance commissioners and insurers to testify as to the amount of the premium dollar that was going to injured persons in no-fault states, answering one of Eckhardt's major concerns. Given Eckhardt's strong ego and interest in getting to the bottom of issues, while he knew what I was trying to do, he never failed to call on me.

My efforts to influence Eckhardt also extended outside the hearings. One time I arranged for him to meet with some key insurance reps, Les Cheek of Crum & Forster and Peter Connell of Aetna, as well as Kathleen O'Reilly of CFA and Mike Gildea of the AFL-CIO. Of course, Eckhardt knew exactly what was going on. As the meeting was breaking up, he turned to Gildea and said, with a twinkle in his eye, "I'd like to thank you all for coming in to lobby me on behalf of my counsel!"

9. Eckhardt, Carter, and Cannon Support No-Fault, Only to Be Betrayed by Sen. John Durkin (June 1977–June 1978)

With the field hearings in Boston, Fort Lauderdale and New York City completed, the subcommittee started the first of six hearings in DC, on June 13, 1977. The focus of the hearing was to contrast compensation under no-fault with that under fault. Ted Johnson, Sutcliffe's outstanding press person for the Committee for Consumers No-Fault, identified through stories in the *Chicago Tribune* two victims, one injured in a no-fault state and one in a tort state. The first, Rosemary Pryor, was a nineteen-year-old State Farm insured who had been injured in the no-fault state Michigan. The second, Tom Tuzzolino, had been seriously injured in the tort state Illinois. We decided to put them on a hearing panel, along with Tom's mother, Karen, to contrast the consequences of their accidents. We also invited the two reporters to testify.

At the hearing, Pryor testified that she had been in the back of a pickup truck when the girl who was driving lost control and hit a tree.[1] She was paralyzed from the waist down. Her insurer paid all her medical costs and then told her to call a rehabilitation center for therapy. When she called, the center told her they had no openings. When she told them she had been injured in a car crash and was a State Farm insured, they changed their tune and said they could take her right away. The reason for the change was that Michigan's no-fault law included unlimited medical benefits for medical and rehabilitation expenses. Because she had been injured in a single car crash, she would not have been eligible for any recovery had she been injured in a tort state.

By contrast, Tom Tuzzolino was injured at age five when he stepped off a curb and was hit by a car. He suffered a serious brain injury, with major expenses. Because he was injured in the tort state Illinois, his family had to sue the driver. It took six years to recover damages, and the recovery was limited to $20,000 because that was all the coverage the driver had. In the meantime, Mrs. Tuzzolino had to go to work to help pay some of the bills, even though she had six other children. The story only got worse from there, but the two experiences showed just how much better the no-fault system was.

The two reporters who wrote the stories about the injured persons, William Gaines and John McCarron, fleshed out more completely the differences between the Michigan and Illinois laws. It created a nice echo chamber, with the reporters then reporting on the hearing at which they had testified in their newspaper.

The rest of the hearing focused on the performance of the Michigan no-fault law. The Michigan commissioner of insurance, the director of the Michigan United Auto Workers, and a representative of the Michigan Bar Association all testified in support of the federal bill, citing the positive experience with the similar law in Michigan. A representative of the Michigan Trial Lawyers Association testified in opposition.

With the state no-fault hearings completed, Eckhardt put summaries of each hearing in the *Congressional Record*, a common way to educate/lobby other representatives for support. These, of course, were narrowly aimed at the undecided members of his own subcommittee. They all appeared under the name "Hon. Bob Eckhardt." He submitted the first statement, "Massachusetts No-Fault Hearing," ten days after the Michigan hearing.[2] Eckhardt subsequently submitted three additional statements in September 1977: "Florida No-Fault Hearing,"[3] "New York No-Fault Hearing,"[4] and "Michigan No-Fault Hearing."[5]

The successful Michigan hearing was one example of the inside-outside coordination between congressional staffers and the outside Committee for Consumers No-Fault coalition. For the better part of 1977 and 1978, the two groups met regularly to share information about substance and ideas for hearings and advocacy documents as well as the latest information on the positions of the members. The coalition helped identify witnesses for the hearings, secured many newspaper editorial and columnist endorsements, and helped devise strategy, It even solicited the signatures of well-known lawyers on a letter to Congress from a self-created group, Attorneys for No-Fault. The letter, which was sent to all congressional offices on April 26, 1977, was signed by many legal luminaries of the time, including Erwin W. Griswold, solicitor general of the United States and dean of Harvard Law School; Guido Calabresi, John Thomas Smith Professor of Law, Yale University Law School; two chairmen of the FTC, Calvin J. Collier and Michael Pertschuk; Roger Henderson, dean of the College of Law at the University of Arizona and coreporter of UMVARA; Rhoda H. Karpatkin, executive director of Consumers Union (CU); Francis T. P. Plimpton, president of the Bar Association of the City of New York and ambassador to the United Nations; William Ruckelshaus, deputy attorney general of the United States and administrator of the EPA; and Robert E. Montgomery, counsel to the special assistant to President Nixon for consumer affairs.

Sutcliffe was far more effective than his predecessor in lobbying members, particularly in the Senate, where he had worked for many years, and helping to coordinate the effort among the House and Senate and the White House. Even with his considerable legislative skills and Johnson's considerable newspaper skills, the outside effort was hamstrung by the lack of sufficient funds to mount major grassroots campaigns in the districts of the undecided members. They knew what to do and how to do it, but because of the lack of funds, it was like being in a fight with one hand tied behind your back.

Meanwhile, there was a parallel effort to get the support of President Carter. He came into office having supported the Georgia no-fault bill (a weak one, but a no-fault bill nonetheless) but taking the position that he wanted to review state no-fault experience before deciding whether to support the adoption of federal legislation, even though the 1976 Democratic Party platform included a plank calling for federal legislation (another effort orchestrated by Sutcliffe). Sutcliffe had also managed to get the White House to hire Mary Schuman, a highly competent young Senate Commerce Committee staffer whom I had helped educate on no-fault (paying it forward from Bob Joost's assistance to me, albeit in much less time).

Fortuitously, Joost had moved over to DOT, where he wound up as the key player in a 1977 update of the original DOT report that focused on state experience, the president's concern. After analyzing how the sixteen no-fault states, with widely varying benefit levels and tort thresholds, met the goals of more timely compensation of more losses for more people and examining the cost experience, the report found:

> In summary, State experience with no-fault automobile insurance would appear to confirm the basic soundness of the theory and the feasibility of the theory's implementation. No-fault plans of sharply varying objectives and character are widely seen as successes. No problem has arisen in the implementation of no-fault for which there does not appear to be a readily available and feasible solution, *given the political will to make the necessary change* (emphasis added).[6]

The report concluded emphatically, "No-Fault insurance works."[7]

With knowledgeable and supportive people in the administration, no-fault advanced far faster than either Carter or Eckhardt anticipated, and probably faster than they would have liked. Schuman's job was to gather the views of relevant federal agencies and then write an action memo for the president. As part of that process, she conducted a meeting at the White House on June 22, 1977, with the key agencies as well as congressional staff (me; Mike Mullen, who had assumed Senate responsibility for no-fault after Joost went to DOT and Sutcliffe into the private sector; Mark Raabe, Chairman Staggers's counsel; and Cindy Douglass, Ranking Minority Sen. James Pearson's staff). All ten or so federal agency reports were positive.

Schuman then wrote a five-page memo recommending that the administration endorse federal no-fault legislation. She reported that President Carter, who liked to know all the details, without keeping in perspective the competency of his staff and the larger requirements of his job, read not only the five-page cover memo but also the roughly one hundred pages of agency reports—and then endorsed the House and Senate bills in July 1977.

The timing of the president's endorsement dovetailed nicely with the conclusion of the subcommittee's field hearings on June 12, 1977. On July 21, 1977, DOT secretary and former member of the House Brock Adams testified in favor of the House bill on behalf of the Carter administration. After the usual August congressional recess, with the end of the first session in sight, we decided to let the Senate move first to build momentum in advance of House action. Little did anyone know that this time the bill would be sabotaged by one of its strongest supporters.

When new Senate Commerce Chairman Howard Cannon (D-NV)

convened a markup on S. 1381 on February 28, 1978, he was blindsided by questions from Sen. John Durkin (D-NH) about the accuracy of studies showing that the Michigan no-fault law, the one that most resembled the federal bill, was working well. Durkin demanded a new cost study, indicating that he wouldn't vote to report the bill until he got his study. Chairman Cannon had little choice but to acquiesce to Durkin's "request" because of the change in the composition of the committee between Congresses. The previous Congress's membership had voted to report its no-fault bill by a broad bipartisan margin of 15–3. Chairman Cannon knew he needed Durkin's vote to get the bill out of the new, narrowly divided committee.

No-fault supporters were caught off guard by Durkin's request because he had previously been a strong supporter. As insurance commissioner in New Hampshire, he had supported no-fault, and he had touted his support for no-fault in his successful run for the Senate. In the Senate, he had been a floor manager of the bill in the Ninety-Fourth Congress and was a cosponsor of S. 1381. The resulting study by Philip Presley, a New Hampshire actuary and friend of Durkin, confirmed the efficacy of the Michigan law (a fact Durkin initially challenged before conceding it), but the time it took to complete the study delayed the markup until May 2, 1978. After the study met Durkin's satisfaction, he agreed to vote to report the bill, but at the same time, he launched an attack on how rates would be set under the bill (basically, that job would be left to state regulators). Why did Durkin become no-fault's Benedict Arnold? Arnold was given a military commission by the British and money. As for Durkin, he was in a tough reelection campaign, and Tom Boggs agreed to serve on his reelection committee. That was probably worth a lot more than Arnold received. As I mentioned about Representative Broyhill's change of heart, the top priority for almost all members of Congress is getting reelected.

The Senate Commerce Committee finally reported its bill on May 9, 1978, but only by a 9–7 margin. The effort had lost two months and a lot of momentum. The situation was then exacerbated by a trial lawyer–inspired May 24, 1978, letter from fourteen senators to Majority Leader Robert C. Byrd threatening a filibuster. Among other things, the letter raised the common argument that the Senate shouldn't act because the House wouldn't (even though that was not true):

> It should be noted that the House has never taken action on national no-fault proposals, and it appears unlikely that the full House Interstate and Foreign Commerce Committee will report a bill this Congress.
>
> We feel most strongly that the Senate's deliberate action to defeat a similar proposal in the last Congress, and the closeness of the vote by which S. 1381 was order reported (9–7) demonstrate the highly controversial nature of this proposal. Without a doubt, this controversy will lead to a thorough exploration of every question surrounding the no-fault issue, as it should, if S. 1381 is scheduled for floor action.
>
> We felt it incumbent upon us to advise you of this fact, and to suggest that *a time agreement on this bill would be very unlikely* (emphasis added).

These developments badly hurt the House Commerce Committee's willingness to proceed. Nevertheless, Eckhardt scheduled a markup of H.R. 6601. As the subcommittee was preparing for the markup, the ABA, which had issued a report calling for more study of no-fault in February,[8] suddenly proposed five tort changes and an increase in the required amount of bodily injury liability coverage as an alternative to H.R. 6601. We viewed the report as less a serious proposal than a political one, a last-ditch attempt to derail no-fault to assure the continued role of both plaintiff and defense attorneys in resolving auto personal injury cases. Nevertheless, it presented a clear and present danger to the bill in that it threatened to provide some members a fig leaf to use as an excuse to oppose no-fault. It was important to provide a speedy and effective response.

The five proposals included in the package were a change from contributory to comparative negligence, abolition of host/guest statues, removal of statutory limits in wrongful death actions, universal compulsory automobile liability insurance with mandatory uninsured motorist coverage, and an increase in the required bodily injury coverage from $10,000/$20,000 to $50,000/$100,000. Many states had already adopted the first four changes and raised the required limits, but not as high as the ABA recommended.

Whatever its merits, and its proposals would have improved compensation for injured persons, we thought it was a poor substitute for no-fault, and the subcommittee members needed to know why. The first part of a rebuttal was easy. Even if all the changes were adopted, an injured motorist still would have no recovery in single-car accidents, such as skidding off an icy road and hitting a tree, because no one else was at fault. Such accidents are a significant portion of all accidents—about 30 percent. Moreover, it would offer less compensation to seriously injured people than the no-fault bill did. Under the ABA proposal, if an injured motorist recovered the full $50,000, the net recovery after the standard one-third attorney's fee would have been $33,500. By contrast, H.R. 6601 mandated a minimum of approximately $120,000 in no-fault benefits, with no offset for attorneys' fees, and permitted a seriously injured person to sue in tort for any excess economic loss and, in the case of a serious and permanent injury, noneconomic damages (pain and suffering) as well.

It was also obvious that adoption of the ABA proposal would raise costs because, unlike the threshold limiting lawsuits for pain and suffering under no-fault, there were no provisions to offset the increases that would come from more people being able to recover more compensation. The unanswered question was how much would premiums increase?

Fortunately, there was an easy way to obtain a reliable estimate—call Dale Nelson, State Farm's brilliant chief actuary. Throughout the 1970s, Dale provided critical technical assistance many times, often information that we were able to convert into political gain. Our conversations followed a pattern—I would ask Dale what the impact would be on auto insurance premiums if we changed some provision in the bill. I would be met with total silence for about a minute. Then, Dale would give me a precise answer, such as 1.8 percent or $3.32! Experience had shown he was always on target, a good thing given his position at State Farm. I envisioned Dale's brain working as a computer processing information, which wasn't far from the truth. This time Dale needed more than two minutes to calculate the increase. He estimated that the *adoption of all the ABA changes would increase the average premium by 58 percent.*[9] Dale's estimate blew the ABA proposal out of the water as a viable alternative to no-fault.

The increased costs were particularly problematic for low-income people. The higher premiums that would have resulted from adoption of the ABA proposal would have confronted low-income people with a Hobson's choice—forgo necessities to afford insurance or buy necessities and drive uninsured. Were drivers to choose to go "bare," to not carry insurance, they were at risk of severe penalties, including fines and the loss of their drivers' licenses, if caught.

This choice was worsened by the movement of jobs from central cities to the suburbs, where a car was often the only way to get to a job.[10] Also, to the extent that higher prices led some low-income people to drive uninsured or underinsured, not-at-fault insured injured motorists would have had to resort to their own UM or UIM coverage for compensation, thereby raising premiums for all insured drivers.

By failing to propose measures to offset the additional costs and leaving some innocent injured people without compensation, unintentionally, the ABA package of reforms brought into relief the choice between tort reforms and no-fault. The two central questions were (1) how well would injured motorists fare? and (2) at what cost?

When the ABA proposal did not gain traction, despite the uncertainty in the Senate, Eckhardt persevered, and the Consumer Protection Subcommittee reported its bill on May 23, 1978, with the support of Eckhardt, Carney, Metcalfe, Scheuer, and, this time, Rinaldo. The Hollings letter threatening a filibuster came the day after. It was timed to discourage further action in either the Senate or the House, although it had failed to get anywhere near the forty votes required to continue a filibuster in the face of a cloture motion to cut off debate. It did not discourage Eckhardt. On June 8, 1978, he introduced a new bill, H.R. 13048, which incorporated the amendments to H.R. 6601 that were agreed to in subcommittee, and the bill was ready for full committee markup. However, the full committee wasn't ready to mark up H.R. 13048. It first had to dispose of the Hospital Cost Containment bill, which occupied another six weeks of the full committee's time. It wasn't until mid-July that the committee was ready to act on no-fault.

Despite a 2–1 + 1 majority in the full committee, the markup was destined to be close because, in a "pre-echo" of the position Senator McConnell was to take in the 2000s to oppose all of President Obama's legislative initiatives to make him a one-term president, Republicans had decided to oppose all Democratic bills in an effort to make President Carter a one-term president. That said, what happened—actually, what didn't happen—next may have been the single best lost opportunity to pass no-fault.

In December 1977, Bob Joost had become concerned that the federal standards bills couldn't pass because of the increase in antifederal government sentiment. In June 1978, Senate Counsel Mike Mullen and I agreed on the need for a fallback in case there was insufficient support for H.R. 13048 and S. 1381. Joost drafted our agreement into a bill. The redrafted bill called for insurers to offer consumers a no-fault choice, with the focus on just the essential elements of no-fault, the benefits and tort threshold. It would have meant abandoning the provisions that would have regulated the daily business of insurers, such as the imposition of restrictions on cancellation and nonrenewal of policies. These provisions were peripheral to no-fault but important to Democrats. They reflected a deep distrust of insurers—a distrust Eckhardt shared—and were viewed as consumer protections against insurer overreach.

10. One Last Chance

Eckhardt Rejects Late Compromise and Goes to Full Committee Markup (July 25, 1978–August 1, 1978)

While we were working on a compromise fallback bill, Eckhardt was working to garner support for the subcommittee-reported bill. On June 2, 1978, Eckhardt circulated a memorandum to all committee members entitled "Standards for No-Fault Motor Vehicle Accident Benefits Act." The memorandum included a section-by-section analysis of the measure and a background summary paper on the need for basic standards for no-fault insurance. Between June 2, 1978, and July 31, 1978, Eckhardt worked from a memorandum I prepared entitled "The Political Reality of Passing a No-Fault Bill in This Congress." After citing the members' main concern about taking a tough vote if the bill didn't stand a chance of passage in the Senate, the memorandum explained why the bill could still pass the Senate if it was reported from the House Commerce Committee and then listed six suggested calls for him to make—to Reps. Henry Waxman, Barbara Mikulski, Richardson Pryor, Paul Rogers, Tom Luken, and Phil Sharp.

At the same time, I created a 111-page briefing book to prepare Eckhardt for the markup. The book had five major headings—(1) "The Fault System," (2) "No-Fault: Advantages and State Experience," (3) "H.R. 13048: Need and Contents," (4) "No-Fault: Impact on Different Sections of Society; Cost Information," and (5) "Miscellaneous: Impact on Small Insurers; Effect on Accident Rates; ABA Study"—covering twenty-six topics. It was designed to address all the issues that might come up, particularly arguments against the bill, and included voluminous details on state experience with no-fault.

With the Senate facing a filibuster and the vote in the full House Commerce Committee still too close to call, on July 25, 1978, a week before the markup, Steve Perles, a legislative assistant to Republican Senate Minority Whip Ted Stevens (R-AK), took the stripped-down compromise bill to Representative Broyhill on behalf of Senator Stevens. Broyhill, who had devised many compromises with Eckhardt to move legislation, indicated to Perles that this version was acceptable to him and that he would offer it if Eckhardt told him he would accept it. Broyhill told Perles that most Republicans on the House Committee would follow him in supporting it.[1] However, Eckhardt, who had no liking for insurers, chose to stick with the comprehensive original bill.

With all the substantive preparation completed and as much political work done as possible, it was time for markup. On July 31, 1978, with neither side knowing whether it had the votes, the full House Interstate and Foreign Commerce Committee started marking up H.R. 13048, the Standards for No-Fault Motor Vehicle Accident Benefits Act. The first day, the members sparred over the general concept, the implications of the state no-fault experience for the federal bill, and the need for federal legislation. Then, the opponents offered a motion to recommit the bill to the subcommittee, which would have stopped committee consideration and killed the bill. To Eckhardt's surprise, the motion was defeated by a vote of 24–18. However, several Republicans who opposed the motion made it clear that their goal was to resolve, rather than postpone, the matter.

The next day, August 1, 1978, was to prove decisive. It was time to vote, and still neither side was sure where the votes lay. Let me set the stage. The day itself was a typical sweltering, muggy day in Washington, DC. Most of the forty-three committee members, Democrats and Republicans, sat on three elevated carpeted platforms behind dark wooden panels that crossed an expanse of some forty-five feet. As subcommittee counsel, I sat at a long wooden table in front of the members, some ten feet below the top row and many credentials below all of them. I was joined by the minority subcommittee counsel and the committee clerk, whose job was to call the roll on votes and to keep any proxies members left to vote when they weren't present. As counsel,[2] my job was to answer members' questions about the legislation. This was one of the rare times when staff was supposed to be heard as well as seen.

Democratic Rep. John Dingell of Michigan, the third most senior Democrat and a bear of a man, started peppering me with questions about the bill's cost implications for the federal government. The dialogue went something like this:

> DINGELL: Counsel, this bill will cost the federal government millions of dollars! The committee shouldn't proceed without a cost estimate from CBO (the Congressional Budget Office).
>
> ME (APPEARING FAR CALMER THAN I FELT AND A LITTLE SNARKILY): Mr. Dingell, if you will just look at the documents in front of you, you will find a copy of the CBO report, which indicates that the federal government will *save* $6.8 million annually if this bill is enacted into law.

That was a good beginning. We had been prepared for the question and had put the CBO report on the members' desks just that morning, so most of them, including Dingell, had not read it in advance. We had fended off an attack, but Dingell wasn't the biggest concern. He had long since switched sides, opting to side with General Motors (GM) against the United Auto Workers (UAW),[3] and he wasn't going to vote for the bill no matter what the CBO found.

The bigger problem was that no one knew how the undecided members would vote. All the Republicans, except Representative Rinaldo, and seven Democrats had long since committed to support their private sector friends and oppose the bill. It was a simple maxim followed by most members, Republicans and Democrats alike: Your "friends" support your reelection financially, and you reciprocate by supporting their positions on legislation. The public interest was too often a secondary consideration—or not a consideration at all. In this case, the Republicans' "friends" were most of the nation's automobile insurers, and the Democrats' "friends" were the trial lawyers. The reasons were pure self-interest. The insurers feared that the lower premiums the bill promised would mean lower profits for them (lower costs with the same profit margin yield fewer dollars, which, in turn would lower the value of their stock). The loss of revenue was even more certain for lawyers, as the no-fault bill would have replaced a system of fault dependent on lawyers with one similar to health insurance, where most claims are resolved without regard to fault and thus without the involvement of lawyers.

As a result of such powerful opposition, two weeks out from the markup, we had counted 20 leaning for, 19 leaning against and 4 undecided. With no deal with Broyhill, we viewed our narrow path to report

H.R. 13048 as requiring 21 votes from the Democratic side of the committee (Rinaldo's single Republican vote would give us a majority twenty-second vote), and we could count only 16 solid Democratic votes.

With Eckhardt working the members directly by phone and in person, I and other subcommittee staff working the members' staffs and some members we knew well, and no-fault's outside public and private sector supporters reaching out to their member friends, we started adding supporters one at a time. The unions and consumer groups pushed freshman Rep. Al Gore of Tennessee hard. Shortly thereafter, late one morning, he called me to his office to answer a few final questions. He then "asked" me to stay in the room while he spoke with his friends in the Tennessee trial bar. Gore put me on speakerphone while he delivered the bad news, to loud objections on the other end of the phone. That brought the supporting Democratic members total to 17.

The next one was a surprise. I got a call from Ed Greelegs, the legislative assistant to Rep. Marty Russo of Illinois. Russo had been ambivalent at best, somewhat hostile at worst. On the other hand, Greelegs had become a big supporter, and we had talked a lot. Ed was upset. Russo had scheduled a meeting for 2 P.M., a couple of hours away, with Tom Boggs, the lobbyist son of the former majority leader of the House. Armed with his family pedigree, a friendly personality, and, most importantly, the ability to direct trial lawyer contributions to members, Boggs was the most effective trial lawyer lobbyist. Concerned that Boggs might convince Russo to vote against the bill, Ed asked me to come over a little early. When Boggs showed up shortly thereafter, he was (not happily) surprised to see me. Russo then asked both of us into his office, and we had a thirty-minute debate about the merits of no-fault. I got a call from Greelegs later that afternoon saying that Russo would support the bill. The ambush had paid off, and we had the eighteenth Democratic vote.

Next up was Rep. Tim Wirth of Colorado. A liberal lawyer from Denver, he figured to be a supporter because Colorado already had a state no-fault law that was working well. At the same time, it was fatally flawed because it included a trial lawyer provision that represented a ticking time bomb, namely, a "dollar threshold" that permitted the right to sue for pain and suffering if the injured person's economic losses exceeded $2,500. It was just a matter of time until it became a target for unscrupulous doctors and lawyers willing to run up medical bills to cross the threshold to sue. H.R. 13048 was designed to defuse the bomb by permitting suits only in cases of very serious injury.[4] Wirth was a member of the huge Democratic Class of 1974 that had been elected to reform the Congress in the wake of the Watergate scandal. Tall, handsome, and articulate, he had been chosen by the *Washington Post* as the focus of a series of articles on the new reformers. But he had been strangely noncommittal, and we knew he had been lobbied heavily by Boggs and his home district trial bar. Then, just days before the markup, Wirth called Les Cheek, a friend dating back to their days at Harvard who was a lobbyist for the American Insurance Association, a group of large insurers that supported H.R. 13048. Wirth bragged to Cheek that he had just turned down an offer from a lobbyist of a $5,000 campaign contribution (the maximum permissible amount at the time) to vote against no-fault.

Shortly after the Wirth call, Cheek dropped by my office to report it. I called Spencer Rich, a longtime reporter for the *Washington Post.* Rich, in turn, called Wirth's office. He was given the runaround for several hours before Wirth returned his call. Wirth, no doubt informed by his staff that such an offer was one of the few things for which a lobbyist could go to jail, denied the story. Absent Wirth being willing to confirm the story, my hope for a scandal to break open the issue died. At the same time, Wirth's willingness to share the bribe offer with Cheek made us feel comfortable enough to count Wirth in our column. That brought the Democratic total to 19.

The two—and only—remaining Democratic targets were Rep. Paul Rogers of Florida and Rep. Jim Florio of New Jersey. While the outside supporters were lobbying Rogers, I got a surprise call from Jeff Schwartz, a member of full Committee Chairman Harley Staggers's staff. One member of the full committee chairman's staff was assigned to assist each subcommittee, and Schwartz had been assigned to work with Rogers's Health Subcommittee. Jeff and I had become friendly, and now he was offering to talk to Rogers about supporting no-fault. It was a very generous offer, and I took him up on it. Through these efforts, we found out that Rogers was in a tough political position. Because his district was conservative for that of a Democrat, Rogers tended to limit his more liberal votes to the health care issues in his subcommittee. Rogers indicated that he would vote against the bill except under one condition. If his vote were the one needed to report no-fault, he would vote for it. So we didn't have our twentieth Democratic vote, but we had our twenty-first and enough to report the bill if we held all others—if we could find our twentieth Democratic vote from another member.

With these developments, the day before the vote, we felt pretty confident we could count on 21 of the 22 votes we needed (Rinaldo being the lone Republican vote). It would have been nicer if we had been sure of a majority and, preferably, had some margin for error, but time for action in the Ninety-Fifth Congress was running out. The House and Senate would be adjourning in a week for their annual five-week summer vacation (which they euphemistically described on the official calendar as a "district work period"), and when they returned after Labor Day, the House would be in session for only another month before adjourning in early October so the members could go home to campaign for reelection. If the bill didn't move out of committee now, it would, for all practical purposes, be dead for the year, and the whole process would have to start over again on January 3, 1979, with the new Ninety-Sixth Congress.

The last vote we thought we needed, and the only remaining possibility, was that of Representative Florio. Florio had professed support for the bill, but only if it included his amendment. The amendment, which the trial bar admitted to drafting, would have put the federal government into the business of detailed regulation of the auto insurance industry, including setting rates. Federal regulation was anathema to insurers, and the inclusion of the Florio amendment would have driven away all our insurance industry support. That, in turn, would have led to the death of the bill, as a united industry would have exercised its power to get moderate Democrats to vote against it.

We had a very narrow eye of a needle to thread—give Florio enough of what he wanted to get his vote but not so much as to drive away the limited industry support we had. The best shot lay in finding a way to get Florio to abandon the portion the industry hated most, which would have given the federal government the authority to determine the rates insurers could charge for auto insurance, while preserving the rest and then hoping that was enough for the industry. The trick lay in giving Florio some "cover" for dropping the rate-making portion of the amendment. The night before the vote, I discussed the problem with Eckhardt. It was his job, as the chairman of the subcommittee that had reported the bill to the full committee, to lead the full committee effort. The problem was that Eckhardt supported federal rate-making of the insurance industry! It took some convincing on my part, but Eckhardt finally agreed that the no-fault portion of the bill was more important than an amendment that never would become law anyway, as its inclusion would take the whole bill down. Eckhardt told me to draft an amendment that would give Florio all the elements of his amendment except for the rate-making portion. Eckhardt then placed a call to Florio, and I went to my office to draft the language. I followed an old formula, taking most of the Florio language *verbatim* but leaving out what he wanted most. Almost all the fifteen or so pages I drafted came straight from his amendment; the only thing missing was the rate-making portion. It was still going to upset insurers, but with the promise of removal later in the process, we were hopeful that our supporting insurers would grumble but not withdraw their support. When I informed them of what we were going to try to do, they did indeed grumble, but they agreed to stay with us.

Meanwhile, Eckhardt arranged to meet with Florio the next morning, before the second day of markup started, in the anteroom just off the full committee meeting room. I joined Eckhardt in the meeting, but Florio made a mistake; he came without staff. Eckhardt brilliantly convinced, or confused, Florio into accepting the amendment, leaving us to think we had the 22 votes needed to get the bill through Committee. But, as Robert Burns so wisely observed, "The best laid schemes o' mice an' men / Gang aft agley."

Shortly after the Florio meeting, the markup resumed. As Dingell railed at me and Eckhardt effectively defended the bill against all challengers, we saw the first signs of trouble. Three of the members whose votes we were counting on were not in attendance. Rep. Jack Murphy of New York—who had supported no-fault when he chaired the Consumer Protection Subcommittee two years before; had introduced a no-fault bill of his own; was a cosponsor of two no-fault bills in the Ninety-Fifth Congress, including the bill being marked up, H.R. 13048; and had given powerful testimony in favor of no-fault at the subcommittee's September 16, 1977, hearing in New York City—was nowhere to be found. Nor was Rep. Fred Rooney, a Democrat from Pennsylvania. Seated at the staff table, I could also see that they had not left proxies.

Moreover, Rep. Tim Wirth of Colorado was absent and, worse yet, had left a proxy to cast his vote against the bill! The plan was in deep trouble. I informed Cheek about the Wirth problem. Furious, Cheek tracked Wirth down at a hearing in another committee and confronted him. Wirth told Cheek there must have been some mistake and gave Cheek a proxy to give to the clerk to vote in favor of the bill.

We had avoided one disaster, but Murphy and Rooney were still AWOL, and we were running out of both time and votes. Lobbyists went to Murphy's office to ask him to come or send a proxy, but they couldn't get past the receptionist. Murphy was hiding and did not intend to be found. At the same time, they saw Representative Rooney walking down the hall past the committee room! They hailed him, but he just kept walking at a faster pace.

Back in the committee room, Boggs signaled to Representative Scheuer to meet him in the hall. While some of our supporters panicked when Scheuer left the room, there was no reason to worry. As Scheuer had previously flaked during subcommittee markup in the prior Congress before finally voting for the bill (after the bill's supporters had reached out to his rabbi), we had taken precautions to prevent a recurrence. While Boggs and the trial lawyers kept Scheuer out of the room, I was confident that he was okay because I could see his proxy in favor in the clerk's pile of proxies.

While Scheuer was not a problem, Murphy and Rooney were. As debate on the bill was ending, I informed Eckhardt that the votes were not there, but there was nothing he could do. All discussion being over and no more amendments being offered, Eckhardt moved to report the bill. The clerk called the roll, and Murphy and Rooney did not respond, either in person or by proxy. Without supporting votes from Rooney and Murphy, Representative Rogers's vote would not be the deciding one. Eckhardt's motion to report the bill failed, with 19 ayes and 22 nays. As expected under the circumstances, Rogers voted no, as his vote would not have been the decisive one to move the bill forward and it was politically better for him to oppose it.

As close as the vote was, it would prove to be the high-water mark for no-fault legislation in the House in the 1970s. What had happened to Rooney and Murphy? The answers came quickly, but they were far from satisfying. Cheek, who had tried but failed to stop Rooney in the hall outside the hearing room, reported that Rooney had committed to vote for both sides, to the Pennsylvania trial bar and to DOT Secretary Adams. The commitment to Adams seemed to be a lock, as he had the administration's lead on most of the programs in the jurisdiction of Representative Rooney's Transportation Subcommittee. However, to avoid alienating one side or the other, Rooney took a walk. That probably left more people angry at him than had he voted either way, but that was the explanation.

While we had thought Rooney was a bit squishy, no one had seen Murphy's pass coming. That turned out to be a Speaker Tip O'Neill special. We knew O'Neill was close to the trial bar and Boggs, whose father had been majority leader when O'Neill was rising through the ranks. We had long known that O'Neill was opposed. In 1975, when supporters had convinced his son, Tom O'Neill, Governor Dukakis's lieutenant governor and a no-fault supporter, to make a pitch to his father, Tip had stood his ground. When Van Deerlin had sent a letter to Tip the same year, the answer had been quite negative, citing all the arguments of the trial bar. What no one expected O'Neill to do was to intervene in a committee markup against the full committee and subcommittee chairmen. O'Neill did so stealthily and effectively. While Murphy had authored two no-fault bills and was a cosponsor of the no-fault bill that was being marked up, he had no personal investment in the outcome. On the other hand, he cared deeply about one of his own bills, the Endangered Species Act. When O'Neill told Murphy that if he voted to report no-fault, his Endangered Species bill would itself be endangered (it would not be considered on the floor), taking a walk was an easy decision for Murphy.

Even had we known of the threat in advance, we would have had no ability to counter the move. Simply, the House supporters and the outside groups that favored no-fault lacked the necessary clout with both Murphy and O'Neill. Supporters were able to generate some support from unions in their districts, but we had no internal clout in the House to match that of the speaker. Eckhardt was a brilliant man whose intellect gave him great influence in small settings, such as subcommittee markups and House-Senate conferences. However, unlike the dominant Texans of his day, Lyndon Johnson and former House Speaker Sam Rayburn, he was not an arm twister. I once asked a Republican member, Rep.

Manny Lujan of New Mexico, why Eckhardt wasn't more effective on the House floor. Lujan replied, "Because he's always talking about the Constitution!" Unlike Lujan, I took that as a compliment, but on August 1, 1978, it was a disadvantage.

I have said little about the Carter administration because it said little about no-fault. Active support by any president can raise the visibility of an issue, making special interest pleadings somewhat less influential and making the general interest more powerful. The problem is getting an administration's attention when there are always many issues competing for presidential time. While administration support can greatly improve the prospects of legislation, an administration can push only so many issues at once. In the case of no-fault, the official Carter administration position was in favor, and DOT Secretary Brock Adams did testify for it, but it was not one of the administration's top priorities, and according to a magazine article at the time, Adams was the lowest-rated member of the Carter cabinet: Secretary Adams was "largely ignored by [the] White House."[5] Moreover, in Commerce Committee matters, the administration was focused on transportation deregulation—for airlines, railroads, and the trucking industry. Alfred Kahn, chairman of the Civil Aeronautics Board, was a highly respected economist who was a charismatic voice in the airline debate. His strong arguments that airline passengers would save money helped overcome opposition by every airline. Kahn was so effective that he became known as "the father of airline deregulation." His was just the kind of administration voice that was missing on no-fault. To be fair, the Carter administration did win major victories in all three areas of transportation deregulation.

Still, a modest degree of support might have helped get the no-fault bill reported from the House Commerce Committee. Even that minimal amount was not forthcoming. The Carter administration, as was not uncommon, was a day late and more than a few dollars short. In fact, it was 173 days late to the battle. Strong support in July 1978 might well have produced success in the markup, as the administration had much to offer both Rooney and Murphy. Instead, it did little or nothing when no-fault was fighting its last battle. Seven months after the denouement, President Carter offered his strongest endorsement of no-fault in his January 25, 1979, State of the Union Message to the Congress:

No-fault systems have proven to be far more efficient in delivering benefits to the victims of automobile accidents than the current tort system, and they also provide real opportunities to coordinate and reduce overall insurance costs. Too great a percentage of the premiums paid by policyholders goes for the administration of the current wasteful tort liability system. No-fault would save money and court time. It deserves Congressional support.

11. Decompression, Depression, Introspection, and a Failed Effort to Secure Support for a Choice No-Fault Bill (Fall 1978)

After a period for decompressing, for which the August congressional recess came in handy, and some depression, which lasted a lot longer, supporters started thinking backward and forward—backward to why the bill had failed and forward to what, if anything, could be done to secure enactment in the next Congress. In the fall, Lynn Sutcliffe, Les Cheek, and I all wrote after-action memos in the hope of finding answers.

John F. Kennedy once said, "Victory has a hundred fathers, but defeat is an orphan." In this case, I believe defeat also had a hundred fathers. In our analyses, we started with the positives, which were also relevant to answering the questions about what, if anything, could be done differently to change the outcome the next time. On the right side of the ledger was the widespread belief that the outside intellectual and the internal congressional efforts couldn't have been better. The professorial work defining the problems and developing a solution was the best I saw during my twenty-five years on the Hill. The advocacy materials encouraging support for the bill were excellent, externally by the Committee for Consumers No-Fault and internally on both the Senate and House sides.

In the administration, Dick Walsh educated Hill staff with the details of the findings of the original DOT study. In addition, Bob Joost made another major contribution by being the lead author on the second DOT report that analyzed state no-fault experience, "State No-Fault Automobile Insurance Experience, 1971–1977." The study would probably not have been done as rapidly as it was but for pressure from the congressional committees. Even then, DOT did not use its findings nearly aggressively enough. Mary Schuman used the substantive knowledge and political skills she had learned while working for the Senate Commerce Committee to help secure support from the Carter administration.

Overall, I think it's fair to say that no-fault supporters won the substantive argument hands down, say 90–10. But good, even outstanding, staff and academic work can push legislation only so far. Getting it across the finish line usually involves at least enough private sector support to offset opponents' efforts so that members will listen to the merits. Anything more is even better. On the congressional side, the more powerful congressional supporters are, the more likely the bill is to move.

In the no-fault fight, it proved impossible to match the outside efforts of the key opponents, the trial bar and many in the insurance industry. Believing its economic livelihood was threatened, the trial bar raised huge sums of money for extensive lobbying efforts by well-connected insiders Boggs, Timmons, and Korologos. More importantly, the trial bar made campaign contributions to members of Congress (including to all House Commerce Committee members who voted against the bill before the vote). Probably as or more important was the impact of the trial lawyers' ability to weaken the thresholds in many state no-fault laws. They used the subsequent, predictably higher premiums to argue to the Congress that no-fault was a failure. Their arguments were buttressed by a major unrelated event that added to higher premiums, the high inflation during the Carter administration, with a rate of 6.5 percent in 1977 and 7.59 percent in 1978. The trial bar conveniently ignored the fact that inflation had the same impact on rates in tort states, leaving supporters to make a more complicated counterargument. The final component of their cost argument was to compare rates in no-fault states—such as Massachusetts, New Jersey, New York, and Pennsylvania—with those in tort states. It was another red herring, as a disproportionate number of the no-fault states were high-density states, which skewed the comparison.

On the pro-no-fault side of the ledger, no private sector supporter believed adoption of the bill would have provided a financial advantage large enough to warrant matching the opposition's financial effort. That left Sutcliffe, for all his considerable political skills, unable to raise enough money to have the resources to counter the opponents. Had supporters had even half the money the opposition had, no-fault might well have passed.

There was significant support from consumer groups, particularly CFA, as well as unions and from State Farm and the member companies of the American Insurance Association. All expended considerable effort lobbying members and generating grassroots support. Unfortunately, the AARP, which strongly supported the bill, had yet to become the powerful lobbying force it is now, and Nader's silence undercut the support from other consumer groups. It also sidelined Public Citizen, the consumer organization Nader had founded, whose resources could have helped the effort. Perhaps most importantly, the trial bar had an effective counter-argument to liberal Democrats who generally supported consumer and labor issues—they could keep labor and consumer support with votes on other issues, but this was the only issue for the trial bar, and it would run and finance candidates against members who voted for no-fault. Given its resources, this was not a hollow threat. That left supporters to rely on the merits of their argument, which, in the end, did not stand up to the political threat to members' reelection.

Supporters did succeed in putting an end to the cost argument. Early conflicting cost estimates by State Farm and Allstate, the country's two largest auto insurers, had created uncertainty as to the likely outcome of enactment. Allstate had initially estimated that the 1975 bill would increase costs, while State Farm had predicted lower costs. The difference was in the assumptions, with State Farm's costing based on the minimum no-fault benefits required by the bill and Allstate assuming that higher benefit levels would be chosen. To resolve the differences, the subcommittee sent Allstate a letter asking it to cost the bill using the actual requirements within it.[1] The result was that both companies projected nationwide cost savings, with an Allstate projection of 15.8 percent versus a State Farm projection of 11 percent. Their state-by-state projections varied more widely, but the cause was in their books of business, with Allstate's more urban and State Farm's more rural. It also helped that the 1977 bills reduced the level of medical and rehabilitation benefits from unlimited to $100,000, which reduced Allstate's anxiety and thus the intensity of its opposition.[2] In 1976, Allstate invited me to visit its research facility in California and then to meet with a number of Allstate vice presidents at company headquarters in Northbrook, Illinois. In addition to the bill changes, the trip seemed to ease some of its concerns and may well have contributed to Allstate not doing a cost estimate for the 1977 bill. With only State Farm projecting premiums for the impact of no-fault, and projecting lower ones, the debate over costs was effectively over.

As a result of efforts by insurer opponents, with small-company lobbying being the most effective, and state officials, only one Republican voted for the bill in the subcommittee and the full committee. I think it is fair to conclude that the near-unanimous Republican opposition was due far more to the influence of insurers than to philosophical support for states' rights given Republican support in the Senate. There, the bill enjoyed broad bipartisan support, including from Sen. Ted Stevens, who became minority whip in 1977, and Sen. James Pearson, the ranking minority member of the Commerce Committee. In 1974, when the number of Democrats to Republicans was 55–45, the no-fault bill passed by 53–42, with 15 Republicans voting in favor. That represented 35 percent of the Republican caucus. In sharp contrast, only one Republican out of fourteen voted in favor in the House Commerce Committee. Even then, one Republican vote should have been enough, given the 29:14 majority of Democrats to Republicans on the committee, but it was not because of the influence of trial lawyer money. As detailed earlier by Common Cause, the trial bar's PAC spent more money on campaign contributions on this single issue than any other PAC on any other issue. Because its funds went primarily to Democrats, the trial bar was able to peel away many Democrats who would normally have voted for no-fault. While the money was enormously important, it does not excuse Democrats who favored no-fault in private from caving to trial lawyer pressure when it was time to be counted.

Ralph Nader also deserves special mention, as his opposition probably gave two or three moderate-to-liberal Democrats[3] on the House Commerce Committee cover to vote against the bill. More was said about Nader's opposition earlier, and much more will be said later in the context of the Auto Choice effort.

While the inextricable tie between money and politics explains a lot but excuses little or nothing, there were broader factors at work. First, while the high cost of auto insurance had been what first inspired Senator Hart's early hearings, the legislation focused more on the inadequacy of compensation for seriously injured victims than on lowering rates. While this was a worthy goal, the high benefits limited savings estimates to the low double digits and unquestionably narrowed political support. The authors of Auto Choice did not make that political mistake, but the high savings estimates created other problems, as outlined later.

Second, legislation tends to have a limited shelf life for congressional attention, and no-fault was around too long before it had a real opportunity to move in both houses in 1978. During that time, from 1967 to 1978, the climate that favored consumer issues early on faded under an onslaught of consumer legislation and regulation and disaffection with Washington after the Watergate scandal. With hearings starting in 1967 and the first Senate Commerce Committee markup in 1971, the failure of the House Commerce Committee to act until 1978 also gave the opposition way too much time to organize.

Of course, money cannot be overlooked. It can buy an awful lot of help to cover up a weak substantive position. In the case of the most effective opponent, ATLA, money resulted in the full employment of the political playbook—relocating its headquarters from Boston to Washington, DC; hiring a full-time congressional lobbyist, Tom Bendorf (kind of a poor man's Boggs, with the physical but not the political heft, as it were); and hiring the most prominent Democratic lobbyist in town, Tom Boggs, and then the most prominent Republican lobbyists, Bill Timmons and Tom Korologos, all of whom had personal access to senators. Korologos still had the mantle of the White House, having recently been the chief Senate lobbyist for the Ford White House, and Boggs's father had been the House majority whip. Moreover, while the White House didn't actively lobby against no-fault in 1974, it did so in 1975–1976. During this period, ATLA lobbyists worked with White House congressional staff out of the vice president's office to plan strategy for the recommittal vote in the Senate. Boggs supplemented that effort by encouraging House members to contact their senators to argue that Senate passage would present political problems for them, i.e., if they were forced to a recorded vote in the House.[4]

As effective as the trial bar's lobbying effort was its biggest asset: money. The funds raised from its members financed a major grassroots operation and, most important, funded huge campaign contributions from the largest single-issue PAC of the time.

The natural counterforce to the trial bar's grassroots operation would have been the independent agents force of the insurance industry had the industry not been divided and had agents not been fearful that no-fault would bring new competitors. Auto insurance is sold by people who work directly for insurers and "independent" agents, who may work for one or more companies. Historically, the benefit to insurers of using independent agents was lack of benefits, that is, that insurers did not have to provide benefits to their workforce if they were agents (independent contractors) instead of employees. The agents were split because the companies that paid their commissions were divided. They were also split because the agents feared that switching to a primarily first-part no-fault system would make it easier for health insurers to compete for the same business. They were also fearful of facing competition from health insurers and companies such as Aflac that sold supplemental insurance that covered losses not covered by mandatory coverage, i.e., no-fault benefits for such things as loss of individual body parts.

Second, while three administrations supported no-fault, two of them opposed the federal legislation and the one that supported it did not weigh in aggressively. The Nixon administration walked up to the edge with its very strong DOT study endorsing no-fault, but it undercut that support by deferring to the states for action. The Ford administration continued to support no-fault but, again, deferred to the states. When an administration—that of President Carter—finally endorsed federal no-fault, it did not place a high enough priority on it to devote the resources necessary to secure the votes.

Third, bad luck or timing seemed to dog the legislation. The impeachment of Nixon led to a halt of all major legislation in the House in 1974, after a bill had passed the Senate. Attorney General Levi outfought an initially unprepared DOT Secretary Coleman to secure President Ford's opposition in 1975. President Ford's political team's misreading of Ronald Reagan's position led Ford to oppose no-fault and change six Republican votes in 1976. Then, the feckless presidency of Jimmy Carter and his ineffectual secretary of transportation, Brock Adams, failed to exercise the power of the presidency in 1978. A change in any of these four events could well have led to the passage of no-fault legislation.

That said, as discussed previously, Eckhardt missed an enormous opportunity with the Perles/Stevens/Broyhill (Joost/Kinzler/Mullen) proposal. In fairness to Eckhardt, his position on industry regulation was within the mainstream of the party's thinking at the time (and, perhaps, more so now), and he would have had to overcome some Democratic pushback had he worked out this compromise with Broyhill. On the other hand, Eckhardt had worked out several bipartisan deals with Broyhill in the past, and Broyhill's credibility among his fellow Republicans was so high that any deal he agreed to would have brought enough Republican support to overcome any Democratic defections. At the end of the day, it is hard to move any significant legislation without bipartisan support.

Nevertheless, the work on no-fault choice was to lay the groundwork for another major no-fault effort eighteen years later. In the short term, in 1978, as depressed as we were by the defeat of no-fault, I was intrigued by choice. Building on the Broyhill proposal and on previous no-fault choice proposals by Keaton and O'Connell (in the appendix to their original book) and by Yale Law School Dean Guido Calabresi, Mike Mullen and I developed a more detailed proposal for a choice no-fault bill. In November 1978, I circulated the proposal and convened a meeting of no-fault supporters. The idea was to strip away the trial bar's most powerful argument, that insureds who wanted to remain in the tort system and sue could not do so, by offering drivers the option of remaining in their state's tort system. At the meeting in December, the insurers questioned the workability of such a system, and the consumer and labor groups showed their inherent suspicion of insurers, questioning whether they would manipulate the system to discourage consumers from choosing the no-fault system. When no-fault's outside supporters could not agree, the eleven-year effort to enact federal no-fault came to an end.

12. Experience with Other Liability Reform Issues Leads to a Surprise Return to No-Fault (1981–1996)

With no-fault supporters unwilling to consider a no-fault choice bill, I decided it was time to stop pushing the same boulder up the same hill (a lesson Sisyphus never learned).

In the next Congress, the Ninety-Sixth, no member of either house introduced a no-fault bill. Since 1978, no member has introduced a federal standards bill like the bills of the 1970s. Moreover, shortly after no-fault died, so did the three subcommittee chairmen who had worked for its adoption—not literally but politically. Van Deerlin and Eckhardt lost in the Reagan landslide election of 1980, and Murphy went off to jail because of his involvement in the Abscam scandal.

As disheartening as the failure of the Congress to pass no-fault was, to everyone's surprise, that was not the end of the no-fault fight. But the road back was a long and winding one that took nearly twenty years. While I remained interested in the subject, I moved on to other areas of work. One place I did not move to was the Health Subcommittee of the House Commerce Committee. After Eckhardt lost, he volunteered to help the staff get jobs. I asked him if he would talk to Rep. Henry Waxman (D-CA), who was assuming the Health Subcommittee chairmanship, on my behalf. He readily agreed to do so. Two weeks later, I ran into Eckhardt in the Cannon House Office Building. I asked him if he had had a chance to speak with Waxman. Eckhardt stared at the ceiling for about forty-five seconds in silence and then responded, in vintage Eckhardt style, "I don't rightly recall if I did or didn't, Peter, but I know if I did, I said very good things about you."

I survived the 1980 Reagan landslide by moving to the Senate, where job opportunities for Democratic staff were limited by the fact that the election had also brought the Senate into Republican hands, with only two new Democrats elected. Moreover, the Republican takeover meant the elimination of many Democratic committee staffers. Fortunately, I was able to secure one of the few jobs for Democratic staff in the office of newly elected Sen. Christopher J. Dodd (D-CT). The job was as minority counsel to the Consumer Subcommittee of the Senate Banking Committee. Because the Banking Committee had different consumer jurisdiction than that of the Commerce Committee, the issues were completely different.

Serving on a committee with no jurisdiction over liability issues, I never anticipated that my expertise on first-party, no-lawyer insurance systems would lead to involvement in two other major liability reform fights: product liability and vaccine injury compensation. What I learned, substantively and politically, working on these two issues was to prove useful when no-fault returned in 1996.

Starting in 1981, I worked mostly on banking issues for Senator Dodd while on the payroll of the Senate Banking Committee. However, in 1984, I seized another "opportunity" to become involved in liability reform. This time, the subject was product liability. During the 1970s, the costs of product liability insurance had skyrocketed for many products. The increases had had a particularly negative effect on vaccines, dangerously reducing the number of suppliers, but they had affected multiple other industries as well. An Interagency Task Force on Product Liability documented the shortcomings of state laws in 1977. The author of the report was Victor Schwartz, a law professor at the University of Cincinnati who was hired by the US Department of Commerce to chair the task force. Schwartz and I became acquainted when he contacted me to see how product liability cases would be handled under the no-fault bill. Later, we discussed how separate legislation might address the product liability crisis. As is common in DC, Victor went from his government position into the private sector and created the Product Liability Coordinating Committee, a coalition of manufacturers lobbying for changes in product liability law. The result was S. 44, the Product Liability Act, which was reintroduced with the same number in succeeding Congresses from 1979 through the mid-1980s.

S. 44 differed in two significant substantive respects from the approach taken in no-fault: (1) It addressed the issue of frivolous lawsuits only by changing the legal standards to make it harder to recover, and (2) it did not address the deficiencies in compensation for injured persons with legitimate claims at all. The politics were different as well, as product liability manufacturers opened their wallets in support while consumer groups and trial lawyers lined up in opposition. The result was a different political alignment. Almost all Republicans supported the legislation, while most Democrats opposed it. A few more conservative Democrats with important home-state manufacturers did support the bill. This different political alignment proved no more successful in securing adoption than the nearly polar opposite alignment that had supported the no-fault effort.

In 1984, after the bill had gone nowhere, Victor called to solicit my advice on how to make the bill more attractive to Democrats. Initially, I told him that it was unlikely that the bill would have its intended effect, even if it could be passed in its present form. My view was that if his analysis of the problem was correct—that juries were ignoring legal standards in order to find for sympathetic plaintiffs—then juries could just as easily ignore the more restrictive standards in the bill. I told him I would review the issue. I reread his Department of Commerce report, S. 44, and a study by the Insurance Services Office, "Product Liability Closed Claims Survey: A Technical Analysis of Survey Results" (1977).[1] Looking at the materials through the eyes of injured persons as well as aggrieved manufacturers, I discovered a pattern of recovery similar to that of people injured in auto accidents: people with small economic losses recovered, on average, far more than their losses (482 percent when the losses were between $1 and $1,000), while people with significant losses recovered only a fraction of their losses (6 percent when the losses exceeded $1 million). These returns were even worse than those in auto injury cases, and the delays in recovery were again worse than in auto, taking an average of five years to pay a claim for the average loss. The one constant was that plaintiff attorneys continued to do well, taking almost as much as the injured parties.

I suggested to Schwartz that he needed to include provisions to help people with legitimate claims in order to gain support from enough Democrats to pass a bill. But Schwartz had built a coalition around the idea that each involved industry would be helped, so he was unwilling to risk splitting that coalition by switching to a first-party compensation system to provide assurances to both injured persons and manufacturers—at the expense of the lawyers. I had no similar constraints, so, with

Senator Dodd's blessing, I drafted a bill for him using the same basic approach as for auto no-fault: provide assured recovery of economic loss in return for limits on noneconomic loss.

The bill ran into an immediate challenge. The Senate parliamentarian, Bob Dove, indicated that he would refer the bill to the Judiciary Committee, as it involved the judicial system, even though similar bills—no-fault auto insurance bills and S. 44, the product liability bill—had been referred to the Commerce Committee. Dove said that those bills had been incorrectly referred by the previous parliamentarian. Thus, the issue reached a critical juncture even before a bill was introduced. If the bill was referred to the Judiciary Committee, whose membership was almost entirely composed of lawyers, it stood no chance of going anywhere.[2] However, by Senate rules, any amendment to a bill must follow the underlying bill; i.e., if the bill was drafted as an amendment to S. 100, the new Kasten product liability bill, the parliamentarian would be required to refer the amendment to the Commerce Committee because the underlying bill had been referred there. Thus, on March 19, 1985, Senator Dodd introduced a complete bill as Senate Amendment No. 16 to S. 100, and Dove was forced to refer it to the Commerce Committee.

The new bill initially split the business community, as two key players favored the new approach. Supporters of the traditional products bill gave it one more try, only to fail in the Commerce Committee. Sen. John Danforth (R-MO), chairman of the Commerce Committee, then directed his staffer, David Zorensky, to work with Dodd's staff (me) to craft a bill that would attract broader support than S. 100. Senator Dodd graciously agreed, as long as I was able to meet my responsibilities to him on Banking Committee issues. Zorensky and I spent months refining the Dodd amendment (as had been the case with regard to redrafting the House no-fault bill ten years before) into a new draft for a Danforth-Dodd bill (Danforth, after all, was the chairman of the committee and so would be the sponsor, with Dodd as the lead cosponsor). A first draft was released for comment on July 15, 1985, and then a second on November 22, 1985. A new bill faced the same problem of jurisdiction as before. However, on December 20, 1985, Danforth accidentally dropped what was intended to be a new amendment in as a bill instead. Probably because it was the end of the year with the holidays approaching, Dove wasn't paying close attention and accidentally referred the bill, S. 1999, the Product Liability Voluntary Claims and Uniform Standards Act, to the Commerce Committee!

I think it's a common work anxiety dream that something you have worked on for a long time fails while you are on vacation and can't do anything to save it. If it isn't, it should be. I rarely took vacations far from Washington, except when the Senate was out of session in August, and I never went on junkets (day trips to speak at conferences in Newark, NJ, are not junkets). The one true junket I took was a one-week trip to Taiwan. It was in the spring of 1986, while the Congress was in session, and it proved disastrous to the product liability effort in that Congress. The problem began with Sen. Slade Gorton (R-WA). He had expressed support for the effort, but he dragged the process out by revising his position each time Danforth and Dodd agreed to his demands. This game of legislative Whac-A-Mole lasted for months. Then, in May 1986, while I was away on my junket, Danforth agreed to several revisions suggested by Senator Gorton that undermined the structure of the bill both substantively and politically. When I returned, I shared my concerns with David and he with Danforth, but the damage was done. Danforth was forced to postpone the markup in order to secure majority support for a new amendment that then passed the committee, without Gorton's support. The result was a good bill (S. 2760, the Product Liability Reform Act), but it was not reported until June 26, 1986, and the committee report was not filed until August 14, 1986, leaving only a short window for action before the end of the Congress. The bill was considered on the floor in September but failed to secure the votes to cut off a threatened filibuster, in large part because it was too late for the House to act even if the Senate did. This fact enabled the trial lawyer lobbyists to argue to Senate Democrats once again not to take a tough political vote because the House wouldn't act (a version of the adage "Never strike a king unless you are sure you shall kill him"). Then, in the elections of 1986, the Democrats won back the Senate, and interest in the bill waned when an avowed opponent, Sen. Ernest "Fritz" Hollings (D-SC), assumed the chairmanship of the Commerce Committee. However, my involvement in the product liability issue would return in 1991 when Sen. John D. "Jay" Rockefeller IV (D-WVA) took over the chairmanship of the Consumer Subcommittee and changed from an opponent to the major proponent.

While the product liability bill had not passed, I was able to use some of the concepts we had developed for products to help advance legislation to establish a vaccine compensation system. This time the issue was within the jurisdiction of one of the committees Senator Dodd served on, the Health, Education, Labor and Pensions (HELP) Committee.

As indicated previously, lawsuits against vaccine manufacturers had increased dramatically, as courts had started holding them liable in cases where they previously had not been found liable under the "unavoidably inevitable accident" doctrine. This doctrine held that companies were not liable in situations where a product would inevitably injure a small number of those who used it while benefiting many. That had been the case with vaccines, but some courts had stopped applying the doctrine to help the small percentage of people whom vaccines injured get compensation. Because of several large verdicts, many companies had stopped selling vaccines, and the remaining companies were considering doing the same. That created a serious risk to the supply system and to the health of the country. At the same time, the small percentage of people who were injured by vaccines were struggling to obtain compensation, experiencing many of the same issues with no compensation or long delays and under-compensation in serious injury cases as in auto and other product injury cases.

Having helped develop compensation systems for no-fault auto insurance and product liability, I had some ideas that I thought would apply well to vaccine injuries. Not only did I have access to the HELP Committee through Senator Dodd, I had a personal interest because Jeff Schwartz, my friend and fellow House Commerce staffer, had a child who had suffered a severe injury from a diphtheria, pertussis, typhoid (DPT) shot. Jeff had organized a group of the families of children who had arguably been injured by the problematic DPT vaccine to lobby for federal compensation. He called the group Dissatisfied Parents Together (DPT), cleverly mimicking the name of the suspect vaccine.

Unlike the situation for auto and product injuries, the politics came together for the vaccine compensation legislation. The manufacturers wanted relief from recent large verdicts, the federal government wanted a reliable source of childhood vaccines, and the families sought speedy and sure compensation to care for their injured children. The families' support of the final legislation prevented the trial lawyers, who represented the families, from publicly opposing what their clients wanted.

Because of my expertise and the fact that I worked for a committee member, I was welcomed by the HELP staff who were working on legislation on behalf of Sens. Ted Kennedy (D-MA), Orrin Hatch (R-UT) and Paula Hawkins (R-FL). We developed legislation for the senators that was similar to that contained in the Danforth-Dodd bill. The consensus helped advance the issue in the Senate with the focus on first-party, health insurance–like compensation instead of on fault through the tort system. Ultimately, a variant of this approach became the National Childhood Vaccine Injury Act of 1986.

In the spring of 1991, the issue of product liability came alive again. I had not worked on it since the Danforth-Dodd bill had failed in 1986. Then, in 1991, Senator Rockefeller, the new chairman of the Consumer Subcommittee of the Senate Commerce Committee, changed his position and joined with Sen. Bob Kasten to introduce a product liability bill. Rockefeller's support gave the bill new life, as he provided bipartisan support. After the bill was reported from committee, Rockefeller started looking for more Democratic support. Given Dodd's prior interest, Rockefeller's office reached out to take Dodd's temperature on the new bill. I told Rockefeller's legislative assistant, Lynley Ogilvie, that I thought it was better than prior bills but didn't do enough for consumers, as the Dodd bill would have. Then, in the late spring, Lynley left Rockefeller's office to go to the University of Virginia School of Law. She also left me with a surprise—that Rockefeller had asked if I would be willing to staff the bill for him, so long as Dodd agreed. Dodd agreed to this highly unusual arrangement, and suddenly I was working pretty much full-time for Rockefeller.

Rockefeller decided that the best strategy for passing the bill would be to shift the focus from its benefits for businesses to its benefits for consumers. As Rockefeller prepared for floor action in the fall, he was anxious about having to debate fellow Democratic Sens. Fritz Hollings and Howell Heflin (AL) on the Senate floor. Both were lawyers, and Heflin had been a judge as well. I tried to reassure Rockefeller by pointing out that neither of them had taken a course in product liability in law school. The reason was simple—law schools hadn't taught courses in product liability when they had been in school because it wasn't a large enough area of law to warrant a separate course. Hollings and Heflin were starting from the same place Rockefeller was, and I assured him that he would be better prepared than they were.

To help Rockefeller get ready for the floor fight, I spent my August recess break writing a forty-five-page memo. The memo contained sections on the purposes of the bill and the background and need and a summary of the provisions.[3] Each provision included a section with the proponents' arguments, followed by one with the opponents' arguments and then a rebuttal to the opponents' arguments. In late August, Senator Rockefeller invited me to his home in West Virginia to prepare for floor consideration. He had read the briefing book thoroughly, as every line on each page was colored in yellow highlighter, and some lines were colored over in orange.

This time when the bill, S. 640, the Product Liability Fairness Act, went to the floor on September 8, 1992, the opponents mounted a filibuster. Senator Rockefeller argued effectively, but he needed enough votes to invoke cloture in order to get a vote on the bill. At one point during consideration, there were 60 votes for cloture, only to see Sen. Alfonse D'Amato (R-NY) and one other senator change their votes before the vote was closed. Senator Rockefeller kept the clerk's tally sheet with that "winning vote" in his desk for a long time afterward. Alas, there were only fifty-eight votes for cloture when the voting ended, so the bill did not pass. My work on product liability ended when I moved to the House in March 1993. The products bill died the next year when the business community refused to accept a compromise with the Clinton administration. The refusal so angered Senator Rockefeller that he refused to make any further effort. No product liability bill has been considered since then.

My twelve years in the Senate and involvement in two more liability reform efforts gave me insights into both how differently members operate in the House and Senate and how a no-fault bill might be crafted and supported politically to garner enough votes from both sides of the aisle to pass. But I didn't get a chance to put what I had learned into effect for four years. The first two I spent back on the House side, and then, when the Republicans won control of the House in 1994, I decided to try my luck in the private sector.

After twenty-five years on the Hill, I was nervous about leaving. At

NEWS/TRENDS

selves. But they think the new CDs may help revive the original videodiscs, which produce better picture and sound quality than ordinary videotape.

Return of the IPO?

■ Maybe. The market for initial public offerings has been icy since October 19. In January, 29 of 30 companies that had planned to go public found the market so forbidding they dropped the idea. By late February, however, a warming trend had appeared: That's when the first of three high-tech companies took the plunge.

Octel Communications, a manufacturer of voice-messaging systems based in Milpitas, California, had hoped to go public last fall, according to President Robert Cohn. The five-year-old company finally made its debut February 25, selling 2.1 million shares at $7 each—the first high-tech offering since the crash. By the end of the day Octel's stock had floated up to $9 a share. That's encouraging. According to *Going Public: IPO Reporter*, which tracks the performance of IPOs, the 100 newest IPO stocks recently traded at 3.7% below their initial offering price.

Another Silicon Valley company, **Maxim Integrated Products**, a manufacturer of analog semiconductors, went public at the beginning of March. The market quickly snatched up 2.3 million shares, 300,000 more than Maxim had originally planned to offer. The price has been holding steady at around $5.75.

Vitalink Communications, a California outfit that makes so-called wide area network bridges that link local area networks, was expected to go public by mid-March. If that offering does well, some 50 companies may bounce into the IPO pool.

Cohn's Octel broke the IPO barrier.

Glass-Steagall: a nail in the coffin

■ A minor miracle: The Senate Banking Committee brought forth a bill repealing parts of the Depression-era Glass-Steagall Act, which bars commercial banks from most securities activities. The legislation, called the swan song of committee chairman William Proxmire (D-Wisconsin) who is not seeking reelection, would give banks the power to sell most securities but would limit their ability to peddle insurance.

The free-the-banks momentum may meet more resistance in the House. Fernand St Germain (D-Rhode Island), head of the House Banking Committee, has blocked reform for years, but may introduce a limited bill. John Dingell (D-Michigan), chairman of the Energy and Commerce Committee, has expressed worries about broader bank powers.

Dodd: the insurance agent's friend

Still, the jousting in the Senate shows just which financial services have the most lobbying clout. The not surprising answer: It's the insistent independent insurance agents—"at least one in every district," as the 126,000-member Independent Insurance Agents of America boasts. Their point man on the committee was Christopher Dodd (D-Connecticut), from the land of big insurance companies. "Independent insurance agents have always prevailed legislatively," says veteran Bill Bailey, head of his own agency in Waco, Texas. "The battles we lost were with regulatory agencies."

Over the years, regulators in about a dozen states have permitted state banks to sell insurance. The compromise Dodd pushed through the committee would require that both the bank and its parent company be located within a state before officials could grant permission to sell insurance.

So what about the bankers? Charles Pistor, president of the American Bankers Association, says: "We are very disappointed that the insurance provision, unlike the rest of the bill, runs contrary to the consumers' best interest. We will continue working to modify these restrictions."

NEC among the pyramids

■ How far will the Japanese go to protect their export markets? Pretty far. In Egypt, where electronics behemoth **NEC** controls half the local market for TVs, Cairo officials asked if they couldn't get some help selling Egyptian vacations in Japan.

NEC got busy. By April, it will have rounded up almost 700 Japanese tourists and sent them off to marvel at—and presumably videotape—the pyramids.

Here's how the deal works: NEC agrees to export tourists (target: 3,000 a year) with Egypt Air as the carrier. Egypt, which badly needs hard foreign currency, uses half the air fare plus all the money spent by tourists to buy TV parts from NEC. Over the past year, Egypt ordered enough components for 260,000 sets, which a government-controlled company assembles.

Changes in Japanese lifestyle may make tourist deals more popular. Traditionally, Japanese workers have put a far lower value on time off than have their American and European counterparts. But hourly wages in Japan, measured in dollars, are already among the world's highest, and at least one union, girding itself for spring bargaining sessions, has curbed wage demands and asked for more holidays.

Rising again

■ "It is amazing," wrote H. L. Mencken, surveying Dixie culture in 1917, "to contemplate so vast a vacuity. One thinks of interstellar spaces . . . Nearly the whole of Europe could be lost in

12 FORTUNE MARCH 28, 1988

Figure 12.1. Sen. Christopher J. Dodd and Peter Kinzler (Senate Banking Committee staff to the senator), March 28, 1988. Photograph by Brad Markel for *Fortune* magazine.

the same time, I was excited by the prospect of speaking for myself after so many years of speaking on behalf of senators and representatives. While working for Senator Dodd, I cut out and framed a March 28, 1988, picture from *Fortune* magazine that perfectly captured the relationship between a senator and staff. It shows the senator in the foreground with me in the background whispering into his ear (Figure 12.1). It was time to stop being the guy behind the guy and be my own person.

I thought the move to the private sector would involve less interesting but more lucrative work. I was wrong on both counts. To my surprise, it was little more than a year after I left the Hill and started a "consulting" (lobbying) business that I read that Sen. Mitch McConnell was working on a bill to give motorists the option of purchasing no-fault insurance instead of the single kind of insurance mandated by their state. Before I turn to those events, let me describe what the states had done, or not done, since the first congressional no-fault effort that warranted reconsideration of the no-fault concept.

13. Two Decades of Changes in State Auto Insurance Laws Fail to Fix the Major Problems

While I was working on other issues, efforts to secure more state no-fault laws stalled. As we had anticipated, with the end of the threat of passage of federal legislation, much of the incentive for states to act dissipated, and states stopped adopting new laws. The other key factor that stopped state action was the explosion of the ticking time bombs of weak thresholds that the trial bar placed in the laws. The most common device was to permit suits after a person's medical bills reached $500 or $1,000, or as little as $200 in New Jersey. The ease of reaching the thresholds gutted the fundamental trade-off involved in no-fault—paying for everyone's economic losses, without regard to fault, in return for eliminating lawsuits in all cases but those with the most serious injuries. With low thresholds, it was possible for even honest motorists and lawyers to meet them. The answer was not higher dollar thresholds. They proved to be worse, as they became targets for the unscrupulous, with many lawyers working with doctors who would bill for unnecessary tests or tests never given. The cost of this additional fraud was passed along to motorists through higher premiums. By skillful efforts (if political contributions are a form of skill), the trial bar was able to maintain much of its previous auto accident business by turning no-fault into a system that financed tort suits as well. Having gutted the intentions of the authors of no-fault, the trial bar, with a straight face, then turned around and argued for repeal of state no-fault laws on the grounds that they weren't working.

Despite the lack of clean hands, the trial lawyers' actions stopped or undermined the state laws. Since the mid-1970s, no state that didn't already have a no-fault law has enacted one, although Pennsylvania and New Jersey have made major revisions, creating systems that give motorists a choice between fault and no-fault bodily injury coverages. Connecticut, Georgia, Nevada, and Colorado repealed their laws and returned to the tort system.

While the trial bar was hard at work undermining no-fault, Bob Joost and Jeff O'Connell were working to counter its efforts and find a more politically attractive vehicle for federal legislation. I had stayed in touch with Bob after the federal legislation died in 1978. In May 1985, from his position at DOT, Joost was back at it, writing a new DOT study, "Compensating Auto Accident Victims: A Follow-up Report on the No-Fault Auto Insurance Experience."[1] Like the 1977 DOT study, the 1985 study concluded that no-fault was meeting its compensation goals—that significantly more motor vehicle accident victims were receiving more compensation far more swiftly in no-fault states than in tort states. It also found that no-fault laws did not lead to more accidents.[2] To address the fact that premiums were rising faster in some no-fault states than in fault states, Joost introduced the concept of "balance" in a no-fault system. By that, he meant whether the threshold (the restriction on the right to sue for pain and suffering) was tight enough to pay for the new no-fault benefits without raising the costs of the system. In general, he found that states with high benefits and a tight threshold were in balance, as were those with low benefits and a weak threshold. Premium increases in these states were in line with those in fault states. Not surprisingly, the systems with high benefits and weak thresholds (the trial lawyer special) were not.[3]

At the same time, Joost was working to devise a way that motorists could choose between a no-fault insurance option and a liability insurance option. His challenge was to find an equitable and easy-to-understand way to handle intersystem accidents between people who chose no-fault coverage and those who elected to stay under the old tort and liability insurance system. His solution was simple but elegant. It was to add a new coverage for tort system drivers, which was to be called Tort Maintenance Coverage (TMC). It worked just like UM or UIM coverage: namely, a TMC driver injured in an accident with a no-fault, renamed Personal Injury Protection (PIP), driver could sue the PIP driver on a fault basis to recover both economic and noneconomic damages, but, if successful, he or she would recover from his or her own insurer. Since, under the choice approach finally agreed upon, a PIP driver could sue a TMC driver only for excess economic damages and not for pain and suffering, the additional cost of TMC coverage would be offset by the savings from being immune from lawsuits for pain and suffering by a

PIP driver. A few years later, Dan Miller of the JEC staff devised the chart shown in Figure 13.1 to show how accidents, including intersystem accidents, would be handled under a choice system.

This concept went a long way toward addressing what we believed was the most effective substantive argument against no-fault, that it deprived motorists of the option to stay in the existing tort system (although that argument ignores the fact that the tort system had been a motorist's only choice in every state until 1971). Of course, there was still much more work to be done to solve the political problem before no-fault would become a viable political possibility.

After devising this "connector" coverage, Joost needed to find a way to get the idea into the public domain. The answer was simple: Write a law review article with Professor O'Connell, who had also not given up on no-fault and was teaching at the University of Virginia School of Law. Thanks to O'Connell's academic and no-fault credentials, in 1986, the *Virginia Law Review* published an article describing the choice system Joost had devised.[4]

To formulate the best possible no-fault proposal, it was also important to consider the changes in state auto accident laws that had occurred since the publication of the 1971 DOT study. Most state tort laws had been revised, by court decision and statute, to enable more injured people to recover, and changes in liability insurance coverage had increased the amount they could recover. In addition, seventeen states had adopted no-fault laws in various forms, which provided valuable information[5] about what worked and what didn't.

By 1970, with millions of accidents and 52,627 fatalities annually, and with so few people able to recover for their injuries, something had to give. What gave was the tort and liability insurance system. It wasn't a hard sell to convince judges and politicians that the restrictions in the tort system that denied 54 percent of all people injured around 1970 were unfair to injured persons. As a result, starting in the late 1960s, most states and courts took actions to make recovery easier. They modified the doctrine of contributory negligence to help the person who was generally free of fault and, sometimes, even the person primarily at fault. In addition, almost all states repealed family immunity and host/guest statutes for passengers and swept away other antiquated doctrines such as governmental and charitable immunity statutes that restricted recovery

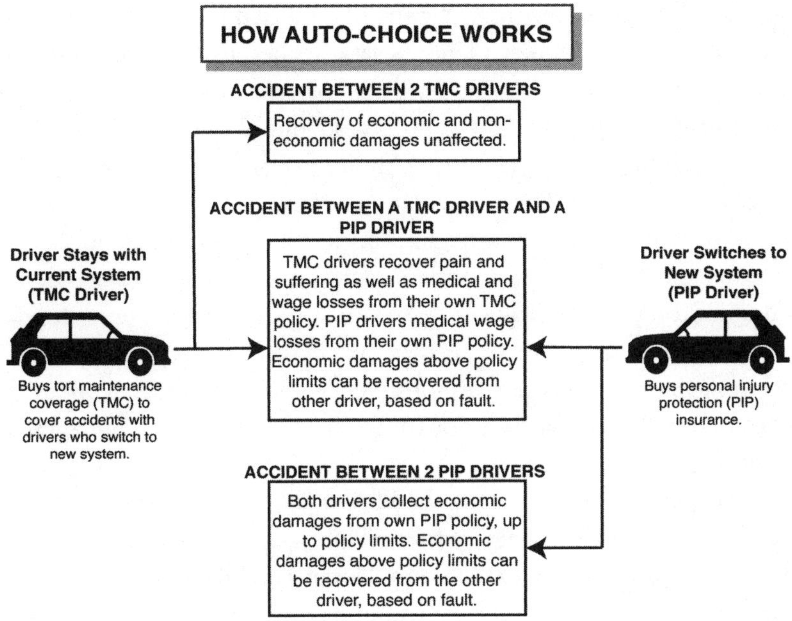

Figure 13.1. Graphic explanation of how the different auto accident scenarios involving PIP (no-fault) and TMC (tort) motorists are handled under Auto Choice.

for injured persons. Most states also removed statutory limitations on recovery in wrongful death actions.

In short, there was a shift in priority between the two main principles underlying tort law—compensation and deterrence—with more focus on compensation. Not coincidentally, the changes also proved highly beneficial for the lawyers who represented both the injured party and the insurance company. The changes were particularly beneficial to plaintiff attorneys because they typically took cases on a contingency fee basis (if I win, I get one-third of the recovery; if I lose, I get nothing).

Many of the changes took place through legislative action, but some were the result of court decisions. The changes that took place through legislation were not the usual business-versus-consumer contests that so often frame legislative battles. In those, typically, consumer supporters try to secure more money from the businesses that cause harm, while the businesses try to limit their liability. These were atypical legislative battles in that there were no battles. All players in the system favored more compensation for injured persons—injured people so they could recover in more situations, plaintiffs' lawyers because they made money only when their clients won, and insurers because more recoveries meant higher insurance premiums and profits (so long as they could pass along their increased costs in the form of higher premiums).

Change was swift. The most prominent change in the legal system was the move from contributory negligence[6] to comparative negligence. The doctrine took two forms: "modified" and "pure" comparative negligence. Modified comparative negligence, the most common type, provides that the person filing suit can still recover even if he or she is partially at fault so long as he or she is less responsible (less than 50 percent) than the other driver. The injured person's recovery is reduced to the degree of his or her fault.

To see how the new system would change recoveries, let's go back to the original accident scenario, where Jill hits Jack and causes him $80,000 of injuries, while Jill suffers $12,000. Under contributory negligence, if Jack were 20 percent at fault, he would have recovered nothing. Under the modernized version, he would recover to the extent that he wasn't at fault, or $64,000. Jill would still recover nothing under modified comparative negligence because she was more than 50 percent at fault.

This result comes with three caveats. Jack would still recover nothing if Jill were a hit-and-run driver and he couldn't identify her. Even if Jack got a court judgment for $64,000, his recovery would be less if Jill had insufficient insurance to pay the full $64,000 (it is rare for lawyers to go after personal assets in auto insurance cases). Finally, like death and taxes, any amount Jack recovered would also be reduced by his attorney's one-third fee. If his attorney's fee were the only deduction, then Jack's bottom-line recovery would be $42,688. That's about half his loss but still far better than the $0 he would have recovered under the contributory negligence doctrine.

As indicated previously, some states went further, adopting the doctrine of "pure" comparative negligence. This doctrine permits each injured person to recover damages based on his or her degree of fault. Let's take Jack and Jill for a spin under this system. Jack would still recover $64,000. Now Jill, too, can recover some $2,400—20 percent of her loss because Jack was 20 percent at fault. Tweaking the assumptions a little can lead to bizarre results. Consider, for example, a situation where Jill's losses exceed Jack's. If you reverse the loss figures while retaining the same fault percentages, this is what you get: Jack, only 20 percent at fault, gets 20 percent of $12,000, or $2,400. Jill, 80 percent at fault, recovers $16,000, 20 percent of her $80,000 loss. The result seems more than a bit unfair.

While both these tort reforms are fairer to Jack and Jill, they significantly increase systemic insurance costs. What would have resulted in $0 paid out under contributory negligence would result in $64,000 under modified comparative negligence and $66,500 under pure comparative negligence. *The critical point is that improvements in compensation, however well justified, also increased costs for all motorists because almost all the additional costs were passed along to all policyholders in the form of higher premiums.*

At the same time that tort changes were increasing the number of injured people who could recover (and, therefore, how much they could recover), there were changes on the insurance side that also improved how many could recover and how much. Some were driven by consumer demand and some by insurers to increase their business.

UM is coverage you buy to protect yourself against being injured by an uninsured motorist. It is a fault-based coverage. If the uninsured motorist who injures you was at fault, then your UM covers your losses. Thus, UM has elements in common with both health insurance (and no-fault) and fault insurance. Like health insurance, UM is a "first-party" coverage; i.e., you pay for it, and your insurer pays you in the event of an injury. Like fault insurance, and unlike health insurance, it is fault-based. Whereas your health insurer pays for your injuries, without regard to fault, your auto insurer pays you under your UM coverage only if the other driver is at fault. You are paying more to protect yourself against an at-fault driver not buying the mandatory liability coverage.

UM is of limited value for two reasons. Only twenty states require motorists to purchase it, although all states require insurers to offer it.[7] Even so, as of 2015, only 13 percent of motorists carried UM.[8] Moreover, UM coverage usually provides minimal benefits, not nearly enough to cover losses in the event of a serious injury.

It was a short leap from insurers offering UM coverage to offering UIM coverage. UIM is like UM on steroids. It pays when the other driver's liability coverage is insufficient to pay for *all* your loss. Like UM, it is a coverage that you, not the at-fault driver, pay for and is also fault-based. Although of more value than UM coverage, as of June 2013, even fewer states—thirteen—mandated the sale of UIM.[9]

Insurers also now sell, and most states require drivers to purchase, Medical Payments (MedPay) coverage, which, unlike UM and UIM, pays for medical losses without regard to fault. Auto insurers offer different levels of coverage, typically ranging from $1,000 to as high as $25,000. MedPay is more valuable than UM or UIM because it is a first-party coverage that pays without regard to fault, just like your health insurance. If this sounds familiar, it is because MedPay is just no-fault by another name. The difference is that in the fault system, you pay an additional amount for this assured protection, whereas in no-fault, it is (or at least is supposed to be) the primary form of coverage. In the fault system, if you already have health insurance, the coverage is largely redundant with the health insurance you already pay for.[10] It is worth repeating that collision and comprehensive coverages, two of the three coverages for damage to your car, also pay without regard to fault.

As with changes in the doctrine of contributory negligence, UM, UIM and MedPay coverages increased both the number of injured people who could recover and the amount they could recover.

Now let's return to the adventures of Jack and Jill to see the implications of these insurance system changes. As I indicated before, regardless of the tort system in effect in a state, a not-at-fault injured motorist would still have no recovery if the other driver drove away without being identified—but for UM and UIM coverages.

Assume, again, that Jill was 80 percent at fault for causing Jack's $80,000 of injuries. If Jill drove away undetected or was uninsured, UM coverage would come into play. If Jack carried $25,000 of UM, then he could recover 80 percent of that, or $20,000. If he also had $25,000 of UIM, he could recover another $20,000, for a total of $40,000.

While $40,000 would not fully compensate Jack, it would increase insurance system costs for all motorists by the same amount. The point is simple—a more generous tort system combined with more insurance coverage provides both better compensation and higher costs.

By the late 1970s, most states had, by legislation or court decision, changed their tort systems to ease the restrictions on recovery for people injured in auto accidents. Many also had mandated that motorists purchase UM and MedPay coverage. These changes were quite similar to those that the ABA had recommended back in 1978 as an alternative to no-fault. These legislative fights had not really been fights because almost everyone favored changes to improve compensation. The trial bar had an additional incentive in its desire to ward off efforts to enact no-fault laws. But, as the previous chapter shows, these reforms came with a cost.

These changes had occurred outside the normal legislative paradigm of many of the historic fights between Republicans and Democrats. In them, Republicans would fight for "fiscal responsibility," focusing on systemic costs but largely ignoring unfairness to individuals. Democrats, on the other hand, would focus exclusively on the unfairness of the system for injured people, largely ignoring any fiscal impact. Part of the reason that costs did not become an issue during the efforts to modify the harsh rules of the tort system is that they were hidden by the insurance coverage, and insurers didn't mind the additional costs so long as they could pass them along to their policyholders. Of course, it was also relevant that state governments were not paying for the additional costs, so neither party had to worry about either budget deficits or possible tax increases.

However, as the last few chapters show and as Dale Nelson, State Farm's chief actuary, had demonstrated with regard to the ABA's tort reform proposals in 1975, there are no free rides. Improved compensation without changes in the underlying system means higher premiums for everyone. As in almost all such situations, there are winners and losers from these changes. Not surprisingly, the winners tended to be wealthier people, while the losers were largely people of low and modest income. Over time, the cost of insurance became an increasingly larger part of the public policy discussion. To some people's surprise, the costs of paying more injured people more dollars is not borne primarily by the at-fault motorist because the whole point of insurance is to spread the risks of injuries over a large group of people so individuals can afford the premiums. Spreading that risk means that the more people recover, the higher the costs become for all motorists.

The primary losers in these tort system changes were low- and moderate-income people, for two reasons. They benefited least from the changes because they had less to recover when injured (they had less work loss than a wealthy person) and because it was harder for them to find lawyers to take their cases because they made less successful plaintiffs. At the same time, they were the people least able to afford the higher premiums that were passed along to all motorists to pay the higher costs that came with more compensation for more people. However, they had to pay the higher premiums or risk losing their ability to drive because most states effectively make auto insurance mandatory. Low-income motorists who choose to drive without insurance are fined, if caught, and lose their license.

For all the improvements in compensation brought about in the tort and liability insurance system, there is only so much good that playing in a defective sandbox can do. After all these changes were made, the system still left many people deserving of compensation with no or insufficient coverage of their losses. The truth of this statement was best demonstrated in the chart designed by Dan Miller in the late 1990s (Figure 13.2).

While state tort and liability insurance laws were changing to improve compensation for injured persons, albeit incompletely and at the cost of increased premiums, several states were experimenting with no-fault insurance. Between 1971 and 1976, seventeen states adopted no-fault laws. One was ruled unconstitutional, several tightened their thresholds, and four repealed their laws. Two—New Jersey and Pennsylvania—adopted choice no-fault systems that permit motorists to purchase lower levels of PIP benefits to reduce their premiums. The no-fault experience with PIP benefits and different lawsuit thresholds also provided key information for O'Connell and Joost in drafting Auto Choice legislation.

For the most part, during this time, the PIP side of no-fault did not cause major problems. States with low benefits—such as Utah at $3,000—had little abuse because there wasn't much to abuse. Also, there was little incentive to run up costs to be able to sue because the threshold for bringing a pain and suffering lawsuit was only $2,500. On the other hand, PIP fraud had started to become significant in urban areas in states with higher PIP benefits because of inadequate medical cost controls. The additional medical costs, in turn, helped plaintiffs both pierce weak thresholds and then increase the amount they could recover in a tort suit for pain and suffering: "54 percent of suspicious PIP claims appeared to involve buildup for the sake of inflating the general damages settlement, i.e., in response to the availability of pain and suffering damages once one crosses a weak threshold, and 37 percent of such claims were built up to overcome tort thresholds."[11]

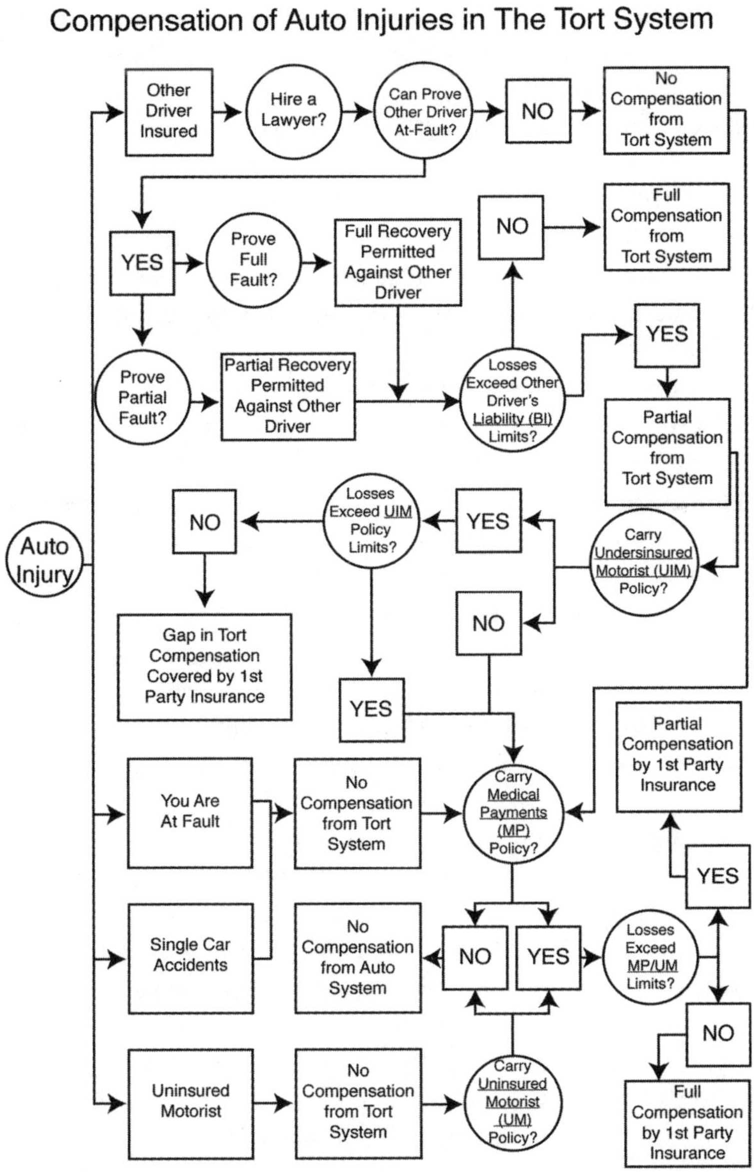

Figure 13.2. The byzantine challenge of recovering compensation in an auto accident under the tort system. For those entitled to a recovery, the chart demonstrates the further challenge of being able to recover enough to cover your out-of-pocket costs. To update a bit, just a bit, the system is not unlike the challenge of directing a frog to cross a busy road in the 1981 arcade game Frogger.

The Keeton-O'Connell plan, the model state law, and the federal no-fault bills had all relied on a tight verbal threshold (one limiting suits to a list including death and loss of a bodily part as well as a catchall of "serious and permanent" injury) to limit costs. The complete text of the threshold in UMVARA, the model state law that closely followed the Keeton-O'Connell plan, reads as follows: "Damages in excess of $5,000, for noneconomic detriment (i.e., pain and suffering, etc. but not punitive damages) if there is permanent significant loss of body function or death or permanent serious disfigurement or more than six months of total disability."[12]

Most of the no-fault states, on the other hand, had adopted simple dollar thresholds whereby an injured person could sue after reaching a certain dollar level. The states did so as a sop to the trial bar and often with the support of the insurance industry because such thresholds were easy to measure. Most dollar thresholds started low, with New Jersey the lowest at $200. The states quickly discovered that they were inadequate to reduce the number of suits sufficiently to pay for the added number of people eligible to recover under no-fault and the cost of adding no-fault benefits. Most states then raised the dollar amount—only, in many cases, to see PIP claims increase to reach the new, higher level.

Several states, especially those with large urban areas, switched from dollar thresholds to verbal thresholds. However, once again, the trial bar succeeded in weakening even the verbal thresholds by decoupling the concepts of "serious" and "permanent." That left the thresholds vulnerable to arguments for damages when there was a minor loss of use to a pinkie, for example, or a short-lived traumatic event. As a result, in a system designed to pay for most injuries without resort to lawyers, roughly 50 percent of the premium was still going to pay for tort damages. In essence, no-fault states such as New York and Florida were and still are operating both a no-fault and a tort system.

By contrast, the Michigan threshold, which was closest to the original no-fault proposals, had kept the cost of lawsuits steady for a long time. For example, between 2005 and 2010, the cost to insurers rose from $51.50 to $53.44, the latter being about 13 percent of the total no-fault portion of the premium. That figure compared favorably to $133.84 in New York and $164.12 in Florida.[13]

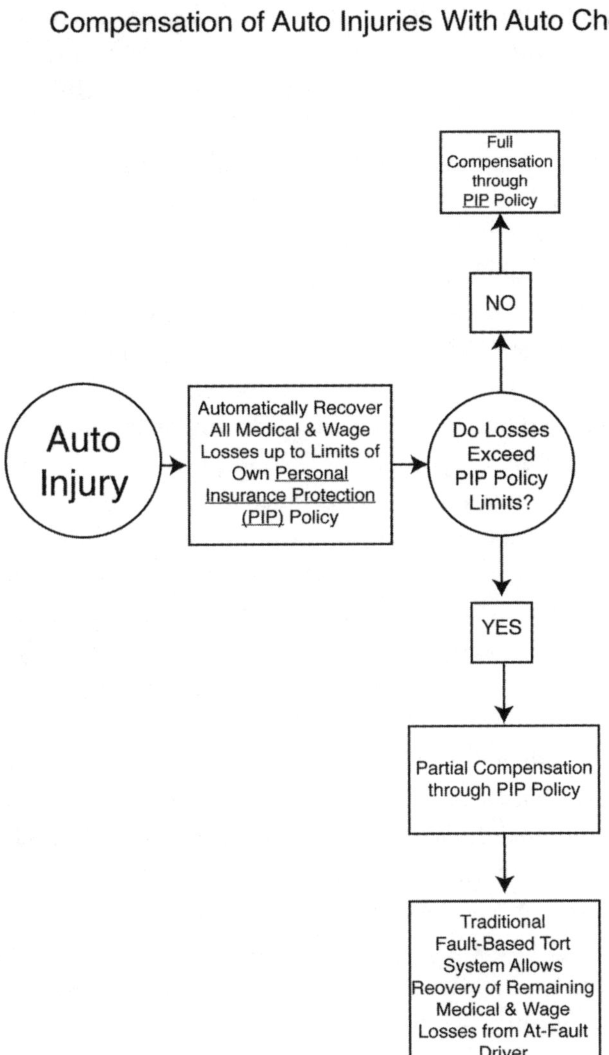

Figure 13.3. The chart shows how much easier it is to recover for your medical bills and lost wages under the Auto Choice system.

In addition to efforts to tighten their thresholds, Kentucky, New Jersey, and Pennsylvania experimented with choice systems. All three adopted no-fault laws in the 1970s. Kentucky's law, in 1975, has always been a choice law, while New Jersey and Pennsylvania amended their no-fault laws in 1988 and 1990, respectively, to offer motorists a choice between the tort system and no-fault. The laws varied widely in their terms, and none contained a mechanism as elegant and logical as O'Connell-Joost for handling accidents between drivers who made different insurance decisions. Of key importance, however, was that New Jersey offered a low-income policy that did not provide coverage for noneconomic damages. Premiums for the policy were much lower than for New Jersey's regular no-fault system, which was saddled with far too many lawsuits owing to the weak threshold.

In this environment of ongoing deficiencies in the tort system and weaknesses in most no-fault laws, the O'Connell-Joost approach became the model for the federal Auto Choice legislation. Its PIP option offered a far easier road to travel to compensation than that offered by the revised, and more costly, tort and liability insurance system. Another Miller chart showed the simpler road to recovery under the no-fault option (Figure 13.3).

Critically, it also addressed the cost problems in state laws on both the PIP and threshold sides. For motorists electing the no-fault option, it would have required them to purchase relatively low levels of PIP benefits, around $25,000 in most states, and eliminated all suits for pain and suffering, preserving only those for excess economic loss (any amount not covered by PIP benefits). Addressing the problems of both the tort system and state no-fault laws also enabled the authors of Auto Choice to promise significant cost savings.

But having a good, even a great, plan in hand is only the beginning of reform. The determined efforts of O'Connell and Joost had solved the key issue for a choice system: how to resolve accidents between motorists in the tort and no-fault systems. But that was just the predicate. The tougher problem to solve was the political one. Here, O'Connell took the next steps.

14. No-Fault Rises Like a Phoenix from the Ashes, Reincarnated as Auto Choice, with a Focus on Lower Premiums and Choice (1992–2004)

Professor O'Connell asked State Farm, a perennial no-fault supporter, to use its position on the board of RAND to secure a series of studies on the cost implications of no-fault. The first study, published in 1991, identified various no-fault approaches.[1] Subsequent RAND studies, which were headed by Stephen J. Carroll, found huge savings for those who chose the no-fault option and some savings for those who remained in the tort system. The first cost study, which was published in 1995, found that "the costs of compensating accident victims on behalf of drivers who elect no-fault would generally be at least 60 percent less than what they would be under the traditional tort system."[2] The study did not analyze the impact on the property damage portion of the premium because it applied only to personal injury, which the authors viewed as more important.

The next piece of the puzzle was more complicated—to find an audience for choice no-fault. Professor O'Connell orchestrated this effort as well by recruiting Michael Horowitz of the Hudson Institute, a conservative think tank. Horowitz, a very bright person with a prickly personality, had a long Republican pedigree, having served as general counsel of the Office of Management and Budget in the Reagan administration. He saw two key Republican values in Auto Choice, as opposed to the earlier no-fault bills: (1) choice, for individual drivers between the fault and no-fault systems, as well as to elect the level of benefits that best fitted their needs, and for states, as they could choose the new choice system or retain their existing law, and (2) the huge cost savings from the no-fault system, which he likened to a tax cut for millions of motorists. At the same time, Horowitz banned the use of the word "no-fault" because it evoked a negative response from Republicans. Of course, the term had been coined not by Keeton and O'Connell but by the trial bar to brand the concept pejoratively. The good news about Horowitz joining the effort was that it brought significant congressional Republican support. That was also the bad news, as substantial support by high-profile congressional Republicans raised warning signals for Democrats.

The first RAND study and Horowitz's support found a receptive audience in the administration of President George H. W. Bush. Jay Lefkowitz, director of the Office of Cabinet Affairs and deputy executive secretary to the Domestic Policy Council, and Charles Kolb, deputy assistant to the president for domestic policy, ran the issue through the policy process. In October 1992, in the middle of the presidential campaign, President Bush announced that his administration would support Auto Choice legislation. Unfortunately for Auto Choice, three months later Bush was a private citizen.

Soon thereafter, O'Connell, Horowitz and the authors of the RAND study teamed up to write three articles that were published in the *Maryland Law Review* between 1993 and 1996. The articles focused on consumer choice and the cost savings available under Auto Choice.[3]

All this work finally paid off in the spring of 1996 when a heretofore moderate and relatively obscure Republican senator from Kentucky, Mitch McConnell, started drafting an Auto Choice bill. That got my attention and started my juices flowing again. As soon as I learned of it, I got in touch with McConnell's staff, Melissa Patak, whom I had worked with on the vaccine injury compensation bill in the early 1990s. I shared both substantive and political information about our past efforts with Melissa. Importantly, I told her of the likely interest on the part of two key Democrats: (1) Senator Moynihan, who had written favorably about no-fault in the 1960s, and (2) Senator Lieberman, whose legislative director, Bill Bonvillian, had been the director of congressional affairs for DOT during the no-fault effort in 1977–1978 (I did not know at the time that Senator Lieberman had been the author of the Connecticut no-fault law).

On June 11, 1996, Senator McConnell introduced the first federal Auto Choice bill, S. 1860, the Auto Choice Reform Act of 1996. To my delight, the cosponsors were Democratic Senators Lieberman and Moynihan and Republican Majority Leader Bob Dole (KS), who was soon to leave the Senate to run for the presidency.

Not long thereafter, Patak left McConnell's office. As he had yet to hire a replacement, I found myself briefing Senator McConnell for his September 24, 1996, testimony before the Commerce Committee, a hearing at which I also testified in favor of the bill on behalf of a coalition I had created to lobby for it.

My experience in the 1970s had made it clear to me that a solid academic foundation, backed up with rigorous cost savings estimates, and some bipartisan support were not enough to defeat the trial bar. That, plus my later work on two other liability reform bills where the academic work was buttressed by significant financial support, had convinced me that there had to be a strong, well-financed operation to raise public awareness and lobby the Congress if Auto Choice were to stand a chance of succeeding. I decided to take on that responsibility.

But first I needed a name for my lobbying coalition. Actually, what I needed more than a good name was a good acronym. Based on my twenty-five years of Hill experience, I knew the importance of a clever, simple acronym that provided instant recognition with the issue. The 1970s coalition name—the Committee for Consumers No-Fault (CCNF)—did not meet this criterion. My initial goal was to have the name reflect the two objectives of no-fault—better compensation and lower premiums. My first stab left much to be desired—the Committee for Comprehensive Automobile Accident Restitution and Rate Reductions (CCAARRR), a kind of stuttered CAR. In my first television appearance, the morning of the September 24, 1996, hearing, the host reinforced the unworkability of the name. He said he believed that this was the longest name for any coalition that had ever appeared on his show (they couldn't fit the full name on the screen)! It was also probably the worst.

I tried to shorten the name and devise a CAR acronym, but the best I could come up with was the Coalition for Auto-Insurance Reform (CAIR). It reminded me of when Banking Committee legislation during the savings and loan (S&L) crisis had renamed the S&L insurance fund from the Federal Savings and Loan Insurance Corporation (FSLIC) the Savings Association Insurance Fund. It seemed to me that depositors would have reservations about putting their savings into an S&L when those funds were protected by a fund (SAIF) whose name the government couldn't even spell properly (the legislation should have devised an acronym whose initials spelled out SAFE). I did not want to make the same mistake in naming the coalition.

I was more successful in recruiting some members. I started by reaching out to people who had been involved in previous no-fault fights. By the time of the hearing, I had signed up Professor O'Connell, former Massachusetts governor and 1988 Democratic presidential nominee Michael Dukakis, Lionel Van Deerlin (the first House chairman I had worked with on no-fault), and Robert Quinn, who had represented Nationwide in the 1970s and gone on to be insurance commissioner of California. That was enough members for the Senate Commerce Committee, as they invited me to testify at the September 24, 1996, hearing.[4]

At the hearing, in addition to Senator McConnell and me speaking in favor of the bill, two witnesses spoke against it, one representing the trial bar and one representing a Nader-supported consumer group, both of whom testified at the request of the Democratic minority. The ranking member was a far cry from the lead Democrat on the committee in the 1970s, consumer champion and chief sponsor Warren Magnuson. It was Senator Hollings, a former trial lawyer, who had led the opposition to Magnuson's bill twenty years earlier.

The other witness at the hearing, Andrew Tobias, was supportive of no-fault. He described his effort to make California a no-fault state via a ballot proposition that he had funded. Tobias was a well-known financial writer, perhaps most famous for his book *The Only Investment Guide You'll Ever Need* (followed later by *The Only OTHER Investment Guide You'll Ever Need*). He made a "vast fortune" developing Managing Your Money, the software predecessor to Quicken.[5] Tobias is both very funny and dogged. His software used to, and his books still do, guide people through challenging financial matters, in part by keeping them laughing. He was dogged in pursuit of issues he was passionate about. He had bankrolled an antismoking campaign on Russian television in 1993 and, against all odds, had won one for Don Quixote. However, his 1996 sponsored no-fault initiative in California proved to be a windmill too far (or perhaps the windmill's revenge?) and failed spectacularly. In California, Tobias managed to add yet another major opponent to no-fault (in addition to most insurers, all trial and defense lawyers and Ralph Nader) in the oil industry when he proposed a pay-at-the-pump ballot initiative. His proposal would have had drivers pay for insurance through higher gas prices, effectively limiting insurers to the claims processing business. The initiative went down in flames by a margin of 65–35. Tobias later served as the treasurer of the Democratic National Committee from 1999 to 2017 (again establishing his bona fides as a masochist or, perhaps, the patron saint of lost causes, with the obvious exception of his important role in the election of Barack Obama to the presidency). Given his background and personality, Tobias was a natural for the coalition and agreed to become a member.

Tobias quickly solved my name problem. While I was lamenting my inability to reach CAR, Tobias said, "Why don't you hyphenate Auto-Insurance?" Voila! I had the Coalition for Auto-Insurance Reform (CAR). My effort reminded me of a bit from my comedy touchstone, *The 2000 Year Old Man* album. In Carl Reiner's interview of the two-thousand-year-old man (Mel Brooks, who initially responds to the question of whether he is really two thousand years old by saying, "Not yet, I'll be two thousand on October 16th"), he asks the old man about some of the jobs he has held. The two-thousand-year-old man cites a Star of David factory. ("I employed six men, see, each with a point. They would run together in the middle of the factory, and in the great speed, they would fuse, thus creating a star. I would make two a day because of the many accidents.") He then says that a fellow had come to him with the idea of a cross, but he had rejected it. ("It was simple. I didn't know then it was eloquent! Two men run together . . . BANG! You got a cross! I could have fired four men!"). Tobias's solution was also "eloquent." and I adopted it. I dropped four words from my original coalition name and had CAR.

After the hearing, I started soliciting contributions from insurers, particularly those that had been supportive of the 1970s effort. On June 10, 1997, I traveled to Columbus, Ohio, to meet with the Personal Lines Committee of the Insurance Information Institute. There I met with eight presidents of some of the nation's largest auto insurers, including State Farm, Allstate, and USAA. As had happened in the 1970s, there was a division between stock companies,[6] publicly owned companies that had to answer to their stockholders, and mutual companies, whose policyholders own the company. State Farm and USAA, two mutual companies, joined CAR. Allstate and the other stock companies once again chose to join the opposition.

Finally, armed with a great acronym and a few dollars, I naively set forth once again to reform the auto insurance system to improve compensation and, this time, to provide significant savings for all motorists, especially low-income people. Before I could do that, I had some catching up to do on how and why Auto Choice differed from the no-fault bills of the 1970s. My focus was on two things: (1) the details of how the Auto Choice legislation worked and (2) making sure it would provide better and faster compensation for injuries as well as substantial savings.

My starting point was the no-fault effort of the 1970s. Although titled "minimum federal standards," the benefits were intended to address the perceived greatest flaw in the tort system—that people with very serious injuries (over $25,000) recovered, on average, only 30 percent of their loss. Thus, the benefit minimum standards in the federal bills (which, for medical loss, ranged from unlimited in the earlier bills to $100,000 in the 1977 legislation) were more generous than those offered in all but the state of Michigan, which had unlimited medical and rehabilitation benefits. To afford to provide such benefits, the bills had a tort threshold that was more restrictive than that of any state, as it permitted suits for pain and suffering only in cases of death or serious and permanent injury. Further, as the 1970s were a time of great federal government activism with Democrats in charge of both Houses of Congress, the legislation was highly proscriptive and would have applied nationally. There were penalties for states that chose not to implement the law, and if a state had not agreed to implement the federal standards, the federal government would have implemented the provisions of the legislation in that state. The bills also contained detailed provisions addressing much of the everyday business of insurers. In short, it was consistent with much other liberal legislation of its time, with the federal government telling the states, private sector insurers, and motorists what they had to do and how to do it.

But what had been fitting for the 1970s was dated by the late 1990s. The 1990s were a time of rising concerns about deficits and skepticism about new government programs (this had been the Republican point of view twenty years before). The Republicans in charge of the House and sometimes the Senate favored consumer choice, tax cuts, and a federalism that preferred local government control. Auto Choice, unlike the 1970s no-fault proposals, was a product of these very different political times. It was grounded in choice: (1) Drivers could choose between the auto insurance system in their state and a federal no-fault alternative, (2) drivers who chose the federal alternative had the freedom to balance benefit levels and costs as they saw best for their particular economic circumstances, and (3) states had the right to reject the federal option and stay with their existing law. In short, as no-fault was a perfect political fit for the 1970s, so, too, was Auto Choice for the 1990s.

Specifically, in states that did not vote to reject Auto Choice, motorists could choose between continuing to buy insurance that had been available in the state and a new federal no-fault option. Unlike in the 1970s, the required level of no-fault benefits was relatively low, averaging roughly $25,000 a person. The threshold for suits for pain and suffering wasn't—people who elected the no-fault system could not sue another motorist for pain and suffering. They could only sue for any uncompensated economic loss. For example, if a person's injuries amounted to $100,000 and the compensation from no-fault benefits was $25,000, then he or she could sue the other motorist, on a fault basis, for the remaining $75,000.

As I mentioned, the key to creating a choice system lay in finding a fair way to treat motorists in accidents between people who had chosen different systems. Joost's solution was simple and fair: (1) The no-fault (PIP) driver would recover economic damages from his or her no-fault policy and could sue the other driver, on a fault basis, for excess economic loss only (that not covered by no-fault benefits), while (2) the tort (TMC) driver could file a claim against or sue an at-fault PIP driver for both economic and noneconomic damages. If the TMC driver prevailed, he or she would not recover the damages from the other driver. Instead, the TMC driver would recover from a new coverage, TMC, that he or she would purchase. The TMC coverage would operate just as UM coverage does, paying damages to the injured driver who can prove the other motorist was at fault.

This way, each driver would get, statistically, what he or she would likely have received had he or she been involved in an accident with a driver who had chosen the same system. As discussed previously, the PIP driver would get compensation for economic loss, regardless of fault, and a much lower premium in return for giving up the right to sue for pain and suffering. The TMC driver would remain in the tort system, with just the source of recovery changed. Importantly, RAND estimated that there would be no cost increase for tort drivers.[7] The reason was that the additional cost to the tort driver of purchasing TMC would be offset by the tort driver's immunity from lawsuits for noneconomic loss when he or she was at fault in an accident with a no-fault PIP driver.

As I compared Auto Choice with no-fault, I began to understand the latter's advantages. The no-fault benefits in Auto Choice would eliminate the compensation gaps in the tort system. While the level of benefits was lower than in the 1970s no-fault legislation, they met my minimum requirement—that the vast majority of injured people would be better off under the new system than under the tort system. The level of no-fault benefits was high enough to cover most injury situations, and in the most serious injury cases, the injured person would have two sources of recovery instead of one—his or her no-fault benefits and any recovery in a suit against an at-fault driver for uncompensated economic loss.

As for the prohibition on suits for pain and suffering, it would have no practical effect in the real world for serious injury cases because the average driver's coverage isn't enough to cover economic loss in serious injury cases, let alone pain and suffering. For those who wanted such protection, the bill would have required insurers to offer no-fault coverage for pain and suffering. Any person who purchased such coverage would get pain and suffering benefits if injured in an accident, without regard to fault.

As I further contemplated the benefits and tort restrictions, I realized that Auto Choice also responded to the lessons learned from flawed state no-fault laws. The lower benefit levels meant fewer opportunities for medical fraud, which was presenting a substantial cost problem in many states with high no-fault benefits. The tighter threshold addressed the problem with flawed state laws that permitted so many lawsuits that they either reduced or eliminated the estimated premium savings.

Finally, Auto Choice reflected the realities of the lives of low- and moderate-income people. The 1970s no-fault bills and the Michigan law essentially required motorists to purchase a Cadillac insurance policy when many of them could barely afford a Ford policy. Even worse, the penalty for driving uninsured is that the motorist cannot recover no-fault benefits, so motorists who are priced out of the no-fault system can't receive any of its benefits. By contrast, Auto Choice would permit motorists to buy coverage that fits their needs, enabling them to decide whether the best use of their dollars is to buy more auto insurance or spend them on food, rent, and other necessities. Because the benefits are lower and the threshold higher, Auto Choice would provide much greater savings than would have been available under the no-fault bills—56 percent on the bodily injury portion of the premium versus 11 to 15.8 percent under the 1970s no-fault plan.[8]

The single greatest beneficiaries of this approach would be low-income people. The reason was simple. Under a first-party insurance system, an insurer knows whom it is obligated to pay in the event of a crash, something it can't know under tort, where the liability is to an unknown other person. Under no-fault, the insurer can set a rate based on what its own insured stands to lose (such as wages) if injured. If the insured is a person of low or moderate income, then the insurer will charge less. Just how much could be at stake was shown by a study of residents of Maricopa County, Arizona, which found that low-income households, those with incomes below 50 percent of the poverty line, spent 31.6 percent of their income on car insurance, with half the residents putting off paying for food, rent, and mortgage payments to pay for auto insurance.[9]

While the advantages of Auto Choice were clear, both substantively and politically, that still left open the question of how it compared to the fault and liability insurance system. The tort and insurance changes that had occurred since the late 1960s to the 1970s had improved compensation for people injured in tort states, but, by definition, they had raised insurer costs and thus consumer premiums.

The RAND studies and work done by the Insurance Research Council (IRC), an entity that collects insurance data, revealed the impact of the tort system changes enacted since the 1971 DOT study. Among the key questions were the following: (1) How many people still had no recovery? (2) How much did people recover relative to their loss? (3) How long did it take to receive payment? and (4) How much of the insurance dollar was paid to injured persons, as opposed to lawyers and insurers?

First, how much had the tort and insurance changes reduced the number of injured persons with no recovery? The 1971 DOT study found that a scandalous 54 percent of all injured person recovered nothing under the tort system.[10] Roughly twenty years later, RAND found that the number had dropped to 30 percent.[11] The single largest category of uncompensated victims remained those involved in single-car crashes (if no one is at fault, there is no one to sue). While the tort changes reduced the percentage of people with no recovery, it still left unacceptably large numbers of injured people with no recovery whatsoever, regardless of fault or the severity of the injury.

Second, compensation for those who recovered remained skewed in the wrong direction, with people with minor losses recovering many times their economic loss and those with serious injuries recovering a tiny fraction of their loss. RAND found, on average, that injured persons with medical bills and lost wages totaling $500 to $1,000 recovered an average of 250 percent of their loss. The picture for those with serious injuries was similar to that in the 1970s: Those with losses between $25,000 and $100,000 recovered only about one-half (56 percent) of these losses. Worst of all, *those with losses over $100,000 recovered just 9 percent of their economic loss and, by definition, nothing for pain and suffering.*[12] (See Figure 14.1)

The upside-down recovery numbers reflected key ongoing factors in the tort and liability insurance system that limit recoveries in serious injury cases: (a) Most states do not have very high coverage requirements, which is understandable given the range of incomes and the cost of higher coverage. As a result, recoveries, for all practical purposes, are limited to the amount of coverage carried by the average motorist. (b) Even with generous comparative negligence statutes, the injured person's recovery is reduced by his or her degree of fault. (c) Many injured people cannot afford to wait months or even years to recover, so they settle for less than they might get if they could afford to wait. (d) Plaintiff attorneys continue to routinely take one-third of any recovery, regardless of how much time they spend working on the case.[13] By contrast, when the loss is small, it is not worth it for an insurer to contest the claim; i.e., the claim has a nuisance value, which means an insurer will overpay to make it go away.

Third, things were no better in the 1990s and 2000s than in the 1970s in terms of the length of time from injury to compensation. If anything, they were worse. Whereas the DOT study found that it took sixteen months for injured people to recover in serious injury cases, in 1999, a US DOJ study of the largest seventy-five counties found that 26.2 percent of auto tort cases took two to four years to resolve and 6.9 percent took more than four years.[14]

A 2003 IRC study also documented how slow the tort system was. It found that only 16 percent of bodily injury claimants received their first payment within thirty days, and only another 15 percent received

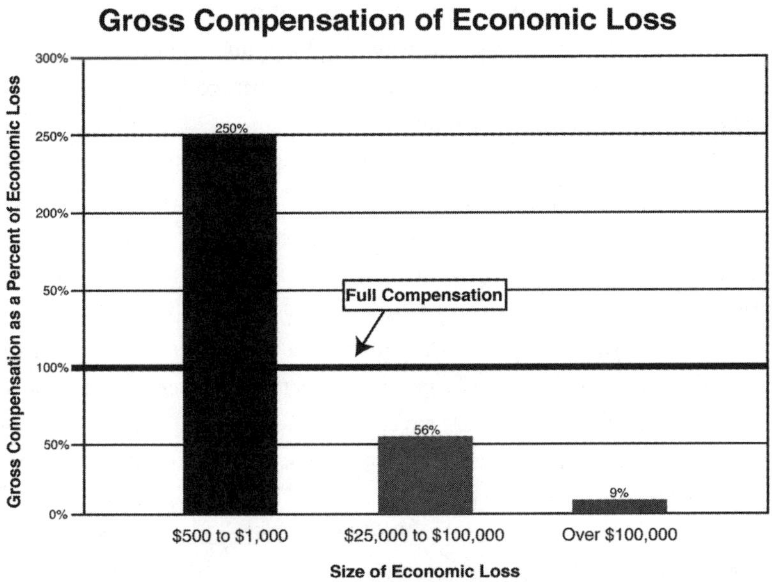

Figure 14.1. The chart shows that the tort system continued to grossly undercompensate seriously injured people in the 1990s, as it had done in the 1970s.

their first payment within thirty-one to ninety days. By contrast, in first-party PIP claims in no-fault states, where losses are paid as they occur rather than in one lump sum at the end of a tort claim, 35 percent of PIP claimants received their first payment within one month of the time they reported the injury to their insurer, and an additional 45 percent received their first payment within thirty-one to 90 days. At the other extreme, 27 percent of bodily injury claimants did not receive their first payment until more than one year later, as contrasted with 4 percent of PIP claimants.[15]

Fourth, Dan Miller teased out the answers for the breakout of where the insurance dollar goes from data provided by the Insurance Information Institute. As the chart on the distribution of the bodily injury premium shows (see Figure 14.2), in 1999, it took 28.4 cents in attorneys' fees (17.4 cents for plaintiffs' attorneys and 11 cents for defense attorneys) to deliver 44 cents of economic and noneconomic damages (including 16.9 cents in fraudulent and excessive claims) to auto accident claimants.[16] Perhaps even more stunning was the fact that attorneys were paid almost twice as much (28.4 cents)[17] as injured people received for their legitimate medicals bills and lost wages (14.5 cents). By contrast, health insurance systems deliver a much higher percentage for medical losses because attorneys are rarely involved.

RAND was also able to quantify the cost of this fraud. In its 1995 study, it concluded that more than one-third of medical costs were excessive or unnecessary—claims for losses that did not occur or for unnecessary visits to medical practitioners. RAND estimated the total bill for fraud at $13–18 billion for 1993.[18]

In addition, the DOJ found that auto cases continued to waste far too much court time. In 2001, tort cases represented 66.7 percent of the civil trials disposed of in the nation's seventy-five largest counties. Auto cases were the single largest category, constituting 53 percent of all tort cases.[19]

After examining the impact of the tort and liability insurance changes in state laws, I concluded that they had improved compensation, but not nearly enough. By definition, no changes to a tort system could ever result in all accident victims being paid for their losses. The system would always be plagued by undercompensation of seriously injured victims, slow payment, the inefficient use of insurance dollars, and lack of choice.

Satisfied that the tort system changes had not rendered no-fault reform unnecessary, I turned my attention to state no-fault laws. I started with a fundamental question that had first been raised in the 1970s: Was there reason to believe that no-fault laws resulted in more accidents than fault laws? Such a result, if true, would raise serious questions about the wisdom of pursuing no-fault in any form.

Not long after the states began adopting no-fault laws in 1971, scholars started investigating this question. Because many factors affected accident rates, the studies needed to make numerous assumptions. Thus, it is not surprising that the many studies reached different conclusions. The first was by Elizabeth Landes, who published an article in 1982 that concluded that no-fault laws had increased fatal accident rates by as much as 10 percent.[20] However, three years later, the DOT reached a different conclusion. It found that the data did not support Landes's conclusions and that there was "no significant difference between the pre/post ratios of no-fault states and the group of tort states."[21] DOT's conclusion comported with common sense—at least my common sense.

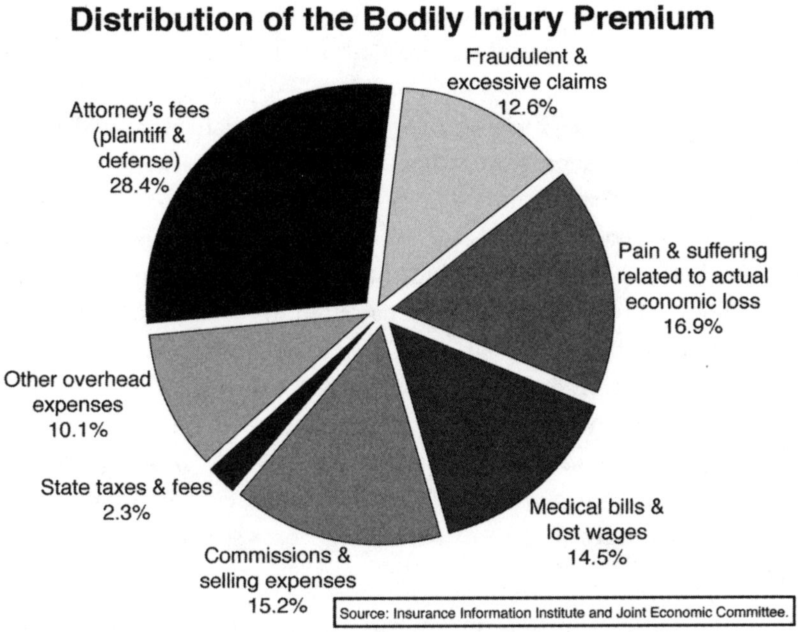

Figure 14.2. The chart shows the ongoing inefficiencies of the fault and liability insurance system in 1999, with more of the premium dollar going for attorneys' fees and pain and suffering, each, than for legitimate medical and work losses. It also shows that almost as much of the dollar was spent for fraudulent and excessive claims as for legitimate economic losses.

As discussed previously, the main deterrent to reckless driving is the risk of doing harm to oneself. The fact that no-fault would pay your medical and work loss bills if you were at fault, which the fault and liability insurance system would not, would hardly seem to provide an incentive to drive recklessly. Moreover, most Americans are covered by health insurance, which would cover your injuries in a fault state. As for third-party liability, to the extent that being liable for personal injuries you caused another provided any additional deterrence, insurance undermined that result by insulating you from paying the full cost of any injuries. That is true under both fault and no-fault systems. The surcharge penalty is the same under either system. Moreover, the at-fault driver under no-fault would still be liable for any property damage his or her negligent driving caused because no-fault doesn't apply to property damage. Given these realities, it seemed illogical that no-fault would increase the number of accidents.

Nevertheless, the issue was certain to rise again during the Auto Choice debate. In 1992, Rose Anne Devlin published a study that found a 9–10 percent increase in fatal accident rates in the no-fault Canadian province of Quebec and in New Zealand,[22] which has a complete no-fault system. While I continued to find the 1985 DOT study and logic more compelling, I knew I would have to pay attention to this issue during the Auto Choice debate.

I was correct. In 1999, Professor J. David Cummins and others estimated a 6.8 percent increase in fatal accident rates in no-fault states.[23] In 2001, David Loughran of RAND published the most thorough analysis of these studies and conducted his own studies, concluding that there was no statistically significant relationship between no-fault and accident rates:

> The previous empirical estimates are not credible, however. The results of the present study show convincingly that not only does no statistically significant relationship exist between the adoption of no-fault and accident rates, but no statistically significant relationship exists between no-fault and accident rates overall or other measures of driver care. Also, no-fault auto insurance as implemented in the United States, even in its strictest form, is unlikely to significantly reduce the expected cost of an auto accident to the at-fault driver. Therefore, even a priori, it seems implausible that no-fault auto insurance could have a substantive impact on driver behavior.[24]

RAND's bottom-line finding was that for the period from 1975 through 1998, "overall, negligence rates are about 2 percentage points lower in no-fault states. . . . If anything, no-fault states appear to have lower overall accident rates and a lower rate of driver negligence generally than found in tort states."[25]

The rest of my examination of state no-fault laws revealed that while they continued to provide far better and more timely compensation, many of them were suffering from unnecessarily high costs. The problems on the PIP side were due largely to fraud and the buildup of unnecessary services, while the problems on the liability side were due to weak thresholds.

If the tort and liability insurance changes did not address the fundamental problems of auto insurance—inadequate compensation, excessive costs, and a lack of choice—and some state no-fault laws were experiencing big jumps in premiums, the next subject to explore was whether Auto Choice would do a better job than these laws in providing better compensation at a reasonable cost. This was a much shorter examination. The legislation would have improved choice by offering people the option of a second form of insurance, a choice that did not exist in forty-seven states. It also would have assured compensation for the 30 percent of injured people who received no compensation under the tort system by guaranteeing payment to all injured people, regardless of fault. By combining assured no-fault benefits and whatever might be recoverable under the remaining tort system (for economic loss only), it would have assured better benefits than the tort system for seriously injured persons (where the average recovery was still way shy of economic loss). It also would have addressed the slowness of recovery, requiring payment within thirty days of submission of a claim.

In addition, the Auto Choice proposal would have paid all injured persons in a timelier fashion more in accord with their losses, with more of the premium dollar going to victims than to lawyers and insurers. By lowering the level of mandatory no-fault benefits, the McConnell bill would have reduced, but not eliminated, the overuse problem particularly associated with high PIP benefits. This would have been a start, although the bill would have benefited from the inclusion of some of the traditional cost-control mechanisms found in health insurance. By eliminating lawsuits for pain and suffering, the McConnell bill would have eliminated the major driver of excessive BI costs. It would also have reduced excessive use of PIP benefits to meet the thresholds. RAND had found that the result would have been a huge reduction in insurer costs. The remaining questions were, how large would the aggregate savings and the state-by-state savings bee? The answers were computed by Dan Miller.

Miller, a libertarian, was the son of a Republican congressman from Florida by the same name. He was brilliant, a member of Mensa, and intellectually honest. Miller and the then politician-to-be Bobby Jindal had been *the* Young Republican Club at Brown (as in pretty much the only members). Though our political philosophies were quite different, we both had respect for where the facts led. While Steve Carroll of RAND had produced studies on the impact of different Auto Choice proposals, it was Miller who used Carroll's work to write several compelling studies for the JEC. The reports analyzed, among other issues, the impact of Auto Choice on the poor, businesses, and other interested parties, as well as on how much lawyers earned, and they provided state-by-state cost savings estimates.[26] Miller was an excellent writer, and his work contributed greatly to generating support for the legislation. We worked closely together to identify key issues and to develop materials to make the case against the tort system and for Auto Choice. Dan, with high-level tech skills, converted the data and information into several highly effective charts, some of which were used as props for the Senate hearings and others in CAR advocacy materials.

In early 1996, the Republicans on the JEC released their first study of Auto Choice: "Improving the American Legal System: The Economic Benefits of Tort Reform."[27] It estimated nationwide savings at $40 billion if all drivers opted for the new PIP option, with an average savings of $221 (28.5 percent) and savings for low-income people of 44.9 percent (Table 14.1).

These estimates were based on the total insurance premium, including the roughly 60 percent for coverages that would not be affected by no-fault. If the estimate had been of savings on the bodily injury portion alone, those affected by the reform, the percentages would have been much higher.

The JEC's 1997 estimate of cost savings under Auto Choice were slightly higher—31 percent (or $243) for the average driver and 48 percent for low-income drivers, with a maximum total potential savings of $45 billion per year.[28] The savings on the 40 percent of the premium that Auto Choice would affect, the personal injury portion, as opposed to the portion that covers damage to the vehicle or its contents, would have been about 63 percent.[29] The magnitude of these savings clearly supported the finding that the existing tort system is overly costly. Both the 1996 and 1997 reports contained state-by-state savings charts as well.

The JEC weighed in with two additional reports between 1998 and 2003. The first estimated total savings at $35 billion,[30] while the second, in 2003, estimated savings at nearly $48 billion.[31]

Armed with well-documented information about the faults of the

Table 14.1 Estimated 1996 Savings from an Auto Choice Plan (in billions)

	Private	Commercial	Total
Total auto insurance premiums	$110.7	$25.0	$137.7
Total available savings if 100% switch	$31.7	$8.3	$40.0
Savings (%)	28.6%	33.3%	NA
Savings for low-income drivers	44.9%	NA	

Source: Abrahamse and Carroll (1995) and JEC calculation.

tort system in the 1990s and the likely benefits of Auto Choice, I developed brochures for CAR in each Congress to explain the need for Auto Choice. The brochures targeted multiple audiences—members of Congress and their staffs, consumer groups and insurers, the press and motorists. Figure 14.3 shows the cover page of the first brochure.

The huge savings estimates from the RAND and JEC work, averaging roughly $40 billion a year if all motorists chose the PIP system, are not surprising when you appreciate what the bill would have done to fix the problems in both fault and no-fault states. Remember, RAND found $13–$18 billion of fraud and buildup annually in fault states. A move to the PIP option would have eliminated most, if not all, of the incentives for bad behavior and the attendant costs as well as the need for and expense of most lawyers. Savings would likely have occurred in no-fault states with compromised thresholds by the PIP option's elimination of all suits for pain and suffering. Additional savings would have occurred by setting the minimum required level of PIP benefits lower than they were in many of the no-fault states with large urban populations, leaving it up to individual motorists to weigh the value of higher benefits against the use of those dollars for other needs.

Using the JEC cost savings estimates, it is possible to project how much consumers could have saved had federal no-fault legislation been enacted during the 1970s. The following very rough calculation assumes that a law similar to Auto Choice had been adopted in 1978. Looking first at the Auto Choice effort, assume a potential annual savings of $40 billion, roughly the midpoint of the JEC savings estimates. Just using the annual figure, before adjusting for inflation and the increasing number of vehicles and premiums, had Auto Choice legislation been enacted in 1998, the American public could have saved $880 billion by

The Auto Choice Reform Act

Overview

In 1997, a bipartisan group of U.S. senators and representatives introduced the Auto Choice Reform Act, S. 625 (McConnell-Moynihan-Lieberman) and H.R. 2021 (Armey-Moran). This legislation ***could save motorists hundreds of dollars a year*** on their insurance premiums by providing a new personal protection insurance (PPI) option. According to the Congressional Joint Economic Committee (JEC), those who choose the PPI option would see an average reduction in their insurance bill of $184 per car, per year. If everyone chose this option, the JEC estimates the plan could save consumers as much as $35 billion a year. Over five years, the savings could total $193 billion.

Under the Auto Choice plan, motorists would have a choice between purchasing an insurance policy similar to that presently available in their state and the new PPI option. Injured motorists who choose the PPI option would be compensated promptly by their own insurer for their medical bills and lost wages without having to prove fault. The injured person could also recover the cost of any medical bills and lost wages beyond the coverage of his/her policy from the driver at fault in the accident. The PPI option would eliminate suits for pain and suffering.

The Auto Choice Reform Act promotes federalism. It would offer motorists a lower cost, more efficient option to existing law. But, if a state does not wish to give its motorists this new PPI option, it can pass a law to prevent the Auto Choice Reform Act from going into effect. Also, the bill would not go into effect in a state if it would not reduce auto insurance premiums for personal injury in that state by at least 30 percent for those who choose the PPI option. Regulation of insurance would remain in the hands of the states.

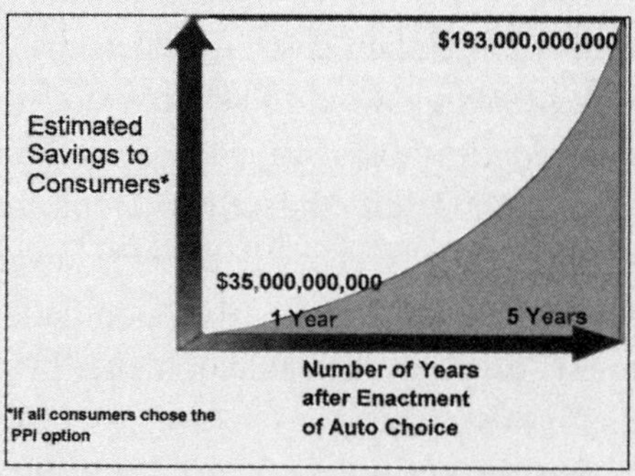

Page 1 — *Coalition for Auto-Insurance Reform (CAR)*

Figure 14.3. First advocacy (primarily lobbying) brochure for the Coalition for Auto-Insurance Reform (CAR), 1997.

2020. Then, go back to when the Congress first considered no-fault in the 1970s. Had the Senate and House sponsors accepted and adopted the Broyhill compromise in 1978, there would have been an additional twenty years of savings. Again, assuming the same level of premiums were written in each year between 1978 and 1998 as were written in 1996 (which would be as inaccurate in the opposite direction as assuming that premiums remained static between 1998 and 2020) would produce another twenty years of savings. Again assuming annual savings at $40 billion a year, that would yield another $800 billion in lost savings in 1998 dollars. If you combine the forty-two years, you get $1.62 trillion. Adjusting that figure for inflation alone from 1998 to 2020 would yield a total savings of $2.62 trillion in today's dollars.[32] That is a sum equal to nearly three times the entire $772 billion US national debt in 1978.

No matter how you slice it, that's real money. The rest of this book describes how the opportunity to start enjoying those savings through the adoption of Auto Choice legislation in the 1990s and 2000s was again thwarted by politicians protecting their jobs, lawyers and insurers protecting their bottom lines, and Ralph Nader siding with the trial bar. The last portion of the book discusses what events might put no-fault legislation back on the federal agenda.

15. Let's All Change Partners and Dance Again

Political Support for Auto Choice Flip-Flops (1996–1998)

Convinced that O'Connell and Joost had invented a better mousetrap, I set out to line up support for Auto Choice among the organizations that had supported no-fault in the 1970s. To say I was surprised at their response would be an understatement. Even though it had been nearly twenty years since consideration of federal no-fault legislation, it was as if I had fallen through the looking glass into an alternative universe. In this new world of Auto Choice, most of my old partners in the 1970s no-fault efforts ran away and hid, fearful of crossing the trial bar and Ralph Nader. On the other hand, many of the previous opponents of no-fault became partners in the effort to adopt Auto Choice legislation.

The sponsorship by Republicans, Senator McConnell and House Majority Leader Armey, was bound to give Democrats pause. The key, and only, public Senate Democratic supporters were Moynihan and Lieberman, whose interest dated back to their involvement in the 1960s and 1970s. Moynihan had written an article supporting no-fault that appeared in the *New York Times Magazine* in 1967, while Lieberman, as a state senator, had been the author of the Connecticut no-fault law in 1973. In the House, the lead Democratic cosponsor was Rep. Jim Moran (D-VA), cochair of the New Democrats, a faction of centrist Democrats most associated with President Clinton. I was able to secure Moran's support the old-fashioned way, by asking for it at a meeting with him. My ask on behalf of CAR was reinforced by being a constituent of his. After listening to an explanation of the substance and politics, Moran agreed on the spot to be the lead House Democrat. Several other Democrats signed on, but two of them took the unusual step of withdrawing their names under pressure from the trial bar.[1]

Overall, in both bodies, there was a mixture of primarily conservative Republicans and moderate Democrats. Conservative supporters of Auto

Choice focused on three things. The first was that the legislation would have expanded consumer choice, something that was denied to motorists in the thirty-six states where the only auto insurance option was the tort liability system. The second was the huge savings it promised consumers. The third was that the bill protected states' rights by giving each state the final say by including an opt-out provision. The Democrats were attracted to the huge savings, particularly for low-income people, and the opportunity to choose a better compensation system. For the most part, they were unconcerned that the federal government was the entity that would make these benefits possible. Given the fact that the Republicans could have used the bill as a political cudgel to attack Democrats for their allegiance to the trial bar as well as to try to defund it, I was pleased and slightly surprised that I never heard any Republican say he or she was supporting the bill to hurt Democrats. Instead, they were constantly seeking Democrat cosponsors in the traditional way one tries to pass a bill.

I expected that securing cosponsorship of the Senate bill from respected Democrats Moynihan and Lieberman would help overcome the knee-jerk reaction to McConnell and Armey being the sponsors, as would my long Democratic track record on no-fault and other consumer issues as a staffer in the House and Senate. These hopes turned out to be naive, to say the least.

I found this out early on when, unexpectedly, I was the lone credentialed Democrat at a June 18, 1997, press conference led by Armey, the new majority leader and one of the leading conservatives in the House. In an attempt to differentiate myself from the Republican speakers, I opened my remarks by saying, "I am surprised to find myself sharing the podium with the man most responsible for ending my political career." My intent was to make people aware that I was a Democrat and that Auto Choice had bipartisan support. Unfortunately, my intended reference to the fact that Armey was part of the new Republican leadership that had caused me to leave the House in 1995 was too arcane for Armey (or perhaps anyone else) to understand. Armey leaned over to his staff and asked, "Did I fire Peter?"

Nevertheless, I dutifully set out to pick up more Democratic support, armed with the history of Democratic, consumer, and labor support for no-fault in the 1970s. In addition, unlike the earlier no-fault bills, Auto

Choice offered huge potential savings for low-income people, which I assumed would be of great interest to Democrats. I wrote two documents to make the case. The first, "Democratic Heritage of Automobile Insurance Reform,"[2] cited the Democratic pedigrees of Keeton and O'Connell as well as Calabresi and the important roles of Dukakis; Senators Magnuson and Hart; Representatives Moss, Van Deerlin, and Eckhardt; and the Carter administration. As persuasive as I thought the history would be, I anticipated the benefits for low-income people would be even more powerful. In a longer-than-usual lobbying document, "The Benefits of the Auto Choice Reform Act for Low-Income Persons"[3] (more than two pages, long enough to test the attention span of many young congressional staffers), I pointed out how many low-income people needed cars to get to jobs in the suburbs and how Auto Choice would help them afford the cost of auto insurance to do so by dramatically lowering premiums as well as giving them more money to spend on other necessities.

Sadly, I discovered that my intended audience was not interested in either my arguments or their history, as a similar political realignment had occurred outside the Congress for largely the same reason—the "generosity" of the trial bar. I reached out to strong supporters from the 1970s, only to see most of them run for cover. I talked with people I knew at the AARP and the unions, both of which had been members of the CCNF, the coalition that had supported enactment of no-fault legislation in the 1970s. They were not particularly responsive, which was a gross understatement. The AARP had "other priorities," although there were none at the time that could have saved seniors the billions of dollars annually that Auto Choice promised. The unions showed a similar lack of interest, although they probably had more important issues to work on as they struggled to halt the dramatic loss in union membership over the intervening twenty years.

I also reached out to former strong supporters among the consumer groups. Everywhere I went, I found Nader's fingerprints.[4] Gene Kimmelman, who began his career as a consumer advocate and staff attorney at Nader's Public Citizen, had assumed a leadership role at CFA, which had been a big supporter of no-fault. CFA had also been a member of CCNF, and its then legislative director, Kathleen O'Reilly, had been one of the most effective and tireless advocates for no-fault. When I approached CFA for support in 1996, I found that the organization had developed a case of collective amnesia. Kimmelman was unwilling to make any commitment. Moreover, his boss and CFA's executive director, Steve Brobeck, backed off an agreement to appear at a January 1997 Auto Choice conference after a *New York Times* reporter, Peter Passell, wrote that "Nader-inspired opposition from consumer groups is crumbling: Stephen Brobeck, executive director of the Consumer Federation of America, has signed on."[5] Passell may have intended that to mean what I had told him, that Brobeck had agreed to speak at the conference, but Brobeck understandably took it to mean that CFA had signed on to support the legislation. Brobeck immediately called me. He was quite angry and refused to accept my explanation that Passell had either been unclear or had misunderstood me. In any event, with his name publicly associated with Auto Choice, Brobeck backed out of speaking at the conference. He later gave me some advice on avenues I might explore to move the issue forward and did invite me to participate in a debate at CFA, but he never publicly supported Auto Choice or authorized CFA to fight for it.

Perhaps most disappointing was the response from Consumers Union (CU), one of the earliest consumer groups to write about and advocate for no-fault. For some thirty years, CU had published numerous favorable articles and lobbied Congress for the adoption of no-fault. Its president, in both the 1970s and the 1990s, was Rhoda Karpatkin. She had signed the Attorneys for No-Fault letter in support of the 1970s no-fault legislation, and CU had been a member of the CCNF in the 1970s. This time not only did CU not support Auto Choice, it actively lobbied against it. In Andrew Tobias's book *My Vast Fortune*, he argued that the likely basis for CU's opposition to Auto Choice and Tobias's Prop. 200 pure no-fault proposition in California in 1996 (opposition to which Nader led) was the receipt of money from the trial bar:

> His [Harry Snyder's] West Coast CU operation, he told *The Wall Street Journal*, gets about 20 percent of its budget from class-action proceeds—not necessarily in cases CU has been party to, but simply "leftover" money where not every member of the class can be found. Rather than let the wrongdoers keep that money, judges frequently give a chunk of it to CU—hundreds of thousands of dollars that CU gets without having to write grant proposals, without having to organize benefit galas. It's about the sweetest money a nonprofit executive can imagine. And were it not for the fine work of the

trial lawyers—much of which *is* fine—Harry wouldn't have had it to augment his budget.[6]

CU and CFA raised substantive objections to both the benefit levels and the limitations on the right to sue. They said the minimum benefit level of $25,000 was too low, as compared to the $120,000 minimum in the no-fault bills of the 1970s. They also argued that the threshold was too tight, limiting suits to cases of excess economic loss only, instead of the 1970s threshold that also permitted suits for pain and suffering in serious and permanent injury cases. These arguments ignored the fact that individuals could choose to purchase higher levels of benefits and that the lower levels of benefits and tighter restrictions on the right to sue would enable low- and moderate-income policyholders to reduce their premiums dramatically. They also ignored the facts that the legislation authorized motorists to purchase no-fault benefits for pain and suffering and permitted people to remain in the tort system and sue for whatever they could get. More fundamentally, their arguments ignored the failures of the tort system and the advantages of no-fault benefits, the two basic reasons for their historical support. CU's focus on the importance of the right to sue sounded just like the argument the trial bar made.

For CU, that was the end of the discussion. On the other hand, CFA tried to engage on the subject because it looked to Bob Hunter, the federal insurance administrator at the Federal Insurance Administration (FIA) during the 1970s, for expertise. Hunter has served for years as a consultant to CFA on insurance issues. Both Tobias and I also had long-standing relationships with Hunter. Hunter and I had worked together in the 1970s to advance no-fault legislation. In fact, Hunter had written memos for the FIA, which was then part of the Department of Housing and Urban Development, endorsing federal no-fault during the Nixon and Ford administrations. Tobias and Hunter had worked together on Tobias's 1996 Pay at the Pump initiative in California.

No doubt at Hunter's urging, CFA arranged for the two of us to debate Auto Choice at a conference held in late 1998.[7] Then, in early 2002, Hunter, Mike Horowitz, and I met privately to see whether we could reach an agreement on a bill with higher PIP benefits. At our request, Steve Carroll costed a bill with higher PIP levels than the $25,000 minimum that motorists would have been required to purchase in most states. Carroll found that $50,000 in PIP benefits would reduce Auto Choice no-fault savings very modestly, from 56 percent to 53 percent, while $100,000 of benefits would still show a savings of 51.6 percent.[8] He explained the reasons why higher levels would have little effect on cost savings: (1) Almost all accident victims had economic loss less than the PIP levels in the existing bills, and (2) economic loss was a relatively small part of the cost of liability premiums compared to the cost of lawyers' fees and noneconomic loss.[9] Not surprisingly, in the meeting, Hunter pushed for $100,000, while Horowitz refused to consider more than $50,000. The meeting was amicable but broke up without an agreement. With the Congress focused on responding to the events of 9/11, however, there was little interest in other legislation, and the discussion went no further.

During our discussions, I asked Hunter if he knew the reasons for Nader's opposition. I had long assumed it was because of his close relationship with the trial bar. Hunter told me he and Nader had debated the merits of no-fault late into the night once during the 1970s until Nader had grudgingly agreed that no-fault might be a better system for motorists than the tort system. But Nader's final point of opposition was that if the trial bar can't get fees from auto insurance cases, where would it get the funds to bring product liability class actions against auto manufacturers for defectively designed vehicles?

Unlike CFA, CU's leadership (other than its lobbyist) refused to even meet to discuss the merits of Auto Choice. Worse yet, it started using trial lawyer talking points about the right to sue as the reason for its opposition to the legislation—the same basic argument that the trial bar had used to oppose no-fault in the 1970s! At that point, I gave up my outreach to the consumer groups, as it was clear that CU and CFA were both in thrall to Nader and/or trial bar money. It was a sad comedown for formerly admirable organizations that once had truly represented consumers.

If the web of connections between Nader and the trial bar weren't clear enough already, Linda Lipsen, CU's chief lobbyist, left CU to become ATLA's chief lobbyist. Then, the remaining CU lobbyist adopted ATLA's talking points against Auto Choice.

The result was harmful in two major respects: (1) Auto Choice lost key potential ground troops to lobby Congress, and (2) CAR lost the ability to cite Democratic touchstones in seeking Democratic cosponsors for the Senate and House bills. I was able to secure some modest funding for CAR, primarily from State Farm and USAA, but it did not compare to that of the trial bar, and we had little or no ground game. The funding was even less than the CCNF had had in the 1970s.

While liberal groups did their best to hide or even change their previous support for no-fault, conservative groups and individuals signed on as supporters of Auto Choice (if not as members of CAR). Jeff O'Connell's recruitment of Horowitz paid off. Horowitz had impeccable Republican credentials from his service in the George H. W. Bush administration and his work at the Hudson Institute. Because he could be short with people, I sometimes had to follow up with people he had offended, including supporters, to keep them on board and to explain things Horowitz didn't have the patience to discuss.

Overall, Horowitz opened far more doors than he closed. He convinced Grover Norquist, of the very conservative and powerful Americans for Tax Reform, to work for the bill. Norquist saw the billions in estimated savings as the equivalent of a tax cut. Norquist helped with the inside game, reaching out to Karl Rove, senior advisor and assistant to Pres. George W. Bush, and to the staff director of the Republican-led House Energy and Commerce Committee. In July 2001, Norquist reported to me that "Rove was supportive and took the two flyers [brochures] you gave me and sent them to the relevant people in the White House."[10] Citizens for a Sound Economy, another very conservative outside group that became Freedom Works, weighed in with an excellent academic article that explained the benefits of Auto Choice to conservative readers.[11]

Interestingly, I found that the Republicans were focused politically on adding Democratic support to keep the bills bipartisan. To address their concern, I drafted and used in my lobbying efforts a document entitled "Bipartisan Heritage of Automobile Insurance Reform Legislation: No-Fault Insurance in the 1970s and Auto Choice Proposals Today."[12] It traced state no-fault laws to both Democratic governors (Dukakis in Massachusetts) and Republican governors (Rockefeller in New York and Milliken in Michigan), cited the bipartisan no-fault bills in the Senate in the 1970s (led by Democrat Magnuson and Republican Stevens) and the support of three presidents—Nixon, Ford, and Carter—among other indicators of bipartisanship. Of course, it also cited the bipartisan cosponsors of the House and Senate Auto Choice bills.

The insurance industry continued to be split, with many "stock" companies (for-profit companies whose stock is traded on the stock exchanges) opposed out of concern about the likely loss of premium income were many people to elect the PIP coverage. As indicated previously, in 1997, State Farm, a "mutual" company (one owned by its policyholders), and USAA did join the coalition and provide some limited funding. The rest of the industry either stayed on the sidelines or opposed the bill, fearful of the impact on their bottom line (a legitimate business concern but not exactly putting their customers first).

Despite my limited success in rounding up the old gang, in late 1997 and early 1998 I made one last attempt to secure more congressional Democratic support, relying on the credibility I had built up with certain senators during my time as a Senate staffer. My hope was that if I could get a few high-visibility Senate Democrats to cosponsor the bill, other Democrats would feel safe in joining them. I first approached the office of Senator Dodd, for whom I had worked for twelve years and who once had signed off on my request to explore the possibility of him introducing an Auto Choice bill. It was not good news when I was able to get a meeting only with his top legislative people but not with him. They listened but made no commitment, and I never got a meeting with Dodd.

I next approached Senator Rockefeller's office. The senator had appreciated the work I had done staffing on the product liability bill, and he later told me that I was one of only nine people for whom he had written personal letters of support in 1996 for a job in the incoming Clinton administration. Unfortunately, after I stopped staffing him in 1993, the private sector refused to agree to a compromise with the Clinton administration on a product liability bill. In response Rockefeller walked away from the effort, saying that he wanted nothing more to do with liability reform. In preparation for my meeting with his staff, I created a document entitled "Why Auto Choice Is Different from Other Tort Reform Issues."[13] The document cited the bill's focus on timely payment of more benefits to more people, particularly the most seriously injured; lower premiums for all motorists, particularly for low-income people; and the long Democratic history of support. I naively even added a talking point about the difficulty of explaining a change in position to constituents! Despite my best efforts, apparently Rockefeller's opposition to liability reform applied to Auto Choice as well, as once again I was unable to get past the legislative staff to make my pitch to the senator.

My last effort was with the office of Senator Harkin. Harkin was a neighbor who had also written a letter endorsing me for a position in the incoming Clinton administration. His longtime staffer Rich Bender told me that Harkin might well vote for the bill if it got to the Senate floor, but there was no way he would cosponsor it. Left unsaid was the fact that cosponsorship would put a target on Harkin's back with the trial bar.

What I hadn't paid enough attention to was the fact that the trial bar had even more sway with Democrats in the 1990s than in the 1970s. They needed them more because Democrats were out of power in both the House and Senate, and they could ill afford to lose the support of one of their largest financial backers. After the meeting with Bender, I knew that the trial bar had locked up most Democrats, and the only way a bill stood a chance of getting their support in either House was if the Commerce Committee were to report one. I still believed that we could get several Democratic votes if they were forced to a public vote on the Senate floor.

Thus, by the end of 1998, the teams were set. Supporters were going to be primarily Republicans and conservative outside groups, and opponents were going to be primarily Democrats and Ralph Nader, consumer groups, and trial lawyers. The insurance industry would once again be divided.

16. The Rubber Hits the Road

Congressional Consideration of Auto Choice (1996–2004)

While the initial effort to secure more widespread congressional support had been disappointing, what we did have was a good story to tell and a first-rate internal effort. As in the 1970s, there was excellent private sector academic work documenting the case for change. In the Congress, there were many very bright, dedicated, and politically astute congressional staff for the key Senate and House sponsors willing to do the tough, unglamorous work required to make the bill workable and to secure votes. This time, however, the staffers were mostly Republicans. Over time, Dan Miller was able to document why the trial bar could afford to be so generous in making contributions to members' campaigns. In a July 2003 JEC report, Miller estimated the trial bar's annual revenue from auto cases in 2001 at nearly $12 billion. The defense bar made close to another $5 billion.[1] There was no way either of them was prepared to sacrifice their income for the good of their potential clients.

After Melissa Patak's departure, Hunter Bates became the lead staffer for Senator McConnell on Auto Choice. Bates had a great combination of substantive and political skills and a useful competitive streak. He demonstrated his political skills early on by insisting on visiting my home to learn more about the issue rather than having me come to his Senate office. It was one of those small things that make a large impression. Bates dug into the substance, even to the point of joining O'Connell and me in writing a law review article that provided a colloquial section-by-section analysis of the bill[2] (I, too, knew how to play the political game, inviting Bates to join us in writing the article). He held up his end of the bargain, doing a lot of work on it.

The most active staffer among the bill's original Democratic cosponsors was Laurie Rubenstein for Senator Lieberman. She brought a rigorous, critical mind to all issues. She was backed up by her legislative director, Bill Bonvillian, whom I knew both from his work on no-fault at DOT in the 1970s during the Carter administration and from when he and I had both served as legislative directors for the two Connecticut senators in the late 1980s, he for Senator Lieberman and I for Senator Dodd.

Lance Bultena was assigned to staff the issue for the committee in 1996 after Senator McConnell introduced Auto Choice. Bultena staffed the first no-fault hearing on September 24, 1996, for then Senate Commerce Committee Chairman Larry Pressler (R-SD). When Sen. John McCain (R-AZ) became the committee chairman in the 105th Congress in 1997, he retained Bultena and gave him the staff responsibility not only for no-fault but for McCain's legislative effort to craft a tobacco settlement. Bultena, despite having just started working on the Hill in 1995, was one of the few people I worked with over the years who understood the unwritten portion of the job—the intuitive sense of the right time to move legislation. For Auto Choice, that meant when to hold hearings and how to arrange them for maximum effect. While much of Bultena's time was consumed with tobacco settlement negotiations in 1997 and 1998, he arranged the two excellent hearings the committee held during the 105th Congress.

On the House side, the key legislative staffer was Gayland Barksdale, chief of staff to Representative Armey, the sponsor of the House bill. Armey had come from the most conservative wing of the party and rose to the position of majority leader in 1995 when the Republicans took over the House for the first time in forty years. Like Bates, Rubenstein, Miller, and Bultena, Barksdale dug into the bill's details, and we spoke regularly about substance and strategy. Given the dramatic increase in partisanship brought to the Congress first and foremost by Newt Gingrich, having Armey as the lead sponsor was a double-edged sword—good with Republicans but poison with Democrats.

I developed close relationships with Bates, Barksdale, and Miller. We regularly discussed the details as well as the politics of Auto Choice. The by-products of these friendships were technically better legislation, powerful JEC reports, and an effective outreach effort, both to members of Congress and to the media, as we shared information and helped create advocacy opportunities for each other. That meant the Hill staff arranging for me to speak to organized coalitions of members and me arranging for them to speak with private sector companies and trade associations. As was the case in the 1970s, there were also regular meetings between the key staffers and my CAR members to discuss substance and strategy.

It is not uncommon for Hill staff and the people they work with off the Hill to develop close personal relationships. It is no different than what happens when people work intensively on any work project. The difference here is that Hill staff must be careful to make sure they are not being manipulated by outside individuals trying to serve the needs of their clients. This situation was an easy one for me because I had only a few paying clients, and none of them opposed the legislation. There is also a built-in check on efforts by private sector groups to mislead Hill staff. If a lobbyist provides misleading information, he or she risks losing access to the staff and, of course, the staff's boss, something a lobbyist cannot afford.

Throughout this time, I also continued to discuss the finer points of Auto Choice issues with Bob Joost, although Joost started experiencing symptoms from Parkinson's disease, and it became harder and harder for him to communicate. He remained a strong advocate of Auto Choice until his death in 2008.

After Senator McConnell introduced the first Auto Choice bill, S. 1860, the Auto Choice Reform Act, on June 11, 1996, the issue quickly attracted public attention. Peter Passell of the *New York Times* wrote the first of several favorable articles on August 11, 1996, and then the Senate Commerce Committee, under the chairmanship of Sen. Larry Pressler, scheduled a hearing for September 24, 1996.

The witnesses at the hearing made the case for and against the bill. Senator McConnell was the lead witness, outlining the case against the tort system and for Auto Choice. He was followed by Professor O'Connell, who explained how the concept had come into being. O'Connell, in turn, was followed by Kathleen O'Donnell, representing the trial bar. She discussed the higher cost of insurance in no-fault states, ignoring the fact that many of the no-fault states were highly industrialized and thus would always be more costly than rural ones. She also ignored the fact that the major cause for higher premiums was the weak thresholds the trial bar had secured, turning "thresholds" into "targets" that led in some no-fault states to retention of almost as many lawsuits as had existed under the tort system. The result was to force so-called no-fault states to, in effect, operate both no-fault and tort systems.

Next, Andrew Tobias discussed the no-fault initiative he had pursued in California, the trial bar's advertising of what he called "outright lies" about the cost impact, and how Nader's opposition had helped kill an initiative that would have saved consumers a lot of money. The last witness, Jamie Court, was Nader's second in command of the effort opposing Tobias's initiative. Court echoed the trial bar's remarks, citing higher costs in no-fault states and claiming that good drivers pay for bad ones. I testified between Tobias and Court, providing a history of the previous federal no-fault efforts and state experience with no-fault. One of the concepts I focused on was that with no-fault, you were trading the right to sue for the right to recover.[3]

In the wake of the hearing, Auto Choice received editorial support from some of the nation's largest and most influential newspapers, including the *New York Times*, *Boston Globe*, *Dallas Morning News*, *Philadelphia Inquirer*, *New York Daily News*, *New York Post*, *Newsday*, *Washington Post*, *USA Today*, and *San Diego Union-Tribune*[4] as well as the *Baltimore Sun*, *Denver Post*, *Des Moines Register*, *Detroit News*, *Hartford Courant*, and New Orleans *Times-Picayune*. In addition, the bill received support from columnists across the political spectrum (from conservatives Steve Forbes and Peter Schuck to moderates Robert Samuelson and Stuart Taylor to liberals/progressives Jane Bryant Quinn and Andrew Tobias). Former House Consumer Protection Subcommittee Chair Lionel Van Deerlin wrote a column in support and joined CAR.

With little time left in the 104th Congress, 1996 came to an end, and it was time to start to prepare for the upcoming 105th Congress, where a new bill would have to be introduced. I used the downtime between Congresses, mid-October of 1996 to January 3, 1997, to work with the University of Wisconsin's Auto Accident Compensation Project to cosponsor a two-day conference in Washington, DC, entitled Auto Insurance Reform at the Federal Level: An Opportunity for Better Compensation for Injured Persons and Lower Premiums for All. The conference took place on January 30–31, 1997. I delivered the opening remarks, and then people from across the political spectrum spoke in favor of Auto Choice. Republican Senator McConnell gave the keynote address and Democratic

Senator Lieberman the luncheon speech. Other speakers included Andrew Tobias from the left, Grover Norquist of Americans for Tax Reform from the right, Al From of the moderate Democratic Leadership Council, and Russ Verney of the third party, Ross Perot's Reform Party. Professor O'Connell and Mike Horowitz also spoke.

Nine senators signed on in 1997 as cosponsors of S. 625, Senator McConnell's Auto Choice Reform Act of 1997, which he introduced in the new Congress on April 22, 1997. On the House side, Representative Armey, with Representative Moran, introduced H.R. 2021, the Auto Choice Reform Act of 1997, on June 4, 1997. The bill attracted twenty-one cosponsors, most of them Republicans, with a few moderate Democrats.

Because the bills were introduced early in the 105th Congress, it was possible to secure earlier hearings in both bodies. The JEC got the ball rolling with a hearing on March 19, 1997. The lead witness, New Jersey Gov. Christine Todd Whitman, testified about choice no-fault legislation she had proposed that would offer New Jersey motorists four insurance options. She commended S. 1860, Senator McConnell's Auto Choice bill, as a model of federalism, leaving the final word up to each state. Stephen Carroll, the author of RAND's no-fault studies, testified about the methodology used in determining that a no-fault alternative would offer consumers huge cost savings, and O'Connell and Horowitz testified about how, despite their philosophical differences, they had found common ground on Auto Choice. Robert Hunter of CFA, a supporter of no-fault in the 1970s, took a different view. He testified that CFA supported a Michigan-type no-fault bill with high benefits but opposed Auto Choice, primarily because of its low mandatory benefit levels.[5]

Senators McConnell, Moynihan, and Lieberman, as well as House Majority Leader Armey, testified at a July 17, 1997, Senate Commerce Committee hearing,[6] the first of the two the committee held during the Congress. It is rare for the House majority leader, or any House member, to testify in the Senate, and it is usually highly effective. Tobias and I testified again, this time with the newly minted CAR acronym, thanks to Tobias.

The hearing proved interesting for more than just the subject matter. Chairman McCain, who was to become a cosponsor of the bill in 1999, delivered opening remarks and then left the room before Senator McConnell testified. Years later, McCain's counsel, Lance Bultena, told me that McCain had planned to do so in advance. The reason was that he was angry with McConnell over his opposition to McCain's campaign finance reform bill. I believe the strained relationship was to play a role in the failure of the committee to mark up the bill.

Senator Moynihan reprised his brilliant take on no-fault, the one that he had first written in his 1967 *New York Times Magazine* article. At the hearing, as in his earlier article, Moynihan said that crashes "are called accidents but . . . are nothing of the kind. . . . [There are] a statistically predictable number of these collisions—they are not accidents, they are foreseeable events."[7] His point was that auto crashes should not be treated as accidents because the combination of powerful automobiles and traffic congestion, and the human limits of drivers make crashes inevitable. Given that, he had concluded that it was best to adopt the legal and insurance system that provided the fastest compensation to injured people at the least cost. He was also deeply concerned about the waste of judicial resources on auto litigation, time that he said could be far better spent on other issues.

The congressional supporters ramped up their efforts in late 1997, starting with an op-ed by Dick Armey and Mitch McConnell, "Tackling the High Cost of Driving," in the December 3, 1997, edition of the *Washington Post.* The Senate cosponsors followed up with a series of "Dear Colleague" letters to other senators on December 12, 1997, January 21, 1998, February 10, 1998, and May 7, 1998. All the materials cited the promise of improved compensation for injuries at far lower premiums.

There was less activity in the House. The only House hearing occurred on May 20, 1998, in the Commerce Committee. When I testified before the Subcommittee on Finance and Hazardous Materials in the full committee hearing room, it was the first time I had sat at the table since August 1, 1978, the day the committee had failed to report the Eckhardt no-fault bill. It was no more pleasant than the previous time, as Democrats Bart Stupak (MI) and Diana DeGette (CO) peppered me with questions that came straight from the trial lawyers' talking points.

Three years later, I learned more about the House Committee's lack of interest. It was part practical, part transactional. A group of supporters met with Terry Haines, the staff director of the Commerce Committee. Here is my report on the meeting:

> His back [*sic*] point was that Auto Choice is a great issue and the committee is prepared to push it, but only to the extent that interested companies and organizations are prepared to make the necessary effort. Terry asked everyone to go back to their bosses and then report to him by early September what sort of effort they are prepared to make.[8]

That the committee took no further action reinforces the point about the lack of a special interest willing to participate fully in the legislative process to counter the trial bar's interest.

The final hearing in the 105th Congress occurred back in the Senate Commerce Committee on September 9, 1998. It focused on the benefits of Auto Choice for different categories of people. Dukakis was the lead witness, and he and Robert DeMichelis, a person with a brain injury who testified on behalf of the Brain Injury Association, made a strong case for the benefits of the legislation for seriously injured people. Prof. Robert Lee Maril made an equally strong case for its benefits for low-income people. Maril described the study he had conducted on the spending habits of low-income people in Maricopa County, Arizona, in which he had found that low-income drivers spent in excess of 30 percent of their income on auto insurance. Last, Wellington Webb, the mayor of Denver, testified about the benefits of Auto Choice for cities.

While waiting for the Congress to act, in 1997–1998, I continued organizing, drafting, soliciting support, and working with the Hill staff. As the president and sole employee of CAR, I gave numerous speeches around the country; participated in television and radio debates with trial lawyers, insurers, and consumer advocates;[9] spoke with newspaper columnists and editorial boards; wrote several articles; and developed informational (lobbying) materials. I also worked to add members to CAR, even some paying ones. The American Trucking Associations joined, as did Auto Nation, a major car-rental company.

Ford Motor Company joined, but GM and Chrysler opposed the legislation on the grounds that it would increase the number of liability suits against them as auto manufacturers. Jim Vondale of Ford invited me to a meeting in Detroit in an effort to persuade GM and Chrysler to change their minds. I supported Ford's position that better compensation from auto insurance was likely to leave injured people more satisfied with their recoveries and thus less likely to sue the auto manufacturer. GM and Chrysler took the opposite view, arguing that faster and more complete auto insurance recoveries would finance product liability suits against them, as injured people would be able to afford to wait longer to sue rather than settle for less money earlier to pay for their injuries. Neither side could convince the other, and the auto industry remained divided. This was quite unfortunate in that it resulted in the powerful US Chamber of Commerce Institute for Legal Reform withdrawing from the fight after it had previously made Auto Choice its top legislative priority.

While I had been unable to secure support from the consumer and labor groups, I thought it might be still be possible to leverage their support if the Clinton administration could be convinced to endorse Auto Choice. Before trying to set up an appointment, I spoke with Guido Calabresi, now a US Court of Appeals judge, who had been a strong supporter of no-fault during the 1970s and a useful ally in the effort to draft legislation to apply similar principles to product injuries when I was working for Senator Dodd. Calabresi summed up the possible interest of Bill and Hillary Clinton, saying, "They didn't take my class" (while they were at Yale). Unfortunately, it looked as if we were dealing with a blank slate.

There were still other ways to get the attention of the Clinton administration. Vice President Gore had voted for the 1970s no-fault bill when he was a member of the House, and we had remained on friendly terms while he was a senator. I decided to hold off contacting him until we had exhausted all other avenues. That meant reaching out to Jack Quinn, Clinton's White House counsel, who had lobbied for no-fault in the 1970s on behalf of State Farm while he was an attorney in private practice with the law firm of Arnold & Porter.

On September 10, 1996, I wrote to Elena Kagan, then a White House associate counsel, following a discussion we had had days before about Auto Choice. The letter described the 1970s effort and its Democratic origins and requested a meeting. The meeting wasn't scheduled until two years later, in September 1998. In the interim, starting in late 1996, I had several discussions with George Wiggers, DOT's lead expert on no-fault after Dick Walsh had retired. Wiggers produced some excellent charts describing how auto accidents worked under Auto Choice and said that he had started to push the agency to support the federal bills. He arranged a meeting with John Lieber, the acting assistant secretary for transportation policy, and then drafted a decision memorandum (undated) for Lieber that concluded as follows:

> We now have an opportunity over the next year to support his bipartisan effort in Congress and lower consumer costs, increase highway safety and provide greater injury recovery benefits to those most in need. I recommend you designate the Policy Office as the Department's lead in working with the White House, Congress, other Federal agencies and other interest groups in supporting automobile insurance reform.

The trail then ran cold at DOT. I never heard whether Lieber forwarded the memorandum to DOT Secretary Rodney Slater. Wiggers told me he had been contacted by Amy Finkelstein, a staff economist for the CEA, and to expect a call from her. In December 1997, she called with three questions, two of which were based on the work of conservative scholars: (1) "Does no-fault insurance induce motorists to drive less safely and cause more accidents?" and (2) "Will lower insurance rates induce driving (and thus more accidents)?" I explained to her both the logic and academic work that debunked the first question. With regard to the second question, one that had been propounded by Yale Law School Prof. George Priest, I explained that insurance rates were only one of many cost factors, such as gas and repairs, that increase with additional driving. I also pointed out that lower insurance premiums would make it easier for many low-income people who live in cities to get to jobs that are often located far away in the suburbs. Of course, in general, the argument that the lower insurance premiums Auto Choice was projecting would encourage more driving and thus more accidents was an argument against ever doing anything to lower auto insurance costs. Ironically, some rates had already declined over the years because mandatory auto safety rules had reduced the number of injuries. If Priest's argument had been correct, then it would have created an ironic circle: federal standards that led to safer cars would result in lower insurance premiums, which, in turn, would lead to more driving, more accidents, and more, not fewer, injuries. In short, safer cars would result in more injuries. Priest did not present any evidence to support his thesis. In addition, I sent Finkelstein a memorandum about victim and attorney compensation under tort versus the PIP no-fault option of Auto Choice. I heard nothing more from her.

Finally, a meeting with White House staff was scheduled for September 1998. Dukakis, Nancy Perkins, an attorney at Arnold & Porter who was representing State Farm, and I met with key White House staff—Bruce Reed, assistant to the president for economic policy; Sally Katzen, chief of staff for the Domestic Policy Council; Paul Weinstein, deputy chief of staff for the Domestic Policy Council; and Jonathan Orszag, economic policy adviser for the National Economic Council—in the Old Executive Building. Dukakis was warmly received, as many of the staff had worked on his 1988 presidential campaign. The meeting lasted an hour and covered both substance and politics. It was clear that the trial bar had been ahead of us again, as the White House staff raised many of its talking points. Specifically, Katzen said she was skeptical about the cost savings estimates in light of the failure of no-fault to reduce premiums in the states and expressed concern that bad drivers would be more likely than good drivers to opt for the no-fault option, which would lower savings. We easily answered those canards, and the staff seemed to listen intently. Afterward, I followed up with further information in September 29, 1998, letters to Reed and Katzen.

Unfortunately, neither support within the lead substantive agency nor our White House meeting generated support from the Clinton administration. We never heard back from the White House staff. I suspect the administration was too dependent on trial lawyer money, particularly with a presidential election upcoming in 2000, to appreciate how good the policy was for many of their supporters as well as for motorists in general.

Once again, another Congress ended with no markup on either the House or Senate side, and the whole process had to start over again with the beginning of the 106th Congress in 1999. This time, I thought we had made enough progress in the past two Congresses to be well-positioned to move a bill. For the second Congress in a row, the Center for Consumer Affairs at the University of Wisconsin–Milwaukee and CAR started off the year with a joint conference, this one on January 28–29, 1999.[10] Prof. Jim Brown, the director of the center, and I delivered opening remarks. Senators McConnell and Lieberman and Representatives Armey and Moran then spoke about the new Auto Choice bill at a sponsors' roundtable, followed by a debate on the Auto Choice legislation, with Mike Horowitz and I arguing in favor against Kathy O'Donnell of the trial bar and Frank Clemente of Public Citizen's Congress Watch. The next panel was on the impact of Auto Choice on victims, cities, consumers, and business, with the mayor of Denver and a representative of the US Chamber of Commerce speaking about the favorable impact and a representative of CU reprising trial lawyer arguments against. It was followed by a panel on the cost projections for Auto Choice with Dan Miller and Steve Carroll. The last panel was a debate on no-fault and accident frequency, with O'Connell and Pierre Gauthier of Quėbec, Canada, arguing that no-fault had no impact on frequency and Priest taking the opposite position. Gauthier provided data from Quebec to support his position. Not only was the quality of the speakers excellent, but the conference attracted a number of Hill staff and reporters.

Then, with great work by Hunter Bates and Gayland Barksdale in particular in revising the legislation, the House and Senate sponsors introduced identical bills on April 20, 1997, just as Sen. Warren Magnuson and Rep. John Moss had done on April 25, 1977. Armey, with Moran, his Democratic colleague, introduced H.R. 1475, the Auto Choice Reform Act of 1999, and Senator McConnell introduced S. 837. The Senate bill appeared to have the ideal sponsors, as, for the first time, Senator McCain, the chairman of the Commerce Committee, joined Senators McConnell, Moynihan, and Lieberman on the bill.

As chairman, McCain determined committee priorities for action. It was encouraging when he scheduled a hearing on S. 837 for June 9, 1999, and it appeared as if the committee would finally mark up the bill. McConnell, Lieberman, and Moynihan testified in favor of the bill at the hearing along with O'Connell, Dukakis, and me.[11]

As was often the case, O'Connell was able to articulate the issue clearly and concisely. He started by reciting the bad news that the issues involved—tort law; liability insurance; and all kinds of data, including actuarial data—are complicated. Then he stated "the good news":

> You don't have to decide [who] is right. All you have to do is decide whether my friends sitting to the right [including Nader] are so right that the system they urge on you should continue to have its monopoly whereby in a state that requires tort liability insurance everybody has to buy it, or whether one should have an option to get out of it [i.e., buy no-fault coverage].

Andrew Tobias was also scheduled to testify in favor, which would have pitted him against Nader, the person who had led the opposition to

Tobias's no-fault initiative in California. After that initiative failed, Tobias wrote an article in 1996 for *Worth* magazine entitled "Ralph Nader Is a Big, Fat Idiot." It was Andy's way of getting people's attention. He explained up-front why he was angry with Nader:

> Okay. Ralph Nader is neither fat nor an idiot. In fact, he's lean and smart and has done some extraordinary things over the years. But recently, he was the linchpin of a deceptive campaign, the outcome of which cost California consumers more than $3 billion a year. This is the story of how he shafted them, despite what were doubtless good intentions, and thwarts reform that could save almost all of us money.

Alas, the interaction between Tobias and Nader that Tobias had long sought did not come to pass. Just before the hearing, Tobias was appointed treasurer of the Democratic Party, and Senator Hollings, as ranking minority member on the Commerce Committee, asked him not to testify and withdraw his testimony so that it would not seem as if the Democratic Party was endorsing Auto Choice. It was an understandable argument, although, given Hollings's long-standing opposition, it was a mere rationalization. Tobias told me about the request and suggested that I make sure his prepared testimony was circulated in advance of the hearing. It was the best he could do to help under the circumstances.

At the hearing, Nader testified against no-fault, again endorsing the arguments of his trial lawyer supporters, ignoring the safety incentives of no-fault and the opportunities to expand consumers' choices and save them money—three of the bedrock principles on which he based his career:

> On its face, no-fault has always been objectionable to me because it does not permit a recovery of compensation for pain and suffering. It dehumanizes the injured person, turns them into so much damaged property. I don't believe in ever trading off constitutional rights for a presumed economic benefit. In this case, there's no guarantee at all of economic benefit. Nothing in this bill would require or guarantee an alleged reduction of $35 billion. They leave it up to the insurance companies and the insurance state.

Of course, Nader's comments ignored the well-documented facts that almost all so-called pain and suffering damages go to people with small or *de minimis* economic loss with, as RAND found, much of it based on excessive, unnecessary, or fraudulent medical claims. Almost never do pain and suffering damages go to the seriously injured unless one is "lucky" enough to be hit by Bill Gates or, for that matter, Ralph Nader, people with the resources to pay a large judgment. As for guaranteeing savings, almost all state insurance departments require insurers to file their rates for the regulators to review, often before they can go into effect. Some state laws authorize the regulators to control the rates, while in other states, highly competitive markets keep insurers from gouging consumers. As Jeff O'Connell once said at another hearing, open the yellow pages in any city directory (he obviously said it a long time ago) and you will find pages of advertisements for different prices for auto insurance. It's a very competitive business. However, should you look for advertisements of different rates for lawyers to take accident cases, you won't find any.

The June 9, 1999, hearing was the fourth one the Senate Commerce Committee had held in three years. Coupled with a very solid body of academic work critiquing the tort and no-fault experiences, the introduction of identical bills in both Houses by a bipartisan group of heavyweight legislators, excellent congressional staff work, and, most important, Senator McCain's position as chairman of the committee, it seemed as if the bill was finally positioned to take the next key steps—a Senate Commerce Committee markup and serious consideration by the White House.

But it was not to be. Auto Choice was just one of many bills competing for the attention of the committee. This situation always gives the minority in the Senate leverage to obstruct consideration, as the ranking member can offer to help the chairman move other bills he or she wants in return for holding up legislation the minority opposes. In this case, the Senate Commerce Committee was also considering many other major bills, so by the time Auto Choice hearings and action on other bills were completed and the bill was ready for markup, it was 2000. With time growing short, Senator Hollings, twenty-two years after threatening to filibuster no-fault, used his leverage as the ranking minority member to prevent a markup by offering carrots and sticks to Chairman McCain. The carrots were his willingness to cooperate to move several other bills

McCain cared about instead; the stick was a very real threat to filibuster Auto Choice.[12] The other bills moved through committee, and Auto Choice was not marked up.

So it was back to it in the 107th Congress. Although it is axiomatic that the bigger the legislative initiative, the tougher and longer the fight, the supporters were understandably becoming discouraged. Initially, it appeared as if Auto Choice had received good political news when George W. Bush won the presidency. As governor of Texas, he had indicated support for the concept. Therefore, we shifted our focus to the new administration. On March 6, 2001, Armey and McConnell wrote a four-page letter to the incoming president, with copies to all relevant key members of the new administration, describing the benefits of Auto Choice and its history of bipartisan support, including from the new president's father. The letter concluded, "As you can see, Auto Choice is a notion that can hold tremendous promise for insurance consumers, and our national economy. We look forward to working with you and the Administration in reaching this and other accomplishments for the good of the country."

Less than three months later, on May 24, 2001, Democrats took control of the Senate when Republican Sen. Jim Jeffords of Vermont became Democratic Sen. Jim Jeffords of Vermont. His switch in parties gave Democrats the majority in the Senate, and with that, Senator Hollings became chairman of the Commerce Committee. As he had been the chief opponent of no-fault for more than twenty-five years, it was clear that the Commerce Committee would not act.

But the House was still in Republican hands, and so was the presidency. That left a different window to success, but a window nevertheless. I shifted my attention to the new administration and was able to schedule a meeting for 9:30 A.M. with key staff, including Jay Lefkowitz and Diana Schacht, both from the Domestic Policy Council, and a young White House staff secretary named Brett Kavanaugh. On the scheduled date, I was at an earlier planned meeting in Washington, DC, having turned down an offer to speak on Auto Choice at a New York State Department of Insurance meeting in downtown New York City. But it was 9/11 in 2001, and the White House meeting was adjourned before it took place when a plane flew into the Pentagon.

With the administration and the Congress focused on combating terrorism, it became impossible to get their attention for Auto Choice or much of anything else. It also hurt politically that we had not been able to secure more Democratic support. They were suspicious of the Republican sponsorship in the House and Senate and, more importantly, so reliant on trial bar contributions that, at best, a few Democrats had indicated that they would vote for the bill if it got to the floor, but they would not stick their necks out by cosponsoring legislation. By the time the White House meeting was rescheduled, it was January 15, 2003, and Auto Choice was no longer on the agenda of either the Senate or the House.

The last whimper came when then freshman Sen. John Cornyn (R-TX) introduced S. 2931, the Auto Choice Reform Act of 2004, with McConnell and McCain, on October 7, 2004. This time, there were no hearings in the Senate and no companion House bill. Members know when it is time to focus on other issues.

The failed effort strongly echoed that of no-fault legislation in the 1970s. The outside experts, key members of Congress and their staff, and the private sector coalition of supporters had all done excellent work. The result was a very good bill and superb supporting materials, but once again, that was not enough. The opposition from the trial bar and the ongoing split in the insurance industry were too much to overcome, as was bad timing. Most importantly, it simply wasn't possible to counter that opposition with support from the people who would benefit most, the general public—at least, not without a lot more money than I was able to raise for CAR and without campaign contributions to members backing up private sector support. Another problem was that, unlike in most other legislative battles, it was not possible to find a place to compromise that would bring the major opponents, the trial bar, to the bargaining table. The threshold was the critical component for both sides, and for the supporters to compromise on the threshold would have been to compromise the bill, leaving more lawsuits in the system and undermining the savings component, just as had happened when such compromises were made in state legislatures.

Recognizing the futility of making another effort without some major change in the political dynamics, Jeff O'Connell, Dan Miller, and I wrote a "time capsule" piece for the inevitable next time the issue arises, as it surely will, given the ongoing gross inadequacies of the fault and liability insurance system and unnecessarily high premiums. The article includes a variety of suggestions for ways to reform both weak state no-fault laws and inadequate state liability laws.[13] The article is also included in my work papers on no-fault and Auto Choice that are housed at the University of Virginia Law Library along with Professor O'Connell's files.[14]

As it turned out, Auto Choice was not the last liability reform bill I worked on in the private sector. Just as the Auto Choice effort was ending, class action legislation was heating up, and one of my other clients wanted me involved. The legislation was a response to abuses by the trial bar in bringing class actions against large corporations. The attorneys had found a way to maneuver around the federal rules that permitted such cases only when the plaintiff and defendant were from different states (diversity jurisdiction) to bring cases in plaintiff-friendly jurisdictions. The resulting flood of large class action suits in these jurisdictions forced companies to settle cases rather than risk huge judgments. Whether and when to settle involved risk/benefit judgments on both sides. Plaintiff attorneys, who handled these cases on a contingency fee basis (with the lawyers getting between 33 percent and 50 percent if they won but nothing if they lost) weighed the risk of losing (no fee)[15] against the benefit of winning (a calculation of the likelihood of recovery and the likely amount of a verdict). By finding a way to work around the diversity rules to maneuver cases into plaintiff-friendly jurisdictions, they had improved the odds of winning. Many companies facing notoriously plaintiff-friendly juries concluded that they were better off settling the cases than risking a "bet the company" verdict in a "hometown" jurisdiction.

From my proconsumer perspective, I found that too many of the settlements provided benefits for plaintiff lawyers and companies at the expense of the consumer plaintiffs. This is how it worked: Plaintiff attorneys' fees would be determined as a percentage of the settlement amount rather than the amount actually recovered by the plaintiffs. This happened because, in return for a guaranteed fee, the attorneys would agree to terms that made it difficult for their clients to recover. Sometimes they did this by devices such as tight timetables for filing claims. Other times they accomplished the same objective by disincentivizing consumers to accept their awards by having the awards be coupons to buy more of the offending product! As you can see, such settlements were really collusive ones won by attorneys and companies at the expense of the members of the class. Finally, the companies decided to go to Congress to end these abusive cases with legislation that they designed to protect themselves but that did not address many of the abuses experienced by consumers.

My main substantive, and political, contribution to the effort was to encourage the inclusion of a "Consumers' Bill of Rights" section in the bill to assure that plaintiffs would get a fair share of any judgment. It, for example, banned settlements where lawyers benefited more than the plaintiffs. It didn't surprise me that some of the companies objected because it would reduce their leverage in negotiations. But the section stayed in, and its inclusion helped make it safe for enough moderate to conservative Democrats to support the bill to overcome a filibuster. S. 5, the Class Action Fairness Act of 2005, became law on February 18, 2005.

The experience reinforced for me the importance of money and the role of private sector lobbying in bringing support from Republicans. The flip side was that business support made Democrats suspicious, a concern that was reinforced by the increasing importance of trial lawyer funding to Democrats. The political challenge of securing enough votes from both sides of the aisle to pass any legal reform legislation seemed to hinge on striking the proper balance between business and consumer interests and procuring enough funding to be heard on the merits.

17. Is There Some Education in the Second Kick of a Mule?

Given the spectacular failure of the two efforts to enact federal no-fault legislation, with first a proposal that appealed primarily to Democrats and liberals and then one that appealed primarily to Republicans and conservatives, is there any reason to believe no-fault might make a third appearance on the national stage? Perhaps no-fault is like the seventeen-year cicadas, only on a twenty-year cycle, and is closing in on another run in 2024. The more serious answer to that question probably lies in the answers to the following questions:

1. What were the main reasons the Auto Choice effort failed?
2. Were there political flaws in the proposal that supporters overlooked?
3. Is there anything to be learned from the success of other legal reform proposals?
4. Are there any external events that might force federal action?

Chapter 11 analyzed in detail why the 1970s effort failed. In performing a similar analysis of why Auto Choice failed, it makes sense to look first at what went right. Once again, I think it's fair to conclude that Auto Choice was a well-conceived and -documented proposal. The intellectual work done by O'Connell and Joost in refining the choice concept and devising a simple, equitable mechanism for resolving accidents between fault and no-fault drivers was brilliant. Moreover, the emphasis on consumer choice—giving motorists both a choice between insurance systems and a choice as to the level of no-fault benefits—and states' rights—giving each state the option to keep its existing auto insurance system—reflected the realities of the conservative, Republican-led Congress of the mid-1990s. Auto Choice was as in tune with the politics of its time as the high benefits/mandatory no-fault bills of the 1970s were with the realities of the liberal, Democrat-led Congresses of the 1970s.

Perhaps the single most important issue the bill got right, substantively and politically, was to offer huge cost savings. This was the result of a shift away from the 1970s approach that would have mandated extremely high benefits. That mandate had limited the cost savings estimates of those bills to between 11 percent and 15 percent. In sharp contrast, Auto Choice, with its lower benefits, promised estimated savings of approximately 50 percent on the bodily injury premium. The Auto Choice approach was consistent with the conclusions of a 2010 RAND study that cited the failure of state no-fault laws to generate substantial cost savings as a reason for loss of support for no-fault:

> We conclude that the decline in no-fault's popularity is a result of (1) its unexpectedly high claims costs and (2) the political debate shifting from an overall assessment of the optimal insurance system to the impact of those high costs on consumers. No-fault's high claim costs are the result of very high medical costs. Further research is necessary to evaluate reforms that some no-fault states have introduced to control the growth of medical costs.[1]

Another important thing the supporters got right was the academic work. The studies in both decades made compelling cases for the proposed reforms. Steve Carroll and his colleagues at RAND and Dan Miller on the JEC staff documented the flaws of the tort system and the likely benefits of the Auto Choice proposal in comprehensive, brilliant fashion, addressing and answering all the arguments by the opposition. The congressional staff work was also first-rate, and I believe the outside coalition efforts through CAR were also quite effective in their substantive advocacy.

What was less effective than in the 1970s, though still highly valuable, was the internal political effort on behalf of Auto Choice by members. This was not from a want of knowledge and effort but rather from a difference in position and power. On its face, the sponsorship by Senator McConnell and House Majority Leader Armey seemed like a powerful combination. But the Senator McConnell of the 1990s was not the dominant force that Majority Leader McConnell was in 2020, and Armey was a polarizing figure with Democrats. Most importantly, neither McConnell nor Armey served on a committee of jurisdiction. By contrast, the 1970s bill sponsors were in positions of leadership on the committees—Magnuson as chair of the Senate Commerce Committee and Van Deerlin and Eckhardt as chairs of the House Consumer Protection Subcommittee . While Senator McCain, a cosponsor of Auto Choice, was for a time in the 1990s the chair of the Senate Commerce Committee, it was never the priority for him that it had been for Magnuson.

That the key congressional supporters were not as well-positioned as their predecessors in the 1970s was not one of the main reasons for the failure of Auto Choice to become law. They were important enough figures. The tribal nature of the Congress was far more relevant. It always makes one side or the other suspicious when there is strong support for legislation by the other party. The partisanship was particularly relevant in the House because Democrats were in shock after losing the majority for the first time in forty years. Their knee-jerk negative reaction to the Republican leadership of the effort was further compounded by the harshly partisan tone of the incoming speaker, Newt Gingrich.

While increasing political polarization played an important role in the defeat of Auto Choice, I believe the single greatest factor once again was the influence of trial lawyers and the absence of a counterweight among supporters to level the playing field. With the Senate and House in Republican hands in1995, Democrats were exponentially more dependent financially on the trial bar than they had been twenty years before. Meanwhile, a divided insurance industry once again was not willing to contribute sufficient resources to the effort to counter the power of the trial bar, although the staffs that State Farm and USAA assigned to the issue worked it hard.

While I knew the trial bar would be a significant obstacle to passage, I was unaware when I started CAR that it had also gained major influence with most of the main consumer groups in the intervening years. It appears to have been a major factor in sidelining CU by encouraging judges to direct funds left unclaimed in class actions to CU. The absence of CU from the list of supporters—in fact, its opposition—no doubt made it safe for other consumer groups to oppose Auto Choice.

To the extent that the consumer groups were not deterred by the trial bar or the opposition of CU, they were intimidated by the open opposition of Ralph Nader, the twentieth century's single greatest consumer advocate. Agree with him or not on specific issues, Nader stuck to his guns and eschewed special interest influence—except on no-fault. Leah Young, Andrew Tobias, and Bob Hunter (unintentionally) have described a deep funding relationship between Nader and the trial bar. Nader has benefited directly from trial lawyer contributions to his public interest organizations and indirectly from their filing of class action suits against auto manufacturers and their participation in rule-making proceedings before the NHTSA over design defects that affect the safety of cars. As a result, Nader was unwilling to break with the trial bar on any issue of importance to it, and Auto Choice was just such an issue because it threatened the trial bar's major source of easy money. No matter how much good Nader's alliance with the trial bar produced in terms of safer cars, his full-throated defense of the tort system left the victims of inevitable motor vehicle crashes to the vagaries of a grossly inadequate compensation system. Moreover, his opposition to no-fault was at cross-purposes with the goals of his other efforts. It denied consumers the ability to have more choices, to have an alternative to the fault and liability insurance system that is their only choice in thirty-eight states. It also has meant higher premiums for low- and moderate-income drivers and senior citizens, who would have benefited most from the lower premiums Auto Choice promised. Last, ironically, Nader's opposition helped prevent the implementation of a system that would have provided private sector incentives for auto safety, as insurers could have offered discounts for safety features that reduced the risk of the driver and his or her passengers being injured.[2] Had Nader focused only on consumer benefits and supported the trial bar when it was pressuring the NHTSA for tougher safety regulations and its opponents (no-fault advocates) when they were working to pass good no-fault legislation, he might have helped consumers experience the best of both worlds—safer cars and better, less expensive insurance.

The loss of consumer group support gave Democrats another excuse not to cosponsor the bills, and it denied the bills' supporters ground troops to lobby the Congress. Perhaps an even bigger factor than the loss of consumer support in terms of the inability to get more Democrats to cosponsor Auto Choice was the loss of union support. It was caused by a dramatic reduction in unions' numbers in the intervening years, which had forced them to focus on issues that were essential to their survival. Labor and consumer groups had played a major role in Senate passage of no-fault legislation in 1974. As author Lee Drutman noted, "Labor unions were much more important, and the public-interest groups of the 1960s were much more significant actors. And very few companies had their own Washington lobbyists prior to the 1970s."[3] Now the unions were missing in action, and the consumer groups had switched sides.

In the 1990s, several other factors beyond increased political polarization and the opposition of the trial bar, and Ralph Nader played a role in the two parties essentially reversing their positions from two decades before. Bad timing plagued the Auto Choice effort, as it had no-fault years before. In 1992, during the presidential campaign, Pres. George H. W. Bush had announced that he would be sending Auto Choice legislation to the Congress at the beginning of the next session, only to lose the race to Bill Clinton. In 1999, Senate Commerce Committee Chairman McCain, who could have moved legislation through his committee at any time, chose not to place a higher priority on Auto Choice, a bill he had cosponsored. Finally, in 2001, the terrorist attacks of 9/11 stopped all legislation when there was a good chance that Pres. George W. Bush might have endorsed Auto Choice.

The failure of many state no-fault laws to lower premiums also played a role again, as many of those laws suffered the inevitable consequences of more lawsuits and higher premiums as a result of weakened thresholds. In states such as New York and New Jersey, the cost of the bodily injury portion of the premium was about the same as that of the portion that paid for no-fault benefits. Weak thresholds had turned the no-fault concept on its head, as these states were forced to operate two systems—a no-fault system and a tort system—and two systems are always more expensive than one.

Ironically, it was the thresholds that had initially facilitated the passage of many state laws. They represented compromise, a middle ground that made legislators comfortable. Even some insurers supported dollar thresholds—as low as $200—in the 1970s, as they knew how to cost a dollar figure, which they couldn't do as easily with a verbal or descriptive threshold (one that often defined the basis for a lawsuit for pain and suffering as a "serious and permanent" injury). The industry was naive, as it proved easy to inflate medical bills, honestly or not, to breach the threshold. The dollar figures became targets instead of thresholds. As in the 1970s, the trial bar then turned around and argued to Congress that the state laws weren't working because they were too costly, even though they were the reason the laws were too costly.

In assessing the roles of the different political parties, despite my Democratic pedigree, I believe Republicans come off looking better than Democrats the second time around. While they had supported their insurance friends in opposing no-fault in the 1970s, to their credit, many of them reversed their positions when presented with a revised bill in the 1990s that fitted their values of consumer choice, lower premiums (tax cuts), and states' rights/federalism. Republicans adopted a more nuanced view of federalism this time, expanding individual choice while protecting states' rights. The Auto Choice Reform Act would have advanced individual choice by giving motorists the opportunity to purchase a second kind of insurance while preserving states' rights by giving each state the final say as to whether to permit that choice. Unlike Democrats who sacrificed their principles for the support of the trial bar, many Republicans supported Auto Choice and their principles over the opposition of their insurer allies. That the bill would also have taken a multi-billion-dollar bite out of trial lawyer revenue might have eased the pain of parting ways with their insurer allies, but I never heard one Republican member or staff mention that as motivation.

In sum, an initial examination of the failure of Auto Choice seems to point to many of the same causes that were responsible for the earlier failure of no-fault, with special interest money the most important, but were there other factors the supporters overlooked? If we had learned nothing from the loss in the 1970s and merely repeated the same mistakes, then, to quote one of Senator McConnell's favorite Kentucky sayings, "there's no education in the second kick of a mule."[4]

I think we did learn some things the second time around. One factor in the defeat may be a gut feeling among many Americans that, when something goes wrong, the other person is always the guilty party, and fairness dictates that they should pay for your injuries, including the intangible of pain and suffering. I've reached this conclusion through years of trying to explain no-fault to friends and foes alike. First conversations often go something like this:

> ME: No-fault auto insurance works just like your health insurance. If you get injured in an auto accident, your insurer pays for your medical bills as well as your lost wages. It's simple. No lawyers, no uncertainty of recovery, and no waiting.

FRIEND (OR FOE): You mean I have to buy insurance to cover myself, that I can't sue the bad driver who hit me? Doesn't that mean that good drivers like me will be paying for bad drivers? And won't bad drivers be encouraged to drive even more recklessly if they don't have to pay for the accidents they cause?

ME: No. Let me explain how bad the tort system is, how more dollars go to lawyers and pain and suffering than to injured people.

FRIEND (NOW, PERHAPS, FORMER FRIEND): Wait a minute, are you telling me that if some driver hits me and breaks my ankle, I can't sue him for my pain and suffering being in a cast for three months?

ME (BEGINNING TO GROW EXASPERATED): Under the tort system, you can sue for pain and suffering, but there's usually barely enough to cover your doctor bills and lost wages and rarely anything left for pain and suffering if you are seriously injured.

FORMER FRIEND (NOW FOE?): Then make them buy more coverage.

ME: Then you would have to buy more, and it would cost you more as well.

FLAT-OUT FOE: Me? Why would I have to buy more coverage? I'm a good driver.

Three things strike me immediately about the respondent in this conversation: (1) a sense that it is unfair to take away the right to sue an at-fault driver, (2) the belief that the other driver is always at fault, and (3) the idea that good drivers will pay for bad drivers. These are the trial lawyers' basic arguments. They do not reflect the reality of the tort system, but they appeal to people's gut feelings. Perhaps Milton Lower put his finger on the effectiveness of these arguments when, as a staffer on the Eckhardt subcommittee in 1977, he came up with what was intended as an amusing acronym for no-fault: National Organization of Fast-driving, Alcoholic, Unrepentant, Liability-shirking Tortfeasors.

A fourth thing that strikes me is that my response to the trial lawyers' one-minute, emotion-connecting argument is a twenty-minute explanation of how the tort system really works. My explanation may prevail in academic journals, but it can be a hard, time-consuming sell to the public and members of Congress who are rushed for time. It was far more effective to respond in writing through the use of a table comparing the fault and no-fault systems, and that was what we did through CAR brochures.[5]

However, that wasn't always possible, and we were often left on the defensive, as the above dialogue shows.

There is one other trial lawyer argument whose power we may have underestimated—that even if no-fault lowered the cost of insurance, insurers would never pass along the savings to drivers. This argument appeals to Americans' hate/love relationship with the insurance industry—they hate it when they have to pay premiums for something they don't use and love it when it pays them for some loss. The consumer groups have long held similar suspicions about the auto insurance industry. In fact, one of the main reasons we were unable to garner support for a choice no-fault idea in 1978 was the consumer groups' concern that insurers would keep any money the system saved. It became one of their main grounds for opposition to Auto Choice.

If my speculation about these underlying reasons for resistance to no-fault is correct, it's possible that the Auto Choice concept solved one problem at the expense of exacerbating another. In solving the cost problem in many state no-fault laws by narrowing the right to sue to excess economic loss only, proponents may have unintentionally strengthened the opponents' appeal to injured persons' gut sense of the fairness of being able to sue the at-fault party for all their injuries, including for pain and suffering.[6] Auto Choice tried to address that concern by permitting motorists to stay in the tort system and recover damages for pain and suffering, but from their own insurer rather than the at-fault driver's insurer. This just led to another trial lawyer argument, that bad drivers would pick the no-fault system and good ones the tort system, leading to good drivers paying for bad drivers.

I'm not sure how important these issues were compared to the raw power of the trial bar, but I believe they played a role. Nevertheless, I still think that a well-financed no-fault effort could have passed the Congress in the 1970s and a well-financed Auto Choice effort could have passed the Congress in the 1990s or early 2000s. But that was then, and this is 2021, a time of intense partisanship and slim margins in a Congress that reflects the divisions in the country. For the foreseeable future, the political center no longer exists. When I started working in the Senate in 1981, its membership strongly resembled a bell-curve graph, with conservative Sen. Jesse Helms at one end, liberal Sen. Howard Metzenbaum at the other, and a large number of members from each party in the middle. In that Senate, Bob Dole was a conservative. In today's Senate, with his traditional conservative views and fierce independence, Bob Dole might be a Democrat or, if still a Republican, be as isolated as another Republican senator who was once the party's nominee for president: Mitt Romney. It would be hard to graph today's Senate. The Democratic side has more progressives and fewer moderates, and the grassroots energy is with the progressives. On the Republican side, moderates are an endangered species, with most Republicans lining up in lockstep with Trump. As the most liberal Republican is not as liberal as the least liberal Democrat, and the most conservative Democrat is not as conservative as the least conservative Republican, there is no point at which the parties intersect.

Before considering four possible scenarios that might bring the issue back before the Congress despite the toxic political environment, I want to briefly examine my experience with other major liability reform issues to see whether they might shed some light on how it might be possible to pass no-fault legislation. I start from the premise that no-fault is *sui generis* among these issues because of its consumer focus. It was designed almost exclusively to improve the compensation system for auto accident victims. By contrast, the other liability reform bills I worked on were designed largely to narrow the circumstances under which an insured business could be liable for injuries. The beneficiaries under no-fault, by contrast, were all injured motorists, and its political appeal was to the public rather than to any special interest. What all these liability bills, including no-fault, had in common was that they would substantially reduce trial lawyer income. Thus, in all three cases, that meant there would be strong opposition. To me, the basic question was whether there would be a strong counterweight.

Let's look at the other three liability issues in some detail. Of the three, the National Childhood Vaccine Injury Act of 1986 was most like no-fault in that it focused more on simplifying the compensation system than on assigning liability. It established a schedule of recovery for different injuries and created incentives for settlement to avoid judicial proceedings. Politically, however, it was far different from no-fault. The vaccine manufacturers were losing costly verdicts in cases that previously had not been winnable for injured people under the "unavoidably inevitable accident" doctrine. That doctrine provided immunity from liability where the product would inevitably injure a few people while benefiting many. Once the courts had effectively abandoned that doctrine and started awarding damages to injured children, the manufacturers were willing to support legislation that paid injured people reasonable certain amounts of compensation in return for limiting their exposure to suit. If they knew their exposure, then they could price their vaccines. Thus, you had both the families of injured children and the manufacturers working to find common ground.[7] Equally important, trial lawyer opposition was muted because the families involved in congressional negotiations were their clients. That was different from the no-fault fight, in which the changed rules would have helped trial lawyers' future, as opposed to present, clients. The vaccine manufacturers' need for relief and the neutralizing of the trial bar by its clients' support of the legislation presented a far different political situation than no-fault.

The other two efforts, product liability and class action, were like one another and different from either no-fault or vaccine compensation. Both bills were initially drafted by industry to protect companies against large verdicts or, in some circumstances, any verdict. They ignored people with legitimate injuries. Let's take them separately. The manufacturers' argument in favor of the products bill was that juries had become too sympathetic to plaintiffs, resulting in their ignoring legal standards for recovery and awarding excessive verdicts to undeserving plaintiffs, making the costs of some products, such as ladders, nearly prohibitively expensive. The bill's solution was to toughen the legal standards for recovery to restore balance to the system.

For a few Congresses, the bill foundered. It was largely supported by Republicans, with some support from moderate to conservative Democrats who represented states that manufactured products that had been the subject of large verdicts. Initially, there was little or no focus on how the system hurt consumers—how people injured by defective products had to wait years to recover a small fraction of any serious loss, if they ever did recover. Later bills I worked on added a component similar to that of the vaccine bill, creating incentives for the two sides to settle cases for economic loss. The consumer benefits would be greater certainty of recovery, higher recoveries for serious injuries, and faster payment. The tradeoff was giving up the potential giant jackpot verdict. While the trial lawyers and consumer groups strongly opposed the bill, the more balanced legislation got 58 votes in the Senate in 1992 and came close to enactment during the Clinton administration. It fell short when the companies rejected a compromise favored by the bill's sponsor and chief Democratic supporter, Sen. John D. "Jay" Rockefeller IV. Why did the bill move further than no-fault? The reasons seem to be (1) deep-pocketed supporters and (2) the provisions that were added to help consumers. As a bill driven by business interests, it received near-unanimous support from Republicans. The well-financed effort and the proconsumer provisions helped bring along several largely moderate to conservative Democrats.[8] Because no-fault was focused primarily on consumer benefits and had no major special interest support, the main lesson from the product liability experience seems to be the importance of special interest money in countering that of the trial bar.

The story of the Class Action Fairness Act is similar to that of product liability, only on steroids. Far more companies were experiencing huge class-action judgments in the plaintiff-friendly jurisdictions into which trial lawyers were able to maneuver the cases. The companies contributed more than enough money to offset that of the trial bar, and inclusion of a consumer bill of rights section helped bring along enough Democrats for the bill to become law. As with products, the bill's supporters had enough special interest money to counter that of the trial bar, and the consumer provisions were sufficient to give moderate to conservative Democrats cover to vote for the bill.

The success of the class-action bill and what should have been the success of the products bill appear to have been the result of having support from a large enough special interest to counter the trial bar and the inclusion of enough proconsumer provisions to attract the necessary number of moderate to conservative Democrats. I submit that the vaccine bill was also unique for liability reform bills and holds no lessons for no-fault.

Is it possible, then, that American individualism, the suspicion of government programs, played a role in the defeat of either or both no-fault efforts? While one sees the increased influence of such views in today's politics, they were more likely to have played a role in the 1970s than in the 1990s. For the most part, Democrats have long been comfortable with more government intervention in the marketplace. However, the no-fault fight dragged on from the early 1970s to the late 1970s, a time when the public grew more suspicious about government after the impeachment of Richard Nixon and the adoption of a slew of regulatory bills. On the Republican side, where suspicion of government has always tended to run high, it did not prevent Republicans from supporting the product liability and class action bills that were intended to help businesses. As for no-fault, Republicans were quite supportive of Auto Choice when it offered consumer and state choice (states' rights) and lower premiums, an analogue to tax cuts. The fact that the federal government would be the author of those major changes in auto insurance gave Republicans little pause.

After reviewing all the liability reform efforts I've worked on, I think the bottom line comes back to money and, more particularly, enough money to match the political efforts of the trial bar. Focusing on cost savings was a major plus, but it did lead to an effective counterargument with Democrats that the savings were coming at the expense of being able to recover from at-fault drivers. Nevertheless, I think money was the key to Auto Choice's defeat, and CAR did not come anywhere close to raising enough to neutralized the influence of the trial bar. As the lack of money to counter the trial bar had been our major conclusion in analyzing the 1970s effort, it appears that there was no education in the first kick of the mule. If no-fault is ever to succeed at the federal level, there had better be education in the second kick of the mule.

Supporters would also be wise to find more effective ways to respond to trial lawyers' arguments about the right to sue, bad drivers paying for good ones, and insurers not passing along the savings. The CAR brochures addressed all these questions effectively but did so in six pages. Any future effort should take a cue from the one-page memos that most senators demand from their staffs. Auto Choice supporters should develop some simple one-pagers. Here are a few possible themes: (1) Auto Choice replaces the right to sue with the right to recover, (2) Auto Choice permits you to stay in the lawsuit lottery system or choose a no-fault system that guarantees payment just as health insurance does, (3) Auto Choice will reduce your premiums by eliminating most portions of your insurance dollar that pay for fraudulent or unnecessary claims and lawyers, (4) state regulators would have the same authority to control rates, and (5) lawyers get as much in fees as you get in compensation under existing law.

Afterword

Does No-Fault Have Another Turn on the Federal Agenda?

Where does that leave the prospects for another, preferably successful, no-fault effort? Assuming that one could replicate the outstanding academic work that supported the two previous efforts and that the conclusions remained the same, as well as the superior congressional member and staff work and the broad media support, what has changed in the past seventeen years that might present a way to counter trial lawyer money? The answer might be found in the development of crowdfunding. For no-fault to stand a chance of passing at the federal level, it would need to be able to raise enough funds in this way to neutralize trial lawyer money.

Such an outcome is uncertain at best but perhaps not impossible. To see the possibility, look, for example, at fund-raising totals for Democrats in 2019 and 2020. In 2019, six million donors contributed $1 billion to Democratic candidates and organizations through ActBlue, the online payment processor for most small-donor contributions to Democrats. Even more stunning were ActBlue's totals for the third quarter of 2020 alone—6.8 million donors made 31.4 million contributions to 14,223 campaigns, with an average contribution of $47 per donation. The grand total was $1.5 billion.

If it were possible to raise enough money to counter the trial bar, any effort would face another huge obstacle. The near-complete polarization of the Congress means that the moderate and conservative Democratic votes that helped other legal reform bills pass are either gone or going fast in a party moving to the left. Worse yet, Democrats and Republicans in Congress are barely talking to each other in the wake of the 2020 presidential election, and that is likely to continue for some time. As hard as it may be to imagine a return to something closer to comity, the Congress has gone through tumultuous times before only to find ways to get along well enough to pass important legislation. Perhaps the January 6, 2021, attack on the Capitol will have sobered the parties enough for them to again seek to find common ground. Whether it is that or other events, whenever the parties start looking for areas of agreement, I think there are several circumstances under which no-fault might return to the national agenda, including two that would involve a bit of political jujitsu to turn less intense but still negative polarization into a positive.

Let's explore how the issue might return to the national agenda. Here are four possibilities, some of which might surprise you. The first, and probably least likely, would involve yet another attempt to create a bipartisan congressional coalition on an Auto Choice bill. The plan would entail securing near-unanimous Republican support based on the bill's Republican principles and using crowdfunding revenue to counter trial bar money sufficiently to secure enough Democratic votes to squeak by. Given all the components that reflect key Republican values that made Auto Choice so attractive to Republicans, it might be possible to line up a substantial majority. What would be the most likely place to seek Democratic votes? The perhaps surprising answer would be from the progressive wing of the party, particularly from members representing districts or states with large cities and large low-income populations. With social justice issues front and center, Auto Choice could help remedy the mismatch between where low-income people often live, in large cities, and where jobs are increasingly located, in the suburbs.[1] With limited mass transit connecting the two, low-income people need cars to get to where the jobs are. That requires auto insurance. Fault and liability insurance is of no help because premiums are based on how much you would have to pay someone else if you hit that person. By contrast, Auto Choice premiums reflect who you are, so insurers can offer lower premiums to people who stand to lose less if injured, which would be the case for people with lower wages. Thus, the huge savings Auto Choice promised, if the data would still support them,[2] could make driving more affordable for low-income people and, at the same time, enable them to use the money they save on auto insurance for other, more essential items. To sweeten the bill for these Democrats, the authors might raise the minimum required medical benefits to $50,000, which could be done with minimal impact on premium savings.[3] The rise of social justice issues makes this a possible path to success, although it would require hard-core conservative Republicans and staunch progressive Democrats to listen to one another. Given Democratic control of the House in the 117th Congress starting in 2021, the challenge would be even greater, as it would require progressive Democrats to take the lead. While there have been plenty of "strange bedfellow" legislative efforts over the years, it is hard to imagine an Alexandria Ocasio-Cortez (D-NY)–Chip Roy (R-TX) bill.

A second path that would be slower, but perhaps stand a better chance of success, would be to fix the defects in state no-fault laws and then use their success to bring the issue back to federal attention. While there is no crisis or other matter of such great importance as to demand federal attention now, things are different at the state level. The forcing issue in most of the twelve no-fault states is the high cost of no-fault. High premiums mean public discontent, which, in turn, keeps pressure on the legislatures to make changes to lower premiums. RAND, the JEC, and the two NAMIC articles I authored (one coauthored with Jeff O'Connell and Dan Miller) have drawn a road map for how to fix the defects in those laws. Should some states respond by fixing their laws to fulfill no-fault's savings promise, then the success might encourage the Congress to take up the issue again. The irony of such a dynamic would be that it would be the opposite of what happened in the 1970s, when the threat of federal action led seventeen states to enact no-fault laws. In this scenario, successful state laws would encourage action on federal legislation.

Before leaving this approach, let's examine in some detail what went wrong with state no-fault laws and what the states would need to do to make them work well enough to attract federal attention. It's important to keep in mind that all of them have proved successful in providing better, faster compensation to injured persons. That is the reason they are worth perfecting. The cost problems that have arisen have occurred on both the PIP (or no-fault) side and the liability side of these laws. The short of it (the long is to follow) is that there were few if any cost controls for medical losses in the PIP system, and the thresholds were not restrictive enough to limit the number of lawsuits sufficiently to keep premiums down. The PIP problems were a flaw in the original design that is easy to remedy substantively. The threshold problem that shows up in the liability premium is largely the fault of the trial bar, which, as I've said probably far too many times, weakened the intended thresholds to preserve more lawsuits. It remains by far the larger cause of high premiums in most states and the most difficult one to solve politically. Now, here is the long of it, starting with the PIP issues.

The 2010 RAND study identified one cause, that "no-fault insurance shifts medical costs associated with auto accidents from the first-party health insurance system to the automobile insurance system."[4] While accurate, the sentence needs further elucidation. Such cost shifting does increase the cost of PIP no-fault benefits, but it reduces health insurance costs. The costs remain the same; all that changes is the system that pays them. From a societal standpoint, it doesn't matter which system pays the losses; all that matters is the combined cost. If no-fault does nothing more than shift the same costs from health insurance to auto insurance, it does not increase the cost of medical care.

Professor O'Connell, Miller, and I examined in more detail the reasons for increasing PIP costs in no-fault states in a 2011 article. In it, using auto insurance industry *Fast Track* cost data, I found that between 1987 and 2010, PIP paid claim frequency (the number of claims filed) dropped by 20 percent. However, PIP claim severity (the amount paid per claim) increased by a whopping 320 percent.[5] The increase was largely due to fraud, or buildup, because of the combination of inadequate medical cost controls and the weak thresholds that provide an incentive to run up medical costs to be able to sue for pain and suffering.[6]

Michigan was unique among the states in that its threshold was relatively tight and thus was not much of a target. However, Michigan experienced huge jumps in PIP severity for a different reason—because it combined the highest PIP benefits (unlimited medical and rehabilitation) of any state no-fault law with probably the weakest medical cost controls.

It is not surprising that most no-fault laws started with few, if any, of the traditional cost controls health insurers utilize to avoid overuse and fraud. Just examine where no-fault came from and who did much of the drafting. The no-fault concept was developed by two law professors who were focused on remedying the problems of the fault system. They also were sensitive to the fact that those who could recover under the fault system were paid for all their medical losses, without any deductibles or copayments, to the extent of the at-fault driver's insurance coverage. Professor Keeton and other law professors then drafted the model no-fault law. Thereafter, the two largest automobile insurance companies, State Farm, frequently, and Allstate, on occasion, played major roles in refining the details of the legislation. Neither of them sold health insurance.

Thus, it is also not surprising that RAND found much higher medical costs for the same types of injuries in no-fault states.[7] That finding suffers from lumping all no-fault states and areas of no-fault states together. For the most part, the abuse of the PIP system occurred in states with major urban areas and aggressive attorney populations. It did not occur in more predominantly rural no-fault states, which also generally had modest levels of PIP benefits. Studies done contemporaneously with the 2010 RAND study provide useful insight into the connection between PIP abuse and weak thresholds. In Florida, for example, PIP coverage was plagued by "escalating claims costs, high utilization rates for expensive diagnostic services, high chiropractor utilization rates, [not surprisingly] high rates of attorney involvement, and high rates of apparent fraud and claim buildup."[8]

A 2010 study found that in New York, PIP claimants with minor injuries in the New York City metro area used far more expensive diagnostic tests (such as MRIs instead of X-rays) and nontraditional medical providers (such as chiropractors and even psychiatrists) multiple times than claimants in other parts of the state. New York City area residents also hired more lawyers to handle PIP claims (53 percent versus 25 percent in the rest of the state) and had a far higher percentage of claims with the appearance of fraud and buildup as, once again, lawyers became involved in the PIP system in order to build claims for lawsuits.[9] A study by the New York Insurance Bureau also found that the no-fault system was attracting a hardened criminal element, both to collect PIP benefits and to aid in breaching the threshold. Many fraud suspects had multiple prior arrests for such crimes as gun possession, narcotics violations, and robberies.[10]

Unlike Florida and New York, Michigan's adverse PIP experience was not driven by efforts to breach its threshold. The nation's tightest threshold (the one closest to the model state law and the federal no-fault legislation) stood relatively firm, even in the face of a 2010 court decision that undermined the threshold component of permanency.[11] The problems flowed from having the highest level of PIP benefits of any no-fault state—coverage for unlimited medical and rehabilitation expenses. This was not a problem from the law's inception in 1973 to 1987. *Fast Track* insurance industry data for 1987 showed that the total personal injury cost (for PIP plus the bodily injury coverage that pays for lawsuits) was $108, lower than the $117 cost for Florida, which had only $10,000 in PIP benefits. While PIP costs were somewhat higher in Michigan, tort costs were much lower, thanks to Michigan's tighter threshold.

This all changed between 1987 and 2010. During this time, PIP costs rose by 250 percent in Florida but skyrocketed by 360 percent in Michigan.[12] *Fast Track* data revealed that the average PIP claim *severity* in Michigan was $32,974, compared to $8,742 in New York and $7,673 in Florida. That is what happens when unlimited medical benefits meet an uncontrolled medical system. Despite the lack of controls, for the first twenty-five years of its existence, the unlimited PIP medical benefit in Michigan was not a problem. As late as 2001, the cost for the most seriously injured was $14.41 per car.

Then, things changed. By 2012, the cost for the most seriously injured had risen to $145 per car. Unlike rising costs in Florida and New York, which were caused by excessive use of nontraditional providers and the high level of expensive diagnostic tests, the source of this dramatic increase resulted from the skyrocketing costs of catastrophic care in general and home health care in particular. In 2012, *the 1–2 percent of no-fault claims that exceeded $500,000 were responsible for between 31 and 45 percent of the PIP premium.* Of this amount, 42 percent was attributable to home care provided by both professional agencies and family members.[13] These huge costs occurred because, unlike other insurance for personal attendant care services, there were no limits on the number of hours for such care, who could provide it, or the total cost. In fact, most health insurance policies don't even provide coverage for personal attendant care services. The Michigan law also contained no fee schedule for medical services or medical protocols for the treatment of injuries.[14] While this was good for the injured individuals, it was a disaster for the other motorists who paid for this care through much higher premiums.

To give one an idea of how generous the Michigan PIP system was, by contrast, Medicare's benefit for home health care generally is limited to eight hours a day, with a weekly limit of twenty-eight hours. More to the point, it pays for skilled nursing and therapy services only and not for the kind of personal attendant care services available under the Michigan no-fault law. Moreover, Medicare has far more generous benefits than most private health insurance. For example, Blue Cross/Blue Shield for federal government employees provides benefits for home nursing, limited to fifty visits per year by a registered nurse or licensed practical nurse, subject to the annual deductible and required copays. It offers no benefits for personal attendant care services.

For nearly two decades, Democrats and Republicans fought over whether and how to reform Michigan's no-fault system while unchecked PIP costs continued to rise each year. By 2019, when the cost of the 1–2 percent of claims over $580,000 rose to $220 a policy, the Michigan legislature finally acted. The new law, which went into effect on July 1, 2020, permits motorists to purchase lower levels of PIP benefits. Most qualify to select $250,000 or $500,000 PIP coverage, while those on Medicaid can select $50,000.

The new law includes other significant changes. Motorists can opt out of buying PIP coverage if they have qualified health coverage that applies to auto accidents. There is a fee schedule for medical providers and hospitals, although it is generous, starting at 200 percent of the Medicare rate before declining on an annual basis. Motorists now also have a managed care option, with deductibles and copayments, in return for a lower premium. Importantly, with regard to the cost of unlimited coverage, the new law limits reimbursement of family members who provide personal attendant care services to fifty-six hours a week.

These changes should begin to bring PIP costs down. Shortly after enactment, the Michigan Catastrophic Claims Association announced that as of July 1, 2020, it would reduce the surcharge for PIP claims in excess of $580,000 from $220 to $145, a 45 percent reduction.

While, as just detailed, PIP costs increased significantly in the period studied, with the exception of Michigan, they were not the major cause of higher no-fault premiums in states with large urban populations. Whatever the level of fraud in New York, PIP costs were less than half the cost of the total personal injury premium (48 percent). The majority of the premium still went to pay for tort claims that exceeded the threshold. In Florida, the situation was the same. PIP benefits constituted only 46 percent of the personal injury premium.[15]

The 2010 RAND report documented the degree of the problem, finding that "BI (bodily injury fault liability) costs have actually been *higher* in no-fault states [than in tort states between 1993 and 2006]."[16] The authors suggest that the higher costs are the fault of no-fault, whereas the fault lies with those who lobbied the states to replace the original tight thresholds with these weaker versions that were destined to fail. Clearly, the thresholds need to be tightened if no-fault is to generate the cost savings it promised.

That BI costs are so high in some no-fault states doesn't negate the necessity to implement cost controls to reduce PIP costs; it just shows that reforms are needed on both the PIP and tort sides if state laws are to be completely successful. Health insurance offers many models for controlling costs that could easily be applied to auto insurance to reduce fraudulent and excessive PIP costs.

The threshold problems could easily be resolved in either of two ways. The first would involve replacing defective trial lawyer thresholds with tight thresholds similar to those in either the original Keeton-O'Connell plan or the federal bills of the 1970s. Such a threshold in the Michigan law has kept the bodily injury portion of the premium around 15 percent, even before the jump in PIP costs. The second, which would solve both the threshold and PIP problems, would be for states to adopt the provisions of the federal Auto Choice bill. Fifty years of state no-fault experience strongly suggests that Auto Choice would operate as intended to realize the promise of lower premiums. If for some reason it didn't, motorists could utilize its fail-safe escape hatch and instead choose the insurance system in effect in the state.

One reason the 2010 RAND study did not find for higher premiums in no-fault states was that no-fault induces less careful driving. RAND examined this long-debated subject, from the 1982 Landes study through studies as late as 2009. It found that

> Although these models [that posit that no-fault may induce drivers to drive more recklessly] are both simple and somewhat intuitive, it is not clear that they describe real-world driving behavior. Fear of death or serious personal injury provides powerful incentives to avoid accidents no matter how generous the insurance. Moreover, the costs of causing an accident include both third-party and first-party personal injury and property damage as well as the costs of being cited, which may include future insurance-premium increases. Although no-fault limits first- and third-party personal-injury costs,

> it does so for only a subset of accidents and leaves other costs largely unchanged. Thus, the total effect of no-fault availability on the incentives for avoiding accidents may be relatively minor.[17]

Unsurprisingly, the study concluded that "the empirical evidence is mixed. The study examining the broadest range of accident types (Heaton and Helland, 2009b) finds no evidence of an effect of no-fault on accident rates."[18]

While the failure of the states to correct the defects for years is not encouraging, the unnecessarily high premiums the defects cause continue to offer motivation for states to act, and the solutions—tighter thresholds and medical cost controls—are well known. New Jersey and Pennsylvania, two states that already have choice laws, would be natural laboratories to see whether making changes that mirrored the refinements in the federal Auto Choice legislation would live up to the promise of the legislation. If the amended state laws worked as expected, particularly by lowering premiums dramatically, then federal legislators might again see the political attraction of Auto Choice.

The third and fourth possibilities for federal action strangely enough would involve narrowly partisan efforts by either Republicans or Democrats, with the House, Senate, and presidency all in the hands of one party. Were Republicans to achieve total control at some point, then the idea of adopting legislation that fitted their ideological framework of individual choice and federalism and whose cost savings (a tax cut for all but trial lawyers) could help defund one of the major sources of Democratic funding might prove very attractive. Of course, such an approach would almost assuredly be feasible only if the Senate eliminated the filibuster for legislation. Given the narrow partisan division in recent Congresses and the strong desire of each party to impose its legislative agenda on the other, it seems almost a foregone conclusion that the filibuster's days are numbered.

The fourth possible scenario assumes Democratic control of both Houses of Congress and the presidency and perhaps the elimination of the filibuster. Given the trial bar's importance to Democrats, why might Democrats be interested in Auto Choice in that situation? The answer is not so much that they would have an inherent interest (other than social justice) but rather that one of their top legislative priorities, universal health insurance, would mean that all Americans would have the equivalent of no-fault insurance for all medical losses, including those that arise from auto accidents. That would force Congress to determine how to deal with medical bills that presently are covered by other insurance systems, such as auto and workers' compensation. No-fault experience with unlimited medical and rehabilitation benefits and few cost controls would also be highly relevant in deciding how generous one can make a universal health insurance program without its costs running out of control.

It would make little sense and be wasteful to have both health and auto insurance pay for the same losses. If some form of national health insurance paid for most or all losses, without any deductibles or copayments (as proposed by Sen. Bernie Sanders and others), then it would be simplest to eliminate what would be duplicative payments from auto insurance. However, a national health insurance law would almost assuredly include some cost-control provisions that limit payment, as does the Affordable Care Act (ACA). In that case, the Congress would have to decide whether the federal health insurance provisions or state auto insurance would be primary, i.e., which coverage would pay first. The one that didn't pay first would be secondary, picking up any costs not paid by the primary coverage.

It would appear simplest to make the health insurance coverage primary. However, there is no easy, absolute answer. There are several, sometimes competing goals: (1) certainty of compensation for all victims, (2) the administrative costs of the system delivering benefits, (3) insurance coverage limits, (4) the kind of auto insurance system, (5) coordination of benefits to prevent duplicate payments, and (5) market allocation through the internalization of accident loss costs. These issues are dealt with most easily when both systems are first-party no-fault systems, as are private health and no-fault auto insurance, because they pay automatically in a timely manner regardless of fault. By contrast, in liability auto insurance states, if auto insurance is primary, health insurers would still have to pay up-front and then track a lawsuit, often for several years, before they would know how much auto insurance paid. Only then would they be able to seek recovery for the duplicative amount they paid.

The best substantive argument for making auto insurance primary is that it would internalize the costs of accidents within the auto insurance system, a universe of policyholders that is different from private health insurance policyholders.[19] However, in a fault state, auto primacy would leave in place all the incentives for inflated claims and fraud as well as the duplicative payments that result from the collateral source doctrine.[20] That would make the total bill for health coverage greater than if health were primary.

The political argument in favor of auto primacy is that it would lower the price tag for legislation to expand health insurance coverage by moving several billion dollars of medical costs into the auto insurance system. If just the costs of auto accidents that are now paid by Medicare and Medicaid were paid by auto insurance instead, the annual savings to the federal government would be approximately $8 billion.[21] While the nature of any expanded health care coverage is unknown, the savings to Medicare and Medicaid would equal 13 percent of the $58 billion annual cost of ACA private insurance market plans in 2020.[22]

That would represent a significant contribution to the cost of any future coverage expansion, but there is good reason to believe that auto primacy could also result in higher savings by capturing some of the private health insurance dollars that are now used to pay for the injuries of auto accident victims.[23]

State no-fault experience, particularly that of Michigan, would also be relevant to the drafters of national health insurance as they sought to balance comprehensive coverage with reasonable limits on payment. The Michigan experience makes it clear that a largely open-ended health insurance system with few, if any, cost controls could be wildly expensive. If RAND is correct that no-fault's popularity declined because consumers focused on the costs rather than on the optimal insurance system, then implementing a similar system for health care might run the same risk of political rejection.

In short, any national health insurance–type plan would raise the issue of no-fault auto insurance. The Congress could do the minimum necessary to coordinate the two systems, or it could do more. One option would be to create incentives for states to adopt no-fault laws, perhaps by increasing the match for federal highway assistance. A second, bolder option would be for the Congress to consider a comprehensive solution of both health and auto insurance. Whatever course it took, should the

Congress consider expanding health insurance no-fault would be back on the federal agenda,

What might happen then is anyone's guess, so let me close with the wildest fantasy I can imagine. Having been on the losing side from each partisan direction, I've learned my lesson. The objective of this exercise, however problematic, is to outline a political and substantive proposal that could result in enough votes from members of each party to pass no-fault. The plan is grounded in past experience and hinges on identifying a way to merge Democratic support for no-fault in the 1970s with Republican support in the 1990s.

Let's start in the 1970s. Then senator, now president Joe Biden voted for every no-fault bill that reached the Senate floor. That is a matter of record. Far less well known is that Senator McConnell in 1968–1970 was then just plain Mitch McConnell, a congressional staffer in the position of what is now called a legislative director. His boss, Sen. Marlow Cook (R-KY), served on the Commerce Committee in the early stages of consideration of no-fault. While Cook believed the issue was a matter for the states, he was a no-fault supporter, testifying before the Senate Judiciary Committee that "the concept of no-fault insurance is a concept whose time has come."[24] Under the circumstances, McConnell had to be aware of the issue.

Next, let's move forward to 1996. Now Senator McConnell was the chief sponsor of Auto Choice legislation from 1996 to 2002. As the bill never reached the floor, still Senator Biden did not take a position. The bottom line is that in one decade or another, both Biden and McConnell supported federal no-fault legislation. The goal would be to get them to support no-fault in the same year.

While past is definitely not prologue in this situation, and this is still just my fantasy, imagine this scenario: President Biden wants to expand the ACA to cover all Americans, and there is sufficient public pressure to do so because the coronavirus has made the public fearful of not having health insurance. Unable to stop expansion of the ACA but able to slow its advance because the filibuster remains in place, now minority leader McConnell finally yields to the inevitable and names his price—the Auto Choice Reform Act of 2022. As for substance, the two longtime negotiating partners and contemporaries agree to split the difference between the two generations of legislation with higher mandated minimum coverage for medical benefits for the most seriously injured—$100,000 instead of $25,000—with a right for low-income people to purchase the lower amount to assure better protection than the tort system at a price they can afford.

How, might you ask, would Democrats overcome the opposition of the trial bar? The answer would lie less in crowdfunding than in securing the support of the most powerful political force in America—the president. The trial bar could not afford to push the president too hard on one of his top issues, and besides, it has diversified its sources of income substantially since the consideration of no-fault. Voila, in five paragraphs, a sixty-year crusade ends with Don Quixote the victor over the windmill with the enactment of the Affordable Care Expansion and Auto Choice Reform Act of 2022. Now, if I could just find a better acronym than ACEACRA.

Appendix 1: Democratic Heritage of Automobile Insurance Reform (1999)

Democrats have been in the forefront of the effort to fix the discredited fault and liability insurance system for auto accidents for 35 years. They led the unsuccessful fight to adopt federal no-fault auto insurance legislation during the 1970s and played a major role in the adoption of 16 state no-fault laws during the 1970s. All of those laws succeeded in meeting their objectives of providing better and faster compensation for more injured people, particularly for the seriously injured. However, too often the state laws' goal of lowering premiums was undermined by "compromises" foisted on the legislatures by the opponents of good reform, the trial bar. Now, after a 20-year hiatus, the U.S. Congress is once again considering auto insurance reform, this time in the form of choice auto insurance. This approach would remedy the defects of the state laws and assure lower premiums along with better compensation.

Today's effort is a bipartisan one. The key senator sponsors in the 106th Congress were Joseph Lieberman, Daniel Patrick Moynihan, Mitch McConnell and John McCain and the key House sponsors were Jim Moran and Dick Armey. Here is a brief history of Democratic leadership on auto insurance reform:

1. In 1965, law professors Bob Keeton and Jeff O'Connell called for reform of the tort system for auto accident cases in a book entitled *Basic Protection for the Traffic Victim*. Professor Keeton was subsequently appointed to the federal judiciary by President Carter. Professor O'Connell might well have been Attorney General in a Dukakis administration. Another early advocate was Yale Law School Dean Guido Calabresi, who wrote a powerful treatise, *The Cost of Accidents*. Dean Calabresi was appointed to the Second Circuit Court of Appeals by President Clinton.
2. In 1971, Massachusetts State Representative Michael Dukakis authored the first no-fault auto insurance law adopted in the U.S. Shortly thereafter, after consulting with Dukakis, Connecticut State Senator Joseph Lieberman authored the Connecticut no-fault law.
3. Senator Phil Hart was a leader in the federal effort. He held the first hearing and authored the first bill. In 1976, he left the hospital where he was dying from cancer to vote for the bill on the Senate floor.
4. Senate Commerce Committee Chairman Warren Magnuson, the leading author of consumer legislation during the 1970s, was the chief sponsor of the federal standards no-fault automobile insurance legislation in the Senate from 1971–78.

5. The chief House proponents were Democratic Representatives and House Commerce Subcommittee Chairmen John Moss, Lionel Van Deerlin and Bob Eckhardt.
6. The 1976 National Democratic Platform called for adoption of the legislation: "We support . . . federal standards for state no-fault insurance programs."
7. Among those who voted to report legislation from the House Commerce Committee in 1978 were then-Representative Al Gore and present Committee Democrats Henry Waxman and Ed Markey.
8. The federal legislation was supported by the Carter Administration. In his message accompanying the State of the Union in 1979, President Jimmy Carter said: "No-fault systems have proven to be far more efficient in delivering benefits to the victims of automobile accidents than the current tort system, and they also provide greater opportunities to coordinate and reduce overall insurance costs."
9. The Coalition for Auto-Insurance Reform (CAR) is headed by Peter Kinzler, who was the chief House Democratic staff person during the 1970s' federal no-fault effort and worked for Senator Christopher J. Dodd for 12 years.
10. CAR members include Michael Dukakis, former Democratic Representative Lionel Van Deerlin, Professor O'Connell and consumer activist and DNC Treasurer Andrew Tobias. Other Democratic supporters include Denver Mayor Wellington Webb, Fulton County Commissioner Michael Hightower and DLC President Al From.

Peter Kinzler, President, Coalition for Auto-Insurance Reform
January 1999

Appendix 2: The Benefits of the Auto Choice Reform Act for Low-Income Persons (1999)

PROBLEMS OF THE PRESENT SYSTEM FOR LOW-INCOME FAMILIES

- A 1999 Progressive Policy Institute study on transportation and welfare reform states the case for access to automobiles in simple and direct terms: "In most cases, the shortest distance between a poor person and a job is along a line driven by a car. Prosperity in America has always been strongly linked to *mobility* and . . . mobility means having the private automobile necessary for the trip." In households below the poverty line, 73 percent of work trips use a private automobile. Owning a car is even more important now as both rural counties and inner cities are isolated from the dispersed job growth of suburban economies.
- Unfortunately, owning an automobile is very expensive for low-income people. For most of them, auto insurance is the single greatest cost of driving. The typical low-income household spends more on auto insurance in two years than the value of their car.
- The cost of auto insurance is regressive. Families in the bottom 20 percent of incomes who buy auto insurance spend 16 percent of their household income on auto insurance. That percentage is seven times the proportion that families in the top 20 percent spend.
- In Maricopa County, Arizona, families with incomes of 50 percent or less of the poverty level spend nearly one-third of their income on mandatory auto insurance premiums. Many of these families put off paying for other major expenses such as food, rent or mortgage payments in order to pay their auto insurance premiums.
- Faced with the need to spend money on necessities, many other low-income drivers choose instead to disobey the law and drive uninsured. They thereby expose themselves to legal punishments, ranging from first-offense penalties of more than $1,300 to impoundment of their cars. Several states have also enacted laws limiting the right of uninsured motorists to sue for compensation for their injuries.
- High premiums add to the transportation obstacles that impede welfare reform. Research in 1996 indicated that welfare recipients who owned a car were 12 percent more likely to work, worked an additional 23 hours per month, and brought home an additional $152 per month more than those on welfare without cars.

- The problem of costly auto insurance is exacerbated for many low-income families because they reside in large cities where liability premiums are already excessively high. For example, the average premium for a 20-year-old male with a clean driving record in Baltimore is $3,214 per year.
- Because high premiums make it more difficult to own a car, many low-income, inner-city workers are unable to access better-paying suburban jobs.
- Finally, the tort litigation system provides lower compensation to poor people than to wealthier people with the same loss. Because low-income families lack the necessary resources to wait for an inefficient tort system to provide compensation, they often settle for a smaller amount rather than hold out for a larger award. Wealthier people fare better because they have the resources to wait out a protracted and costly legal process.

HOW THE AUTO CHOICE REFORM ACT WOULD ALLEVIATE SOME OF THOSE PROBLEMS

- Auto Choice would reduce the average private passenger vehicle premium by 21 percent nationwide, averaging close to $200 per car, according to the RAND Institute for Civil Justice and the Joint Economic Committee.
- Since low-income families often do not purchase optional collision and comprehensive property damage coverages, their personal injury savings represent a larger share of their overall premium—37 percent on average. For a low-income household, these savings are the equivalent of five weeks of free groceries or nearly four months of electric bills. They are also equivalent to four months of auto insurance premiums.
- In cities where premiums are higher, the premium savings would be similarly greater.
- Lower auto insurance premiums will make owning a car more affordable for the poor, thereby allowing them to find and keep better-paying jobs that require a longer commute.
- The first-party insurance option of Auto Choice would enable low-income drivers to receive better compensation for their medical bills and lost wages under a first-party system that pays people for their losses, regardless of fault, just as health insurance does. Under this option, injured policyholders would be paid promptly and in circumstances that would not be covered under the tort system, such as single car crashes. Serious injuries would generally be better compensated, which is important for those with fewer resources. In effect, the first-party option offered under Auto Choice is national health insurance for insured drivers.

FORMER DENVER MAYOR WELLINGTON WEBB ON WHY HE SUPPORTS AUTO CHOICE

- Mayor Webb testified before the Senate Commerce Committee that Auto Choice would mean "that fewer of our working poor will be required to choose between groceries and auto insurance, and fewer middle-class Americans will be forced to choose between their retirement and their children's education. It means a reduced burden for our public hospitals, since a higher percentage of auto accident victims who receive medical care will have insurance to pay their hospital bills. It means lower costs and more success for our small businesses, creating jobs and opportunity. . . . And it means that the unemployed men and women in our communities will have an easier time transitioning from welfare to work because of these jobs and because their transportation costs will go down."

RESOURCES

1. Joint Economic Committee study, *Auto Choice: Impact on Cities and the Poor* (1998).
2. Testimony of Mayor Wellington Webb before the U.S. Senate Commerce Committee, September 9, 1998.
3. Professor Robert Lee Maril, *The Impact of Mandatory Auto Insurance Upon Low Income Residents of Maricopa County, Arizona* (1993).
4. Progressive Policy Institute and Public/Private Ventures, *Working Far from Home: Transportation and Welfare Reform in the Ten Big States* (August 1999).

Peter Kinzler, President, Coalition for Auto-Insurance Reform
1999

Appendix 3: Bipartisan Heritage of Automobile Insurance Legislation: No-Fault Insurance in the 1970s and Auto Choice Proposals Today (1997)

STATE NO-FAULT AUTOMOBILE INSURANCE LAWS

- Michael Dukakis was the author of the first state no-fault law, adopted in Massachusetts in 1971, while Joe Lieberman was the author of the Connecticut law. Other laws were enacted under the leadership of Republican governors, such as Nelson Rockefeller in New York and William Milliken in Michigan.

CONGRESSIONAL LEADERSHIP

- The first Congressional hearing was conducted by Democratic Senator Phil Hart in 1971. In 1976, six months before he died from cancer, Senator Hart left the hospital to vote for federal no-fault standards legislation.
- Democrat Warren Magnuson, the Chairman of the Senate Commerce Committee, was the chief sponsor of federal standards no-fault legislation in the Senate from 1971–78. He was supported by his Ranking Minority Member, Republican Senator James Pearson of Kansas, and Ted Stevens, now the Chairman of the Appropriations Committee.
- The chief House proponents were Democratic Subcommittee Chairmen John Moss, Lionel Van Deerlin and Bob Eckhardt. Mr. Van Deerlin continues to support the concept as a member of the Coalition for Auto-Insurance Reform (CAR). *Then-Representative Al Gore voted to report legislation from the Commerce Committee in 1978.*
- The bipartisan tradition of support for automobile insurance reform legislation continues today. The chief sponsors of Auto Choice legislation are Republican Senators Mitch McConnell and John McCain, Democratic senators Pat Moynihan and Joe Lieberman, House Majority Leader Dick Armey and Representative Chris Cox and Democratic Representatives Jim Moran and Cal Dooley.

PRESIDENTS WHO SUPPORTED AUTOMOBILE INSURANCE REFORM

- The Nixon and Ford administrations supported adoption of no-fault legislation at the state level. Department of Transportation Secretary

William Coleman testified in 1975 that federal legislation would be appropriate if the states failed to act within a reasonable period of time.
- The Carter administration supported the federal standards no-fault legislation.
- Ronald Reagan supported federal no-fault legislation while he was governor of California.
- President George Bush endorsed Auto Choice legislation in 1992.

PRESIDENTIAL CANDIDATE SUPPORT FOR FEDERAL AUTO CHOICE LEGISLATION

- Michael Dukakis is a supporter of the present Auto Choice legislation.
- Bob Dole was a cosponsor of the first Auto Choice bill introduced in 1996.

STATE OFFICIALS SUPPORT FEDERAL AUTO CHOICE LEGISLATION

- Republican Governors John Engler and Christine Todd Whitman and Republican Mayor Rudolph Giuliani have endorsed the federal Auto Choice legislation.
- Democratic Mayor Wellington Webb and Fulton County Commissioner Michael Hightower have also endorsed the federal legislation.

REPUBLICAN AND DEMOCRATIC ORGANIZATIONS SUPPORT FEDERAL AUTO CHOICE LEGISLATION

- Americans for Tax Reform, Citizens for a Sound Economy and the Hudson Institute have endorsed the legislation.
- Democratic Leadership Council President Al From has also endorsed it.

WIDESPREAD PRESS SUPPORT FOR FEDERAL AUTO CHOICE LEGISLATION

- Ten of the top 20 largest newspapers have endorsed the legislation, including *The New York Times*, *USA Today*, and *The Dallas Morning News*.
- Among the national columnists who have endorsed federal auto choice legislation are Michael Barone, Morton Kondracke, Jane Bryant Quinn, Robert Samuelson, Andrew Tobias and Stuart Taylor, Jr.

Peter Kinzler, President, Coalition for Auto-Insurance Reform
July 1997

Appendix 4: Why Auto Choice Is Different from Other Tort Reform Issues (1999)

- *Direct benefits to plaintiffs.* The new personal injury protection (PIP) system provides tangible benefits to injured persons: (1) the minimum of $20,000–$25,000 of PIP benefits for medical bills and lost wages, payable regardless of fault, would be of particular benefit to the 30 percent of injured persons who receive nothing under the tort system, (2) PIP benefits would be payable within 30 days of loss, as contrasted with the average wait of 16–18 months to recover under the tort system, and (3) the average seriously injured person would recoup far more than they would under the tort system by combining their PIP benefits with recoveries from lawsuits for uncompensated economic loss.
- *Lower premiums for all motorists.* A second direct benefit for motorists is the opportunity to reduce their bodily injury premiums by approximately 57 percent or an average of nearly $200 per vehicle per year. If all drivers selected the PIP choice, they could save $40 billion a year.
- *Greatest premium reductions for low-income people.* They would receive the highest percentage reductions. The average per family reduction would be $371, which would represent a 6 percent increase in annual income for a person with an income in the lowest 20 percentile. That is a greater benefit than offered by any federal proposal on the table.
- *Democratic roots in the Senate.* Federal standards no-fault automobile insurance legislation, the forerunner to the Auto Choice bill, was championed in the 1970s by liberal Democratic Senators Phil Hart and Commerce Committee Chairman Warren Magnuson. Three times the committee reported bills by wide margins and once the Senate passed the bill (with the support of Senators Kennedy, Leahy, Biden, Inouye and Byrd).
- *Carter administration/National Democratic Platform support.* The Carter administration endorsed the federal standards no-fault legislation and worked for its passage. The 1976 National Democratic Platform supported it.
- *Prominent Democrats support Auto Choice now.* In addition to Senator Lieberman, who has been a cosponsor of the bill from the beginning, Michael Dukakis, Al From, DNC Treasurer Andy Tobias, Denver Mayor Wellington Webb and Jack Quinn, former White House Counsel in the Clinton administration, all support Auto Choice.

- *The difficulty of explaining a change in position to constituents.* Inasmuch as the tort system has only gotten worse since the 1970s and auto choice would be particularly beneficial for a key Democratic constituency, low income people, it would be difficult for Democrats to explain the change in their previously held position.

Peter Kinzler, President, Coalition for Auto-Insurance Reform
January 1999

Appendix 5: The Current Auto Liability Insurance System vs. the Personal Injury Protection System of Auto Choice (1999)

Fault/Liability Insurance System	Personal Injury Protection (PIP) System
Pays no benefits to more than 30% of all accident victims (often the victims of single-car accidents).	Pays benefits to *all* accident victims.
Pays benefits contingent on other driver's fault.	Pays benefits to *all* accident victims, regardless of fault.
Encourages fraud (more than one-third of all medical claims are fraudulent or for the build-up of claims in response to the incentives of the fault system).	Eliminates the incentives of the fault/liability insurance system for fraud.
Makes recovery contingent on other driver's behavior and auto insurance coverage.	Allows each individual to determine his or her level of guaranteed benefits for injury.
Provides inequitable coverage: Minor injuries are compensated at an average of 2 to 3 times economic losses. Serious injuries are compensated at an average of less than 50% of economic losses.	Affords equitable coverage: All economic losses are compensated up to the level of coverage selected. Permits suits for excess economic loss.
In serious injury cases, pays for losses only after trial or settlement, which can take 2 to 3 years or more.	In minor and serious injury cases, pays for insured losses within 30 days of submission of a bill.
Pays almost twice as many dollars for lawyers as for victims' legitimate medical bills and lost wages.	Eliminates the need for most lawyers. Uses the savings to pay more injured people more equitably and to lower premiums.
Is unnecessarily expensive: $400/yr. for average bodily injury premium, nationwide.	Is affordable: $216/yr. average for personal injury protection benefits and residual bodily injury liability coverage.

Source: Peter Kinzler, Brochure for Coalition for Auto-Insurance Reform (CAR), 1999, 3.

CHRONOLOGY

1896	There are four cars in the United States, with two in St. Louis. The two in St. Louis have an accident, seriously injuring one person.
1900–1968	All state laws apply the rules of fault to auto accidents, narrowly limiting recovery for personal injury to people who did not contribute to causing the accident (the doctrine of contributory negligence). Liability insurance covers motorist's assets if he or she is found at fault and required to pay the injured other person; it does not pay for injuries to the insured driver.
1932	Columbia University study identifies the tort system's multiple deficiencies.
1967	Keeton-O'Connell book proposes replacing the fault (tort) and liability insurance system with no-fault auto insurance that would pay for the medical losses of the insured and his or her family in accidents with health insurance–like coverage.
1969	Democratic Sen. Phil Hart holds the first congressional hearing on no-fault.
1970–1975	Massachusetts is the first state to adopt a no-fault law. Sixteen others follow.
1971	Twenty-six-volume Department of Transportation study documents the deficiencies of the tort system, including the failure to compensate roughly half of all injured persons, underpayment of the seriously injured, long waits for those who can recover, and more money paid to lawyers than insureds. It recommends replacing the tort system with no-fault.
1971	Robert Joost, employee of the trial lawyers' association, surprisingly testifies in favor of no-fault before the Senate Commerce Committee. After losing his job, Joost is hired by the Commerce Committee.
1971	Ralph Nader, consumer advocate, surprisingly remains neutral.

1972	Model state law, UMVARA, calls for high no-fault benefits and tight restriction on the right to sue for pain and suffering ("the threshold").
1971–1974	Democratic Senate Commerce Committee Chairman Magnuson champions no-fault with key assistance from his general counsel, Lynn Sutcliffe.
1974	No-fault bill passes the Senate by 53–42 vote, only to die in a House of Representatives preoccupied with the impeachment of President Nixon.
1975	Democratic Rep. Lionel Van Deerlin assumes chairmanship of House Consumer Protection Subcommittee, with jurisdiction over no-fault. Van Deerlin hires Peter Kinzler, author, as counsel and assigns him to work on no-fault.
1975	AFL-CIO, CFA, State Farm, and the American Insurance Association lead the private sector effort for no-fault. Congressional House majority leader scion Thomas "Tom" Hale Boggs, Jr., leads the trial lawyer opposition.
1975	Attorney General Edward Levi prevails over DOT Secretary William Coleman in a split among presidential advisers, and the Ford administration opposes federal legislation.
June 17, 1975–July 25, 1975	Van Deerlin subcommittee holds nine hearings. One, in Florida, is not a model of decorum.
October 19, 1975	House subcommittee reports "English version" no-fault bill 5–4 with help from a not-so-secret supporter.
March 13, 1976	Senate bill recommitted to committee by a 49–45 vote, as President Ford, faced with a primary challenge by Ronald Reagan, opposes the bill and six Republican senators who had voted for no-fault in 1974 change their votes.
1976	Van Deerlin is succeeded as Consumer Protection Subcommittee chairman by Rep. Jack Murphy.
1977	Murphy is succeeded by Rep. Bob Eckhardt with a little help from Robert Redford.
March–July 1977	Eckhardt subcommittee holds ten hearings.
July 1977	Carter administration endorses no-fault but does little to support it.
February 28, 1978	New Democratic Senate Commerce Committee Chairman Howard Cannon is blindsided at markup by insistence of Senator John Durkin, a longtime sup-

	porter of no-fault, on a study before he will vote for the bill.
May 9, 1978	Senate Commerce Committee reports no-fault by narrow 9–7 margin.
May 23, 1978	Eckhardt's House Consumer Protection Subcommittee reports no-fault bill by 5–4.
May 24, 1978	Democratic Senator Hollings, a former trial lawyer, sends a letter to Majority Leader Byrd threatening a filibuster.
August 1, 1978	Last-minute compromise fails, and full House Commerce Committee votes 23–19 not to report the bill after arm-twisting by Speaker O'Neill against the bill.
1986	Kinzler, having moved to the staff of Senator Chris Dodd in 1981, works with Senate HELP Committee staff to assist in passage of the Childhood Vaccine Injury Act of 1986 to provide relief to children injured by childhood vaccines.
September 9, 1992	Kinzler, on loan by Senator Dodd to Senator Jay Rockefeller, learns what it's like to have a business counterweight to the trial bar, although the product liability reform bill fails by two votes of cloture to end a filibuster.
1975–1995	Changes in tort and insurance laws improve victim recoveries but leave large deficiencies, with many injured people still without recourse, seriously injured people grossly undercompensated, and more money still going to lawyers and excessive or fraudulent claims than to injured victims. Trial lawyer-undermined no-fault laws prove unnecessarily costly, as weak thresholds pervert no-fault into a dual system of no-fault and fault coverages.
1986	Professor O'Connell and Joost devise way to resolve accidents between no-fault and fault drivers, leading to Auto Choice no-fault proposals.
June 11, 1996	Republican Sen. Mitch McConnell introduces the Auto Choice Reform Act of 1996 to give consumers the choice of a no-fault option in all states, with the promise of huge premium savings.
September 24, 1996	Kinzler becomes president of the Committee for Comprehensive Automobile Accident Restitution and Rate Reductions (CCAARRR), mercifully later renamed the Coalition for Auto-Insurance Reform

	(CAR), and testifies at the Senate Commerce Committee's first hearing. Senator McConnell and Andrew Tobias, among others, also testify.
1997	Conservative Republican House Majority Leader Armey introduces a House companion bill.
1997	Previous supporters and opponents switch sides as Republicans and conservatives support Auto Choice, while Democrats, trial lawyers, and consumer groups oppose it. Nader supports the trial lawyer position in open opposition to the no-fault option of Auto Choice.
2001	After multiple hearings in the Senate, House, and JEC, Auto Choice fails to advance in the face of fierce trial lawyer opposition and, finally, the 9/11 attack.
2004	Senator Cornyn sponsors the last Auto Choice bill.
2020	After-action analysis of the failure of Auto Choice points primarily to the absence of private sector support to balance the opposition of the trial bar. The near-universal view of injured people that the other driver is at fault and should pay was likely a contributing factor. The most plausible scenario for the return of no-fault to the national agenda would be a Democratic effort to adopt universal health insurance legislation, which would require Democrats to address the issue of duplicate payment by health and auto insurance for medical losses in auto accidents. It is far easier to do that when both systems are first-party, no-fault systems. Auto primacy could significantly reduce the price tag of health insurance.

GLOSSARY OF PLAYERS

Richard (Dick) Armey: Conservative Republican House majority leader who was the sponsor of the Auto Choice bill in the House.

Gayland Barksdale: Chief of staff for Majority Leader Armey who led the House staff effort for Auto Choice.

Hunter Bates: Led the Senate staff effort on behalf of Sen. Mitch McConnell during the Auto Choice effort. Later became chief of staff to the senator.

Thomas Hale Boggs, Jr.: Son of former Democratic majority leader and powerful lobbyist who led the trial bar's opposition to no-fault.

Mary McInnis Schuman Boies: Democratic Senate Commerce Committee counsel who later, as the assistant director of President Carter's White House Domestic Policy Council staff, had the responsibility for coordinating the administration's position on no-fault.

Herman Brandau: Assistant general counsel for State Farm Insurance Company, which supported both no-fault efforts. Lead counsel for no-fault effort in the 1970s and a key contact for the 1990s Auto Choice effort. He provided detailed information about how automobile insurance works and the political implications of different provisions on support or opposition from other insurers.

Stephen Brobeck: Executive director of the Consumer Federation of America during consideration of Auto Choice.

Jim Brown: Director of the Auto Accident Compensation Project, University of Wisconsin–Milwaukee. Brown put on two major conferences on Auto Choice in Washington, DC, in the late 1990s.

James Broyhill: Ranking Republican on the House Consumer Protection Subcommittee. Twice came close to supporting no-fault, only to be unable to reach a last-minute compromise.

Lance Bultena: Senate Commerce Committee counsel responsible for Auto Choice.

Guido Calabresi: Yale Law School professor and author of *The Costs of Accidents*, a 1970 book that supported no-fault. Calabresi testified in favor of no-fault in the 1970s before becoming dean of Yale Law School and then a judge on the US Court of Appeals for the Second Circuit.

Stephen Carroll: Senior economist, RAND Institute for Civil Justice. Main author of multiple reports during the 1990s projecting the cost savings of changing from fault to no-fault.

Leslie Cheek III: Represented the American Insurance Association and Crum and Forster Insurance Company during the 1970s no-fault effort. Along with Herman Brandau, the most knowledgeable and helpful industry supporter.

William Cohen: Stanford Law School professor. Draftsman and coreporter of the model state no-fault law UMVARA and witness before the House Consumer Protection Subcommittee.

Christopher J. Dodd: Democratic senator who was the author's boss for twelve years and author of a products liability bill in the 1980s that helped broaden support for a later bill.

John Durkin: Democratic senator from New Hampshire. Longtime no-fault advocate who delayed consideration of no-fault in 1978 when he was up for reelection.

Bob Eckhardt: Colorful and brilliant Democratic Texas congressman who chaired the Consumer Protection and Finance Subcommittee during hearings and markup of no-fault legislation in 1977–1978.

Nora Engstrom. Stanford University Law School professor still writing thoughtfully about fault and no-fault insurance in the twenty-first century.

Mike Gildea: Primary AFL-CIO lobbyist for no-fault during the 1970s.

Phil Hart: Democratic senator who held the first hearings on no-fault legislation in the Congress in 1969 and then cosponsored early no-fault bills with Sen. Warren Magnuson.

Michael Horowitz: Senior fellow and director, Project for Civil Justice Reform, Hudson Institute. Conservative activist supporter of Auto Choice.

J. Robert Hunter: Federal insurance administrator who supported no-fault during Pres. Gerald Ford's administration. As director of insurance for the Consumer Federation of America during the Auto Choice effort, he questioned the adequacy of the no-fault benefits but was open to the possibility of compromise.

Ted Johnson: Media specialist for the Committee on Consumers No-Fault who was responsible for generating press and public support for no-fault.

Bob Joost: Lost his job with the Association of Trial Lawyers of America when he testified in favor of federal no-fault. As the legislative counsel for the Senate Commerce Committee, he taught me the ins and outs of no-fault. Drafted two no-fault reports for the US Department of Transportation and developed a key element of Auto Choice with Prof. Jeffrey O'Connell.

Robert Keeton: Harvard Law School professor who cocreated no-fault automobile insurance in 1965 and cowrote a key book in 1967.

Tom Korologos: Senate lobbyist for the Ford administration. Lobbied against no-fault for the trial bar during the 1970s as a member of the firm of Timmons & Co.

Michael Lemov: The author's predecessor on the no-fault issue on the House Subcommittee. Encouraged Rep. Lionel Van Deerlin to hire the author.

Edward Levi: Attorney general during the Ford administration who led the opposition to federal no-fault. Prior to that, he was the president of the University of Chicago.

Joseph I. Lieberman: Senate Democrat who cosponsored the Auto Choice legislation. Previously, he authored the Connecticut no-fault law.

Milton Lower: Staff economist for Chairman Bob Eckhardt's House Consumer Protection Subcommittee.

Warren Magnuson: Democratic Senate Commerce Committee chairman who led the effort to enact no-fault.

John McCain: Among many other things, Republican senator who cosponsored Auto Choice and served as chairman of the Senate Commerce Committee during consideration of Auto Choice.

Mitch McConnell: Republican senator who was the chief sponsor of the Auto Choice legislation. Later became majority leader of the Senate.

Dan Miller: Joint Economic Committee staffer who crunched the consumer savings numbers for Auto Choice and wrote several reports explaining the benefits of Auto Choice for different segments of society.

Jim Moran: Democratic Congressman who was the lead House cosponsor of Auto Choice.

Daniel Patrick Moynihan: Democratic senator who wrote favorably about no-fault in the 1960s and cosponsored Auto Choice.

Mike Mullen: Counsel to both the Senate Judiciary Committee and the Senate Commerce Committee who handled no-fault during the 1970s. Helped convince new Commerce Committee Chairman Howard Cannon to switch his prior position and support no-fault.

John M. Murphy: Democratic US representative who chaired the House Consumer Protection Subcommittee in 1976 and then under pressure reversed his support on a crucial vote in 1978. Served time for taking bribes in the FBI Abscam sting.

Ralph Nader: Famed consumer advocate who remained neutral during the 1970s no-fault debate and then actively supported the trial bar in its opposition to Andrew Tobias's no-fault initiative in California in the 1990s and then to Auto Choice.

Nancy Nord: Republican counsel for the Consumer Protection Subcommittee who marshalled opposition to no-fault.

Jeffrey O'Connell: Cocreated the no-fault concept with Professor Keeton and then cocreated the Auto Choice concept with Bob Joost. He was a professor at the University of Illinois College of Law at Urbana-Champaign and at the University of Virginia Law School. Jeff was a tireless advocate during both efforts.

Kathleen O'Reilly: Leading consumer advocate for no-fault for the Consumer Federation of America.

Robert Quinn: Led support for no-fault in the 1970s on behalf of Nationwide Insurance Company. Became insurance commissioner of California in 1981.

Mark Raabe: Democratic counsel to House Commerce Committee Chairman Harley Staggers. Worked closely with the author to advance no-fault.

John D. "Jay" Rockefeller IV: Democratic US senator who, as chairman of the Consumer Subcommittee of the Senate Commerce Committee, became the chief sponsor of product liability legislation and "borrowed" the author for several months to staff the issue in 1992.

Laurie Rubenstein: Senator Lieberman's counsel for Auto Choice.

Dean Sharp: Judiciary Committee staffer to Sen. Phil Hart who encouraged Joost to testify in favor of no-fault despite the fact that Joost worked for the trial bar.

Craig Spangenberg: Lead trial lawyer opponent to no-fault during the 1970s who testified effectively before the House Consumer Protection Subcommittee.

Ted Stevens: Republican senator from Alaska who worked closely with Senator Magnuson to advance no-fault legislation during the 1970s. Later, he served as the minority whip in the Republican leadership.

S. Lynn Sutcliffe: General counsel to the Senate Commerce Committee during most of the 1970s no-fault effort and president of the Committee for Consumers No-Fault, the supporting coalition in 1977–1978.

William Timmons: White House congressional legislative liaison during the Nixon and Ford administrations. After leaving the White House, lobbied against no-fault as the head of the firm Timmons & Co.

Andrew Tobias: Financial author, sponsor of California Pay at the Pump no-fault initiative, supporter of Auto Choice, and treasurer of the Democratic National Committee.

Lionel Van Deerlin: US representative who chaired the House Consumer Protection Subcommittee when the subcommittee reported a no-fault bill for the first time in 1975.

Dick Walsh: US Department of Transportation staffer responsible for overseeing the 1971 twenty-six-volume DOT study outlining the faults of the fault and liability insurance system and calling for the adoption of no-fault.

NOTES

INTRODUCTION

1. The largest component of "associated costs" was compensation for pain and suffering. As these were intangible losses not subject to quantification, courts routinely awarded them as a multiple of the medical bills and lost wages. This produced an incentive for inflated or fraudulent claims, adding unnecessarily to the cost of premiums for motorists. Ironically, almost all pain and suffering went to people with minor losses, where it was least needed, because most drivers carried insufficient liability coverage to pay for serious injuries.

2. Jeffrey O'Connell, *The Injury Industry and the Remedy of No-Fault Insurance* (Urbana, Chicago, London: University of Illinois Press, 1971), viii.

3. Robert E. Keeton and Jeffrey O'Connell, *Basic Protection for the Traffic Victim: A Blueprint for Reforming Automobile Insurance* (Boston, MA: Little, Brown & Co., 1967).

4. The Commonwealth of Puerto Rico was the first jurisdiction in the United States to enact a no-fault law, doing so in 1968 with an effective date of 1970.

5. Because of these limitations, insurers developed other insurance products to fill some of the compensation gaps. Some, such as Uninsured Motorist and Underinsured Motorist, pay you when the other driver has no insurance or insufficient coverage to pay for your injuries. However, both are fault-based and pay only if the other driver is at fault. Medical Payments coverage does pay for your injuries, regardless of fault, but it is often duplicative of your health insurance and typically provides limited coverage.

6. "State No-Fault Automobile Insurance Experiences," *Hearings before the Subcommittee on Consumer Protection and Finance of the Committee on Interstate and Foreign Commerce, Ninety-Fifth Congress, First Session, on the Experience of Various States with No-Fault Automobile Insurance Laws*, Serial No. 95-41 (Washington, DC: US Government Printing Office, June 13, 1977), 682–683 (hereafter *House State No-Fault Hearings*).

7. *House State No-Fault Hearings*, 677–678. The doctrine that denied recovery to those partially at fault was called contributory negligence. In most states, it denied any recovery if the injured person was 10 percent or more at fault.

8. *House State No-Fault Hearings*, 678.

9. *House State No-Fault Hearings*, 680.

10. The Krakowskis did receive a onetime payment of $1,000 from their own insurer under a minor coverage called Medical Payments that, like health insurance, pays without regard to fault.

11. *House State No-Fault Hearings*, 683–684. Outside the hearing, Pryor told me that when she first called the rehabilitation center to arrange for therapy, the people at the center told her they had no openings. When she explained that she had been injured in a car crash and was insured by State Farm, they changed their tune and said they could take

her right away. The reason for the change was that Michigan's no-fault law meant there was coverage to pay for their services.

12. The only other bar association to support no-fault was that of the city of New York, which did so in a February 6, 1972, report, "The No Fault Principle," by the Special Committee on Automobile Insurance Plans. As in Michigan, the bar's support made it easier politically for New York to adopt a no-fault law.

13. *House State No-Fault Hearings*, 733.

14. The Illinois law was declared unconstitutional within a few days of its activation on January 1, 1972, because it applied only to private passenger vehicles. No other state court ruled its no-fault law unconstitutional.

1. FIFTY WAYS TO LOSE YOUR RECOVERY

1. National Highway Transportation Safety Administration, "Traffic Safety Facts 2017: A Compilation of Motor Vehicle Crash Data" (Washington, DC: US Department of Transportation, 2017), 2.

2. Stephen J. Carroll and Allan F. Abrahamese, *The Effects of a Choice Automobile Insurance Plan on Insurance Costs and Compensation: An Updated Analysis* (Santa Monica, CA: RAND Institute for Civil Justice, 1998), 11n9.

3. Stephen J. Carroll, James S. Kakalik, Nicholas M. Pace, and John L. Adams, *No-Fault Approaches to Compensating People Injured in Automobile Accidents* (Santa Monica, CA: RAND Institute for Civil Justice, 1991), 187.

4. See, e.g., US Joint Economic Committee, "Choice in Auto Insurance: Updated Savings Estimates for Auto Choice," Washington, DC, July 2003, 14–17, which estimated the trial bar's annual revenue from auto cases in 2001 at nearly $12 billion. The defense bar made close to another $5 billion.

5. A 1995 RAND study concluded that *more than one-third of medical costs were excessive and unnecessary*—claims for staged accidents and unnecessary visits to medical practitioners. RAND estimated the total bill for this fraud at $13–$18 billion per year. Stephen Carroll, Allan Abrahamese, and Mary Vaiana, *The Costs of Excess Medical Claims for Automobile Personal Injuries* (Santa Monica, CA: RAND Institute for Civil Justice, 1995), 23.

6. In recent years, some insurers have utilized software, such as the Colossus system, to try to standardize payments for different injuries. Other large insurers informed me that they don't use such software and continue to process claims as they have for years. In any case, there is no public data, at least no significant data, to quantify the impact of such efforts on reducing fraud and lowering payouts in small injury cases.

7. Bureau of Justice Statistics, *Civil Trial Cases and Verdicts in Large Counties, 2001* (Washington, DC: US Department of Justice, April 2004), 2.

8. Jeffrey O'Connell, *The Injury Industry and the Remedy of No-Fault Insurance* (Urbana, Chicago, London: University of Illinois Press, 1971), viii.

9. See, e.g., "The doctrine of fault has to be attributed to the industrial revolution—to the age of engines and machines (which) have a marvelous capacity to cripple and maim their servants." Lawrence Friedman, *A History of American Law*, 2nd ed. (New York: Simon and Shuster, 1985), 300. Friedman went on to argue that judges, fearing that holding businesses strictly liable for all the injury they caused would cripple economic development, reduced tort liability to a standard of ordinary care "to limit damages to some mod-

erate measure" so that capital could "be spared for its necessary work" (469); see also Morton J. Horwitz, *The Transformation of American Law 1780–1860* (Cambridge, MA: Harvard University Press, 1997), 99.

10. Among those were a prohibition on suing a member of your family who was a passenger in the car (family immunity) or even a passenger who wasn't a relative (host/guest statutes).

11. Insurance Information Institute, "Auto: Background on Compulsory/Uninsured Motorists," April 29, 2019.

2. "LAS VEGAS HAS BETTER ODDS THAN THAT"

1. Columbia University Council for Research in the Social Sciences, "Report by the Committee to Study Compensation for Automobile Accidents" (Philadelphia, PA: Press of International Printing Co., 1932), 216–217 (hereafter Columbia University, "Report on Compensation").

2. Columbia University, 217.

3. Robert E. Keeton and Jeffrey O'Connell, *Basic Protection for the Traffic Victim: A Blueprint for Reforming Automobile Insurance* (Boston: Little, Brown and Company, 1967).

4. Connecticut, Colorado, Florida, Georgia, Hawaii, Kansas, Kentucky, Massachusetts, Michigan, Minnesota, Nevada, New Jersey, New York, North Dakota, Pennsylvania, and Utah. Subsequently, Connecticut, Nevada, Colorado, and Georgia repealed their no-fault laws.

5. Magnuson chaired the committee from 1951 to 1976.

6. A joint resolution requires passage by both bodies and signature by the president, just as a bill does. Thus, it, too, has the full force and effect of a law.

7. In 1972 and 1974, the no-fault bills were referred to the Commerce Committee. After the committee reported them, they were sequentially referred to the Judiciary Committee, which killed the bill in 1972. However, in 1974, Magnuson secured an agreement from the chairman of the Judiciary Committee to a time limit on the referral. After the time was up, the Senate passed the Commerce Committee bill.

8. US Department of Transportation, "Motor Vehicle Crash Losses and Their Compensation in the United States, A Report to the Congress and the President" (Washington, DC: US Government Printing Office, 1971), 100 (hereafter DOT study).

9. DOT study, 51–52.

10. DOT study, 36.

11. DOT study, 43.

12. DOT study, 36.

13. DOT study, 53–57.

14. Richard M. Nixon, "Changing Rules of Liability in Automobile Accident Litigation," *Law and Contemporary Problems* 3, no. 4 (1936): 477, 483.

15. Sen. Frank Moss (D-UT) maintained that DOT Sec. John Volpe had prepared a draft statement advocating a national approach: "If basic reparations reform is left wholly to individual state initiatives, it will most likely be exceedingly slow in coming and involve a number of different, perhaps conflicting approaches." According to Moss, Volpe was barred from giving that testimony. Moss also maintained that the "watered down administration position came after several high-level insurance executives of Kemper Insurance

Group, Allstate and Liberty Mutual made a call to Secretary of Commerce Maurice Stans, who intervened on their behalf in the White House decision-making process." *Congressional Quarterly Almanac* 30 (1974): 316.

16. Part IV, "Recommendations for Change," DOT study, 140–142.

17. DOT study, 142.

3. EARLY CONGRESSIONAL ACTION

1. These qualities gave the impression of a much older or more mature person. When I first met Sutcliffe in 1975, he had just turned thirty-two. Because of his impressive skill set and appearance, I assumed he was much older than I. In 1976, I discovered that he was born on March 30, 1943, so I called him and said, "Congratulations, old man." Sutcliffe did not take it well. He responded, "How the hell old are you, Kinzler?" I replied, after some further teasing, "I'm much younger than you, Lynn." "How much younger?" he questioned. Finally, I relented: "I'm much younger. I won't be thirty-three for another nineteen days!" It's been a running joke ever since, and forty-three years later, we still call each other on our birthdays.

2. Senator Hart won this sobriquet for following his view of good policy wherever it led, even when it was not politically advantageous for him. For example, he introduced a bill to break up the Big Three US auto manufacturers on antitrust grounds despite the fact they were headquartered in his state! Because of his willingness to take politically unpopular stands for causes he thought were just and for his integrity, his colleagues named the Hart Senate Office Building after him (it is hard to find anyone who believes the other two buildings, Russell and Dirksen, were named for similar reasons).

3. "Automobile Insurance Reform and Cost Savings," *Hearings before the Committee on Commerce, United States Senate, Ninety-Second Congress, First Session, on S. 945, Uniform Motor Vehicle Insurance Act*, Part 3, Serial No. 92-18, 898 (hereafter 1971 Senate Hearings).

4. 1971 Senate Hearings, 902, 901, 904.

5. 1971 Senate Hearings, 907.

6. 1971 Senate Hearings, 905.

7. Ed Cohen, a fellow staffer on the committee, told me of the time late one afternoon when the staff had been discussing the creation of a major new legislative idea. When Ed arrived for work the next day, he found on his desk a complete draft that Joost had written during the night.

8. 1971 Senate Hearings, 1280.

9. National Conference of Commissioners on Uniform State Laws, "Uniform Motor Vehicle Reparations Act" (Chicago: National Conference of Commissioners on Uniform State Laws, 1972), 3, 5 (hereafter UMVARA).

10. Leah Young, "A Chink in Ralph Nader's Armor?," *New Republic*, September 2, 1972.

11. Representative Moss held fifteen days of hearings between 1971 and 1974 but was never able to move the bill out of his subcommittee. Michael R. Lemov, *People's Warrior: John Moss and the Fight for Freedom of Information and Consumer Rights* (Madison-Teaneck, NJ: Fairleigh Dickinson University Press, 2011), 167.

12. Kinzler interview with Leslie Cheek III, January 27, 2020.

4. HOW TO GET A COMMITTEE COUNSEL POSITION ON CAPITOL HILL

1. The irony of overturning the seniority system as a reform is that the seniority system itself had been adopted in the early twentieth century as a reform to curb the power of Speaker Joe Cannon to appoint all members of the majority party to committees. The seniority system prevented Cannon from keeping members in line with his wishes by wielding his power to deny them choice committee assignments and to remove them from committees when they opposed his wishes.

5. "I'M JUST A BILL ON CAPITOL HILL"

1. Gen. Brent Scowcroft once told *Time* magazine, "I don't have a quick, innovative mind. I don't automatically think of good new ideas. What I do is pick out good ideas from bad ideas." "Brent Scowcroft, National Security Adviser to Two Presidents, Dies at 95," *Washington Post*, August 8, 2020.

2. This is the only time I use the words "inasmuch as" in the book in place of the more commonly used words "since" or "because." I note this because Van Deerlin, having been a broadcaster and columnist, chided me for using the word "since" when the correct words for a causal connection were "inasmuch as." That is now an antiquated usage (as it probably was in the 1970s), but the fact that I unconsciously used the old term brings back fond memories of working for a wonderful man and the only legislator I ever worked for who spoke in complete, grammatically correct sentences.

3. Levitas was a very bright member who had two colossal legislative failures. Each started out promisingly, only to fail spectacularly in the end. The first was the legislative veto. While Levitas was able to secure its inclusion in the FTC legislation, the Supreme Court held it to be unconstitutional. Additionally, Levitas was able to secure funds to build a visitor center at Union Station for the country's two hundredth anniversary celebration in 1976. To construct it, the railroad tracks were moved back a considerable distance, significantly inconveniencing passengers. Then, the center was built at the front of the station. During the bicentennial, pictures of Washington, DC, were shown on the walls. The idea seemed to be that visitors would travel to DC by train, then sit down and watch the pictures in the visitor center—and then, I guess, go home! Instead, they went to see the real sights in DC, leaving the center empty, a giant white elephant. A few years later, the Congress had to appropriate funds again, this time to undo Levitas's expensively flawed concept and move the railroad tracks back into the station.

4. Paul Kane, "Least Deliberative Senate Faces Weighty Task of Holding an Impeachment Trial," *Washington Post*, January 5, 2020.

6. "VAN DEERLIN'S A REALLY NICE GUY, BUT THAT KINZLER'S A SON OF A BITCH"

1. The Watergate Class broke the power of the committee chairman to appoint all or nearly all the committee staff. Many committees, including the Commerce Committee, established separate subcommittee budgets, further diluting the power of the chairman

of the full committee. The result proved semicomical when I went to work later for Rep. Bob Eckhardt. Eckhardt submitted a budget that reflected the subcommittee's needs, while all the other subcommittee chairmen inflated their budgets. The members of the House Administration Committee, which authorized funding, threw their hands up in the air and agreed on a total figure to be divided by the subcommittees according to their percentages of the original total request. Eckhardt never made that mistake again, inflating the subcommittee's needs in case the Administration Committee were to apply the same rule going forward! House Democrats, encouraged by the fact that their numbers had increased so that there were 191 Democrats and 144 Republicans, one more Democrat than a 2–1 majority of all members, overreached by applying a ratio of 2 + 1:1 on each subcommittee. Thus, a 4:2 margin became 5:2; a 6:3 margin became 7:3, and so forth. Adding to the alienation of the Republicans, many Commerce subcommittees established staffing ratios that were far disproportionate to the Democrat/Republican ratio. The Oversight and Investigations Subcommittee, for example, in 1979 had a staff ratio of 87 percent Democrats to 13 percent Republicans. These actions alienated the Republicans, who responded by seeking to obstruct legislation. Worse yet, they found partners in this effort—conservative Democrats who came from historically Republican districts who had been swept in by the Watergate tide. Even worse yet, encouraged by the numbers, the Democrats pushed bills that were often far to the left of many of these newer members. As a result, many bills came out of committee with narrow margins, defeating the purpose of the committee system to reach compromise on major issues and thereby necessitating that the work of the committee be done on the House floor. The result was that many of the Watergate Class of Democrats lost their seats in the Reagan landslide of 1980. Many liberal Democrats, including my four bosses during the 1970s, also lost their seats.

2. Quinn was an intellectual whose worth Nationwide failed to appreciate. He even wrote a book about no-fault entitled *The Lemon Tree*. He drew the title from the Peter, Paul and Mary song of the same name, based on the refrain "Lemon tree very pretty and the lemon flower is sweet / But the fruit of the poor lemon is impossible to eat," to make the point that no-fault was a great idea but impossible to enact into law because of the power of the trial bar. I was probably one of only two people to read it, the other being his wife, Mariann, because it was dense. Nationwide, not knowing what to do with Quinn, took the easy way out year after year, promoting him until he became the head of research. I learned what happened next from Bob Pike, a friend of Quinn's who later became executive vice president and general counsel of Allstate. After Quinn became head of research, Nationwide fired him. Then they immediately invited him to a luncheon seminar on how to get a job! When a waiter came around offering drinks, Quinn took one, saying, "Thanks, I really need one." He was then reprimanded and told that the proper thing to say was "I'll have one if you will." Afterward, Quinn called Mick McCabe, another Allstate friend, and said, "Mick, I just flunked lunch!" Such was the wisdom of Nationwide that Quinn's next job was as insurance commissioner of California for Gov. Jerry Brown.

3. In testimony before the House Consumer Protection Subcommittee on July 22, 1975, Coover's boss, Paul Blume, vice president and general counsel of NAII, argued that "under the traditional concepts of federalism, Congress normally does not act in an area that is covered by State law unless the states have neglected or refused to act. This is just not the case here." No-Fault Motor Vehicle Insurance, *Hearings before the Subcommittee on Consumer Protection and Finance of the Committee on Interstate and Foreign Commerce*

Committee, House of Representatives, Ninety-Fourth Congress, First Session, on H.R. 285 et al, July 22, 1975, Serial No. 94-42, 601.

4. I use the terms "we" and "our" throughout the book to refer to the large number of people involved in developing and working for the passage of no-fault legislation. The plural refers to some or all of the many people who made possible consideration of the bill—the law professors who developed and refined the concept, the labor and consumer groups who lobbied members of Congress on behalf of the public, the few supportive automobile insurers who helped me and other staff refine the legislation so that it would work in the real world, and other House and Senate staff who played major roles. Of course, supportive senators and representatives had to do much of the heavy lifting of convincing their colleagues to support no-fault. Starting in 1975, over the next three years, I was in the position to play a major role because during that time, I staffed the issue for three different subcommittee chairmen, an unusual degree of longevity for the turnover in chairmen. The primary reasons that I was retained by three chairmen were the expertise I had developed on this important Democratic priority and my commitment to policy rather than to individual members. All three chairmen played important roles in this drama.

5. Statement of Hon. William T. Coleman, Secretary of Transportation, *No-Fault Motor Vehicle Insurance, Hearings before the Subcommittee on Consumer Protection and Finance of the Committee on Interstate and Foreign Commerce, House of Representatives, Ninety-Fourth Congress, First Session, on H.R. 265, etc.* (No-Fault Motor Vehicle Insurance bills), June 17, 19; July 8, 14, 17, 22, 24, 25, 1975, Serial No. 94–42, 242 (hereafter 1975 House Hearings).

6. 1975 House Hearings, 254–255.

7. Hon. John A. Volpe, Secretary of Transportation, *Automobile Insurance Reform and Cost Savings, Hearings before the Committee on Commerce, United States Senate, Ninety-Second Congress, First Session on S. 945, Uniform Motor Vehicle Insurance Act, and Others*, Part I, Serial No. 92-18, March 10 and 18 and May 3, 1971, 103–104 (hereafter Senate Hearings).

8. Senate Hearings, 110.

9. 1975 House Hearings, 268.

10. 1975 House Hearings, 284.

11. 1975 House Hearings, 295.

12. 1975 House Hearings. The dialogue between Spangenberg and Van Deerlin occurs at 295–296.

13. 1975 House Hearings, 302.

14. 1975 House Hearings, 306–320.

15. The Hon. Guido Calabresi, Senior Circuit Court Judge of the United States Court of Appeals, Second Circuit, Remembrances of Jeffrey O'Connell (Charlottesville, VA: University of Virginia Law Library, Spring 2016), http://archives.law.virginia.edu/records/mss/1984-3/digital/29261.

16. Add-on laws were the trial lawyers' first backup option when they could not defeat no-fault outright in a state. They were able to convince eight states to adopt add-on laws, but all of them contain low benefit limits, making them no different than if one purchased insurance coverage for medical payments in a fault state. If the trial lawyers' effort to enact add-on failed, their second option was to weaken the no-fault thresholds so people

could sue in more situations. The DOT-commissioned Milliman & Robertson actuarial study that estimated that motorists could save $1.3 billion a year if a no-fault bill with unlimited medical benefits were adopted also calculated the costs associated with simply adding no-fault benefit coverage to existing policies without restricting the right to sue; in all but three states average personal injury premiums increased. Milliman & Robertson, Inc., "Exhibit A-2, Cost Estimate Study of No-Fault Automobile Insurance (Variations on S. 354)," *No-Fault Insurance, Hearings before the Committee on Judiciary, United States Senate, Ninety-Third Congress, First and Second Sessions on No-Fault Insurance, S. 354*, December 4, 1973, and other dates, 1474, 1479.

17. 1975 House Hearings. 635.

18. 1975 House Hearings, 636.

19. 1975 House Hearings, 745.

20. Testimony of John B. Martin, Legislative Consultant, National Retired Teachers Association and American Association of Retired Persons, "Federal Standards for No-Fault Motor Vehicle Accident Benefits Act," *Hearings before the Subcommittee on Consumer Protection and Finance of the Committee on Interstate and Foreign Commerce, Ninety-Fifth Congress, First Session, on H.R. 6601, et al.*, June 14, 15; July 18, 21, and 22, 1977, Serial No. 95–55, 543. (hereafter 1977 House Hearings). Martin's reference to a five-year waiting period to receive compensation for a serious injury was a slight exaggeration of DOT's finding that 26 percent of permanent disability cases handled by an attorney under the tort system had still not been settled after 998 days. US Department of Transportation, "Motor Vehicle Crash Losses and Their Compensation in the United States, A Report to the Congress and the President" (Washington, DC: US Government Printing Office, 1971), 47 (hereafter DOT study).

21. 1977 House Hearings, 543.

22. For background on the automobile insurance reform issue at the national level, see James M. Cannon Files, Gerald R. Ford Presidential Library, box 23, folder "No Fault Insurance (2)," 112, https://www.fordlibrarymuseum.gov/library/document/0039/16988092.pdf.

7. THE HOUSE CONSUMER PROTECTION SUBCOMMITTEE REPORTS A NO-FAULT BILL, ONLY TO SEE THE SENATE BILL FALTER (1975–1976)

1. Rinaldo had introduced his own bill, at the request of Kemper Insurance, which was represented in DC by Mike Dineen, who had worked for Rinaldo. It was nearly identical to S. 354 but had one difference that was designed to help Kemper. Since we couldn't accept Rinaldo's provision without losing the support of our other insurers, securing Rinaldo's vote remained a challenge through the process.

2. The effect of this approach was to add one more Democrat to most committees and subcommittees than a 2:1 majority would have warranted. Therefore, the Consumer Protection Subcommittee became 7:3 instead of 6:3. Democrats overreached with even higher ratios on key committees such as the Ways and Means Committee. Their choices embittered Republicans and came back to bite them when Newt Gingrich and the Republicans took over the House in 1995.

3. *Congressional Quarterly Almanac* 32 (1976): 448.

4. Sarah Havens, "A Legislative History of No-Fault Insurance" (unpublished paper, 1978, prepared for a Hampshire College course while she was working for the Consumer Protection Subcommittee for the summer), 19.

5. Young was truly an intrepid reporter, for which she paid a heavy price. Earlier, on September 2, 1972, she had written an article, "A Chink in Ralph Nader's Armor?," for the *New Republic*, suggesting that Nader's opposition to no-fault was the result of a $10,000 contribution from ATLA (the adjusted value would be over $60,000 today) to a Nader-originated organization, the Center for Auto Safety and a pledge by ATLA "to raise an additional $10,000 from their membership to finance an index of automobile defects." The article also quoted another consumer advocate who championed no-fault as saying Nader was "afraid that if lawyers are wiped out, they won't be around for other things." This comment is similar to the explanation Bob Hunter shared with me in 2002. Nader, at the height of his influence in 1972, retaliated by blackballing Young with the major newspapers in Washington, according to Young.

6. Chairman Staggers did not vote, but Sam Devine, the ex officio ranking minority member of the full committee, voted against reporting the bill.

7. Walter J. Blum and Harry Kalven, *Public Law Perspectives on a Private Law Problem: Auto Compensation Plans* (Boston: Little, Brown, 1965).

8. James M. Cannon Files, Gerald R. Ford Presidential Library, box 23, folder "No Fault Insurance (1)," 1–13, 31–43, https://www.fordlibrarymuseum.gov/library/document/0039/1515888.pdf (hereafter Cannon Files 1). See also Cannon Files, box 24, folder "No Fault Insurance (3)," 79, https://www.fordlibrarymuseum.gov/library/document/0039/1515889.pdf. The files also include a letter from James Kemper to President Ford urging his support for federal legislation. Cannon Files 1, 14–26. Ironically, it was a call by Kemper to President Nixon in 1971 that appears to have been the decisive factor in Nixon's decision to oppose federal legislation. In yet another irony, in 1975, thinking that no-fault would pass in the Ninety-Fourth Congress, the Kemper Insurance Co., along with Prudential and Nationwide, negotiated changes in the Senate and House bills that led to their support.

9. James M. Cannon Files, Gerald R. Ford Presidential Library, box 24, folder "No-Fault Insurance (4)," 2–12, 25–27, https://www.fordlibrarymuseum.gov/library/document/0039/16988094.pdf (hereafter Cannon Files 4).

10. Peter Kinzler, "Background on H.R. 9650, the National Standards for No-Fault Benefits Act," materials developed in 1975 for a Commerce Committee report had the full committee reported the bill, "Papers of Peter Kinzler," Arthur J. Morris Law Library, University of Virginia School of Law, Charlottesville, VA, http://archives.law.virginia.edu/records/mss/2015-03. The figures are Federal Highway Administration data for 1973.

11. *No-Fault Motor Vehicle Insurance, Hearings before the Subcommittee on Consumer Protection and Finance of the Committee on Interstate and Foreign Commerce, House of Representatives, Ninety-Fourth Congress, First Session, on H.R. 265, etc.* (No-Fault Motor Vehicle Insurance bills), June 17, 19; July 8, 14, 17, 22, 24, 25, 1975, Serial No. 94–42, 256.

12. Jack Anderson and Les Whitten (newspaper columnists), "White House vs. no-Fault," *Washington Post*, April 1976, Cannon Files 4, 35.

13. Taft later returned his contribution.

14. "The Political Money Tree Blooms," *In Common: The Common Cause Report from Washington* 9, no. 2 (Spring 1978): 6–7.

8. NEW KEY PLAYERS IN THE NINETY-FIFTH CONGRESS

1. My work on the subcommittee, along with my subsequent jobs in the Senate and then on the Financial Institutions Subcommittee of the House Banking Committee, were cited as the reasons I received honorable mention in the search for "The Ultimate Hill Climber" in the September 20, 1993, edition of *Roll Call*. The award was based on having "held not only many jobs, but also weighty posts."

2. *Hearings before the Subcommittee on Consumer Protection and Finance of the Committee on Interstate and Foreign Commerce, Ninety-Fifth Congress, First Session, on H.R. 6601, et al.*, June 14, 15; July 18, 21, and 22, 1977, Serial No. 95-55 (New York, NY, April 23, 1977), 618 (hereafter 1977 State No-Fault Hearings).

3. 1977 State No-Fault Hearings, June 14, 1977, 268.

4. 1977 State No-Fault Hearings, 182.

5. 1977 State No-Fault Hearings, 183–272. There were two days of hearings in Florida, April 7 and 8.

6. Hon. Bob Eckhardt, *Florida No-Fault Hearing*, House of Representatives, *Congressional Record* 123, no. 143 (September 15, 1977).

7. 1977 State No-Fault Hearings, 551–640.

8. Chairman Eckhardt inserted summaries of the four hearings in the *Congressional Record*, a common and effective way to reach out to other House members. Hon. Bob Eckhardt, *New York No-Fault Hearings*, House of Representatives, *Congressional Record* 123, no. 144 (September 16): 1977.

9. Letter from Jeffrey O'Connell, Professor of Law, University of Illinois at Urbana-Champaign, to Congressman Bob Eckhardt, August 9, 1978, Papers of Peter Kinzler, Arthur J. Morris Law Library, University of Virginia School of Law, Charlottesville, VA, http://archives.law.virginia.edu/records/mss/2015-03.

9. ECKHARDT, CARTER, AND CANNON SUPPORT NO-FAULT, ONLY TO BE BETRAYED BY SEN. JOHN DURKIN (JUNE 1977–JUNE 1978)

1. *Hearings before the Subcommittee on Consumer Protection and Finance of the Committee on Interstate and Foreign Commerce, Ninety-Fifth Congress, First Session, on H.R. 6601, et al.*, June 14, 15; July 18, 21, and 22, 1977, Serial No. 95-55, 677–698.

2. *Congressional Record*, House of Representatives, Thursday, June 23, 1977, 123, no. 109, 20680–20684.

3. *Congressional Record*, House of Representatives, Thursday, September 15, 1977, 123, no. 143, 29559–29562.

4. *Congressional Record*, House of Representatives, Friday, September 16, 1977, 123, no. 144, 29766–29768.

5. *Congressional Record*, House of Representatives, September 22, 1977, 123, no. 148, 30490–30494.

6. US Department of Transportation, *State No-Fault Automobile Insurance Experience, 1971–1977* (Washington, DC: US Department of Transportation, June 1977), 80 (hereafter 1977 DOT study).

7. 1977 DOT study, 80.

8. Special Committee on Insurance Legislation, "Automobile No-Fault Insurance: A Study by The Special Committee on Automobile Insurance Legislation" (Chicago: American Bar Association, February 1978).

9. Letter from Herman Brandau, Associate Counsel, State Farm, to Peter Kinzler, Counsel, House Subcommittee on Consumer Protection and Finance, July 18, 1975.

10. Margy Waller and Mark Alan Hughes, *Working Far from Home, Transportation and Welfare Reform in the Ten Big States* (Philadelphia and Washington, DC: Progressive Policy Institute and Public/Private Ventures, 1999), executive summary.

10. ONE LAST CHANCE

1. Letter from Bob Joost to Rep. Bob Eckhardt, October 6, 1978, Papers of Peter Kinzler, Arthur J. Morris Law Library, University of Virginia School of Law, Charlottesville, VA, http://archives.law.virginia.edu/records/mss/2015-03.

2. In most House committees during the 1970s, legislation was considered at the subcommittee level first. Only if a bill were "reported" (voted out of a subcommittee by a majority of the members) could it be considered by the full committee. Similarly, a majority vote in the full committee was necessary to advance the bill for consideration by the House. The bill had squeaked out of subcommittee in late May 1978 by a one-vote margin and was destined for another close vote in the full committee.

3. Dingell had been the sole cosponsor of H.R. 10, the first no-fault bill ever introduced. The sponsor, Rep. John Moss of California, introduced the bill on January 3, 1973, the first day of the Ninety-Third Congress. The bill number showed the importance Democrats placed on no-fault, as the majority party in the House has the privilege of choosing the first ten bills introduced in a new Congress, while the minority gets the next ten. These bills are the ones that each party considers to be its top legislative priorities. Two years later, Dingell switched sides in response to opposition from the single largest employer in his district, GM. The largest US auto manufacturer was afraid that the limits in the legislation on lawsuits against insurance companies by people injured in car crashes would lead to more lawsuits by injured persons against auto manufacturers. Ironically, Dingell switched sides while the union that represented the GM workers who were Dingell's constituents, the UAW, continued to support no-fault. Michigan's highly respected Sen. Phil Hart took the opposite tack. He, too, was an early supporter of no-fault, having chaired the first no-fault hearing in the Congress in 1969 and introduced the first no-fault bill in 1971. Unlike Representative Dingell, Senator Hart remained a staunch no-fault supporter, bucking GM opposition and even leaving his sickbed at Bethesda Naval Hospital (Walter Reed) when he was dying of cancer to travel to the Senate to cast his vote for a no-fault bill in 1976.

4. The bill included a "verbal threshold" that would have permitted suits only in cases of very serious injury, such as death, loss of a limb or use of it, and "serious and permanent" injury. This threshold was viewed as one that would permit far fewer lawsuits and thus result in lower premiums than a dollar threshold.

5. "Brock Adams is a case of a round peg in a square hole. He should have stayed in Congress." He was "ignored by [the] White House, not a leader. . . no clout." "Carter's Cabinet—How It Rates," *U.S. News & World Report*, October 16, 1975, 25.

11. DECOMPRESSION, DEPRESSION, INTROSPECTION, AND A FAILED EFFORT TO SECURE SUPPORT FOR A CHOICE NO-FAULT BILL (FALL 1978)

1. The major reason Allstate had predicted that the bill would increase premiums was because it used a higher assumption for no-fault benefits for death benefits, ignoring the minimum required by the bill and replacing it with a figure they thought most people would purchase. We insisted it use the figure in the bill. Allstate did so, with a statement that it did not agree with the assumption.

2. Allstate was one of just two large insurers, the other being GEICO, that opposed federal no-fault while lobbying for similar legislation in the states. While modifying the bill in ways that Allstate viewed as improvements did not alter its antifederal stance, the changes put it more at ease and, in turn, lowered the level of its opposition.

3. Reps. Doug Walgren (PA) and Barbara Mikulski (MD) are the two members who I think might have voted for no-fault but for Nader's opposition. Walgren's opposition was also no doubt influenced by the fact that he started his career as a trial lawyer and then worked as general counsel for a company represented in DC by Boggs. Mikulski's opposition might also have been influenced by the fact that she had been hit by a bus and really wanted the company to pay for what it had done to her. "The Political Reality of Passing a No-Fault Bill in this Congress," Memorandum from Peter Kinzler, Counsel, to Chairman Bob Eckhardt, July 1978.

4. S. Lynn Sutcliffe, "Senate Action on No-Fault Insurance in the 94th Congress" (November, 1978), The memorandum also outlines strategic mistakes in the Senate, such as proceeding with the vote when supportive Sens. John Tunney (D-CA) and Henry (Scoop) Jackson (D-WA) were away from the Senate campaigning, and failing to move to table the motion to recommit, a parliamentary move that would have shown which senators needed to be lobbied further before a decisive vote.

12. EXPERIENCE WITH OTHER LIABILITY REFORM ISSUES LEADS TO A SURPRISE RETURN TO NO-FAULT (1981–1996)

1. "Product Liability Closed Claims Survey: A Technical Analysis of Survey Results" (Jersey City, NJ: Insurance Services Office, 1977).

2. Recall that the Judiciary Committee had secured referral of the no-fault bill in consecutive Congresses in an attempt to kill it.

3. The memo, along with my other product liability documents, is in a file labeled "Products Liability" in "Papers of Peter Kinzler," Arthur J. Morris Law Library, University of Virginia School of Law, Charlottesville, VA, http://archives.law.virginia.edu/records/mss/2015-03.

13. TWO DECADES OF CHANGES IN STATE AUTO INSURANCE LAWS FAIL TO FIX THE MAJOR PROBLEMS

1. US Department of Transportation, Office of the Secretary of Transportation, "Compensating Auto Accident Victims: A Follow-up Report on the No-Fault Auto Insurance

Experience" (Washington, DC: US Government Printing Office, 1985) (hereafter DOT study 2).

2. DOT study 2, 3–6.

3. DOT study 2, chapter 3, E., "Balance in a No-Fault Auto Insurance System," 86–92.

4. Jeffrey O'Connell and Robert Joost, "Giving Motorists a Choice between Fault and No-Fault Insurance," *Virginia Law Review* 72, no. 1 (February 1986): 61–89.

5. Only sixteen actually provided information, as the Illinois Supreme Court held that its no-fault law was unconstitutional before it became effective.

6. In 2019, only the states of Alabama, Maryland, North Carolina, and Virginia and the District of Columbia retained the doctrine of contributory negligence: https://www.carinsurance.com/kb/state-list-of-negligence-laws.

7. Insurance Information Institute, "Auto: Background on Compulsory Auto/Uninsured Motorist," April 29, 2019.

8. Insurance Information Institute.

9. Janet L. Kaminski Leduc, senior legislative attorney, Office of Legislative Research, "Auto Liability Insurance Requirements in Other States," 2013-R-0258 (June 27, 2013), https://www.cga.ct.gov/2013/rpt/pdf/2013-R-0258.pdf; see also Insurance Information Institute, "Summary of Uninsured Motorists (UM) and Underinsured Motorists (UIM) Coverage Provisions under the ISO Personal Auto Program," 2018, https://www.verisk.com/siteassets/media/ils/ils8891.pdf?v=1.1.

10. The rationale for buying this coverage when it duplicates the health insurance coverage you already have is threefold: it has no deductibles or copayments, and it covers passengers in your car. This seems like a thin reed for people who could use the money to meet more important needs.

11. Later studies documented the extent of this buildup, which had started by the mid-1990s. Peter Kinzler, "Auto Insurance Reform Options: How to Change State Tort and No-Fault Laws to Reduce Premiums and Increase Consumer Choice," *Issue Analysis: A Public Policy Paper of the National Association of Mutual Insurance Companies* (Indianapolis, IN: National Association of Mutual Insurance Companies, 2006), 13; Insurance Research Council, *Fraud and Buildup in Auto Injury Insurance: 2004 Edition* (Malvern, PA: Insurance Research Council, December, 2004), 16.

12. National Conference of Commissioners on Uniform State Laws, Uniform Motor Vehicle Reparations Act (1972), 5.

13. Independent Statistical Service, Inc., Insurance Services Office, Inc., and National Independent Statistical Service, "Fast Track Monitoring Service Final Report, Form I,—Automobile Report—Private Passenger" (2010).

14. NO-FAULT RISES LIKE A PHOENIX FROM THE ASHES, REINCARNATED AS AUTO CHOICE, WITH A FOCUS ON LOWER PREMIUMS AND CHOICE (1992–2004)

1. Stephen J. Carroll, James S. Kakalik, Nicholas M. Pace, and John L. Adams, "No-Fault Approaches to Compensating People Injured in Automobile Accidents" (Santa Monica, CA: RAND Institute for Civil Justice, 1991).

2. Allan F. Abrahamse and Stephen J. Carroll, "The Effects of a Choice Auto Insurance Plan on Insurance Costs" (Santa Monica, CA: RAND Institute for Civil Justice, 1995), xiv.

3. Jeffrey O'Connell, Stephen Carroll, Michael Horowitz, and Allan Abrahamse, "Consumer Choice in the Auto Insurance Market," *Maryland Law Review* 52, no. 4 (1993), 1016–1062; see also Jeffrey O'Connell, Stephen Carroll, Michael Horowitz, Allan Abrahamse, and Daniel Kaiser, "The Cost of Consumer Choice for Auto Insurance in States without No-Fault Insurance," *Maryland Law Review* 54, no. 2 (1995): 282–35; and Jeffrey O'Connell, Stephen Carroll, Michael Horowitz, and Allan Abrahamse, "The Comparative Costs of Allowing Consumer Choice for Auto Insurance in All Fifty States," *Maryland Law Review* 55, no. 1 (1996): 160–222.

4. See "Auto Insurance Regulations," C-SPAN, September 24, 1996, https://www.c-span.org/video/?75374-1/automobile-insurance-regulations. My testimony begins at 56:30.

5. To read about how Tobias made and spent his money, see Andrew Tobias, *My Vast Fortune: The Money Adventures of a Quixotic Capitalist* (New York: Random House, 1997). It is a deadly serious tale, always told amusingly.

6. The exception to the split in the 1970s was the support by the American Insurance Association, which represented a lot of the old-line New England stock insurers. There was no such split during the Auto Choice effort.

7. See, e.g., Abrahamse and Carroll, "Effects of Choice on Insurance Costs," 26.

8. The 56 percent figure for Auto Choice comes from RAND. Stephen J. Carroll and Allan Abrahamse, "The Effects of a Choice Automobile Insurance System on Insurance Costs and Compensation: An Analysis Based on 1997 Data" (Santa Monica, CA: RAND Institute for Civil Justice, 1999), 23. The lower figures for no-fault come from the 1975 cost estimates of Allstate and State Farm. See the discussion of Allstate and State Farm costings of no-fault above.

9. Robert Lee Maril, "The Impact of Mandatory Auto Insurance upon Low Income Residents of Maricopa County, Arizona," unpublished manuscript (1993); see also Maril's testimony before the Senate Commerce Committee, September 9, 1998, https://www.c-span.org/video/?111275-1/auto-insurance-choice. Two later studies fleshed out just how severe a burden the costly fault system put on low-income people. A 1999 study by the Progressive Policy Institute stated, "In households below the poverty line, 73 percent of work trips use a private automobile. Owning a car is even more important now as both rural counties and inner cities are isolated from the dispersed job grow in suburban economies." Margy Waller and Mark Alan Hughes, "Working Far from Home, Transportation and Welfare Reform in the Ten Big States," (Philadelphia and Washington, DC: Progressive Policy Institute and Public/Private Ventures, 1999), executive summary, 3–4. See also US Joint Economic Committee (JEC), "Auto Choice: Impact on Cities and the Poor: A Joint Economic Committee Report, Prepared at the Request of U.S. Representatives Dick Armey (R-TX), Jim Moran (D-VA), U.S. Senators Rod Grams (R-MN), Joseph I. Lieberman (D-CT), Mitch McConnell (R-KY), Daniel Patrick Moynihan (D-NY) (March 1998)," 30–31: "The poorest fifth of households . . . spends 16.3 percent of their income on premiums when they purchase auto insurance, more than seven times the income share of the richest families. . . . The typical low-income household with auto insurance spends more on premiums in two years than the value of their automobile."

10. US Department of Transportation, "Motor Vehicle Crash Losses and Their Compensation in the United States: A Report to the Congress and the President" (Washington, DC: US Government Printing Office, 1971), 36 (hereafter DOT study).

11. Stephen J. Carroll and Alan F. Abrahamse, "The Effects of a Choice Automobile

Insurance Plan on Insurance Costs and Compensation: An Updated Analysis" (Santa Monica, CA: RAND Institute for Civil Justice, 1998), 11.

12. Carroll et al., "No-Fault Approaches," 187.

13. The IRC estimated the cost of attorneys' fees and court costs for represented plaintiffs at 32 percent. *Paying for Auto Injuries: A Consumer Panel Survey of Auto Accident Victims, 2004 Edition* (Malvern, PA: Insurance Research Council, 2004), 6.

14. Bureau of Justice Statistics, "Civil Trial Cases and Verdicts in Large Counties, 1996" (Washington, DC: US Department of Justice, 1999), 13. In 1970, when US courts were far less congested, it took an average of sixteen to eighteen months for an injured person to receive payment. DOT study, 43.

15. Insurance Research Council, *Auto Injury Insurance Claims: Countrywide Patterns in Treatment, Cost, and Compensation* (Malvern, PA: Insurance Research Council, 2003), 91, 112.

16. JEC, "Auto Choice," 5n16. The footnote states, "The basic breakout of the BI premium is from the Insurance Information Institute (New York, NY: 4/30/97). This analysis uses RAND's lower bound estimate of excessive claiming behavior to identify the component of the BI premium attributable to fraudulent and excessive claiming." See also Allan F. Abrahamse and Stephen J. Carroll, "The Frequency of Excess Claims for Automobile Personal Injuries" (Santa Monica, CA: RAND Institute for Civil Justice, 1999).

17. It is not surprising that plaintiff attorneys' fees continued to constitute a huge portion of the premium dollar. In 2003, thirty-two years after the publication of the DOT study, the IRC found that the vast majority of bodily injury liability dollars were paid out to claimants who retained attorneys: 47 percent of bodily injury liability claimants retained attorneys, and those claimants received 79 percent of all such dollars paid to injured persons. IRC, *Auto Injury Insurance Claims*, 112.

18. Stephen Carroll, Allan Abrahamse, and Mary Vaiana, "The Costs of Excess Medical Claims for Automobile Personal Injuries" (Santa Monica, CA: RAND Institute for Civil Justice, 1995), 23.

19. Bureau of Justice Statistics, "Civil Trial Cases and Verdicts in Large Counties, 2001" (Washington, DC: US Department of Justice, 2004), 2.

20. Elizabeth Landes, "Insurance, Liability, and Accidents: A Theoretical and Empirical Investigation of the Effect of No-Fault Accidents," *Journal of Law and Economics* 25, no. 1 (1982): 49–65.

21. US Department of Transportation, "Compensating Auto Accident Victims: A Follow-Up Report on No-Fault Auto Insurance Experiences" (Washington, DC: US Government Printing Office, 1985), 142.

22. Rose Anne Devlin, "Liability versus No-Fault Automobile Insurance Regimes: An Analysis of the Experience in Quebec," in *Contributions to Insurance Economics*, ed. G. Dionne (Boston: Kluwer Academic Publishers, 1992), 499.

23. J. David Cummins, Mary Weiss, and Richard D. Phillips, "The Incentive Effects of No-Fault Automobile Insurance" (Philadelphia: University of Pennsylvania, Wharton School, 1999).

24. David Loughran, *The Effect of No-Fault Automobile Insurance on Driver Behavior and Automobile Accidents in the United States* (Santa Monica, CA: RAND Institute for Civil Justice, 2001), xvii.

25. Loughran, 34, 37. In 2001, Cummins published another study, revising his previous methodologies. The conclusion was a median predicted increase of 13.8 percent in fatality

rates in no-fault states. Cummins, Phillips, and Weiss, "The Incentive Effects of No-Fault Automobile Insurance." Subsequently, a 2010 RAND study examined the Cummins study and several others, some of which estimated increases and some decreases, and found that "the empirical evidence is mixed. The study examining the broadest range of accident types (Heaton and Helland, 2009b) finds no evidence of an effect of no-fault on accident rates." James M. Anderson, Paul Heaton, and Stephen J. Carroll, "The U.S. Experience with No-Fault Automobile Insurance: A Retrospective" (Santa Monica, CA: RAND Institute for Civil Justice, 2010), 82.

26. US Joint Economic Committee, "Auto Choice: Impact on Cities and the Poor, Prepared at the Request of U.S. Representatives Dick Armey (R-TX), Jim Moran (D-VA), U.S. Senators Rod Grams (R-MN), Joseph I. Lieberman (D-CT), Mitch McConnell (R-KY), Daniel Patrick Moynihan (D-NY)," Washington, DC: March 1998; US Joint Economic Committee, "Auto Choice: Relief for Businesses and Consumers, Prepared at the Request of U.S. Representative Dick Armey (R-X), House Majority Leader and U.S. Sen. Mitch McConnell (R-KY)," Washington, DC, July 1998.

27. Joint Economic Committee Republicans, "Improving the American Legal System: The Economic Benefits of Tort Reform," March 1996, 6–7, https://www.jec.senate.gov/public/_cache/files/4d9850cb-9725-4886-b20d-ec2d865e9fdf/improving-the-american-legal-system.pdf.

28. US Joint Economic Committee, "The Benefits and Savings of Auto-Choice: A Joint Economic Committee Report," Jim Saxton (R-NJ), chairman (Washington, DC: US Congress, April 1997), 8–10.

29. JEC, 8.

30. JEC, "Auto Choice," 34–36.

31. JEC, "Choice in Auto Insurance: Updated Savings Estimates for Auto Choice, Prepared at the Request of Senator Mitch McConnell (R-KY)" (Washington, DC: US Congress, 2003), 12–13.

32. Of course, total vehicles on the road, miles driven, and auto insurance premiums have increased significantly over the years. For example, in 1996, liability premiums totaled $74 billion for private auto insurance and $20 billion for commercial vehicles. JEC, "Benefits and Savings," 8. In 2019, they totaled $138,573,207 for private auto insurance and $27,196,291 for commercial vehicles. Insurance Information Institute, "2019 Insurance Fact Book" (New York: Insurance Information Institute, 2020), 73.

15. LET'S ALL CHANGE PARTNERS AND DANCE AGAIN

1. Rep. William Lipinski (D-IL) withdrew from H.R. 2021 in the 105th Congress, and Rep. Edolphus Towns (D-NY) withdrew from H.R. 1475 in the 106th Congress. Also, Rep. Harold Ford (D-TN), a cosponsor of H.R. 2021 and a rising young star in the Congress, indicated that he had developed reservations about the politics of cosponsoring the legislation, and he would not be a cosponsor of Auto Choice in the next Congress. Representatives Towns and Ford were African Americans whose continuing cosponsorship might have made it easier to secure more cosponsorship from other African American Democrats. In turn, that likely would have made it safer for other progressive Democrats to add their names. In addition, Rep. George Nethercutt (R-WA) withdrew from H.R. 2021 for unknown reasons.

2. See Appendix 1.

3. See Appendix 2.

4. Ralph Nader was officially neutral but quietly opposed to no-fault in the 1970s and actively opposed to Auto Choice in the 1990s.

5. Peter Passell, "Happier Motoring: Choices in Buying Insurance," *New York Times*, January 23, 1997.

6. Andrew Tobias, *My Vast Fortune: The Money Adventures of a Quixotic Capitalist* (New York: Random House, New York, 1997), 111.

7. Consumer Federation of America, "Consumers and Automobile Insurance" debate presented at The Consumer in the Financial Services Revolution: Challenges and Opportunities conference, Washington, DC, December 3 and 4, 1998, C-SPAN, December 3, 1998, https://www.c-span.org/video/?116059-1/consumers-automobile-insurance.

8. Stephen Carroll and Allan Abrahamse, Project Memorandum, "The Effects of an Enhanced Choice Auto Insurance Plan on Auto Insurance Costs and Premiums" (Santa Monica, CA: RAND Institute for Civil Justice, April 2002) (not cleared for open publication). See also emails from Stephen Carroll to Peter Kinzler dated March 22, 2002, and May 23, 2002, and Carroll's later model dated March 19, 2006.

9. Emails from Carroll to Kinzler.

10. Email from Grover Norquist to Peter Kinzler, July 20, 2001.

11. Robert R. Detlefsen, "Escaping the Tort-Based Auto Accident Compensation System: The Federal Auto Choice Reform Act of 1997," *Journal of Insurance Regulation* 17 (1998): 186–212.

12. See Appendix 3.

13. See Appendix 4.

16. THE RUBBER HITS THE ROAD

1. US Joint Economic Committee, "Choice in Auto Insurance: Updated Savings Estimates for Auto Choice, Prepared at the Request of Senator Mitch McConnell (R-KY)" (Washington, DC: US Congress, July 2003), 14–17.

2. Jeffrey O'Connell, Peter Kinzler, and Hunter Bates, "A Federal Bill, with Commentary, to Allow Choice in Auto Insurance," *Connecticut Insurance Law Journal* 7, no. 2 (2000–2001): 511–584.

3. S. 1860, Auto Choice Reform Act, *Hearing before the Committee on Commerce, Science, and Transportation, United States Senate, One Hundred Fourth Congress, Second Session* (September 24, 1996), S. Hrg. 104-613. For video of the full hearing, see "Automobile Insurance Regulations," C-SPAN, September 24, 1996, https://www.c-span.org/video/?75374-1/automobile-insurance-regulations. My testimony begins at 56:30.

4. These were ten of the twenty largest newspapers in the country at the time.

5. US Joint Economic Committee, *Hearing on Automobile Insurance Reform*, S. Hrg. 105-204 (Washington, DC: US Government Printing Office, 1997).

6. The Auto Choice Reform Act of 1997, *Hearing before the Committee on Commerce, Science, and Transportation, United States Senate, One Hundred Fifth Congress, First Session, July 17, 1997*, S. Hrg. 105-873 (hereafter Senate Commerce, 1997 hearing).

7. Senate Commerce, 1997 hearing, 12. Senator Moynihan also mentioned that he had first written in favor of no-fault in "Next: A New Auto Insurance Policy," *New York Times Magazine*, August 27, 1967. In the foreword to Professor O'Connell's book *The Injury In-*

dustry and the Remedy of No-Fault Insurance (Urbana, Chicago, London: University of Illinois Press, 1971), Moynihan described motor vehicle crashes as "the perfectly predictable outcomes of a particular transportation system utilizing a specific technology."

8. Email from Peter Kinzler to Grover Norquist, July 20, 2001, author's personal files.

9. See, e.g., "Automobile Insurance Reform," *Talk of the Nation*, National Public Radio, May 13, 1977; "Automobile Insurance," *Talk of the Nation*, National Public Radio, November 5, 1997; and "Consumers and Automobile Insurance," C-SPAN, December 3, 1998, https://www.c-span.org/video/?116059-1/consumers-automobile-insurance.

10. *Perspectives on Federal Auto Choice Legislation* (Washington, DC: Auto Accident Compensation Project).

11. See "Auto Insurance Options," C-SPAN, June 9, 1999, https://www.c-span.org/video/?124789-1/auto-insurance-options.

12. At a lunch on November 29, 2018, Lance explained the situation to me. It probably didn't help any that Senator McCain was feuding with Senator McConnell over campaign finance legislation at the time, as McCain was a deeply passionate politician who often let his emotions override his reason in the short run.

13. Jeffrey O'Connell, Peter Kinzler, and Dan Miller, "No-Fault Insurance at 40: Dusting Off an Old Idea to Help Consumers Save Money in an Age of Austerity," *Issue Analysis* (Indianapolis, IN: National Association of Mutual Insurance Companies, December 2011). See also Peter Kinzler, "Auto Insurance Reform Options: How to Change State Tort and No-Fault Laws to Reduce Premiums and Increase Consumer Choice," *Issue Analysis: A Public Policy Paper of the National Association of Mutual Insurance Companies* (Indianapolis, IN: National Association of Mutual Insurance Companies, August 2006).

14. See "Papers of Peter Kinzler," Arthur J. Morris Law Library, University of Virginia School of Law, Charlottesville, VA, http://archives.law.virginia.edu/records/mss/2015-03.

15. Plaintiff attorneys were often able to risk losing some cases because their firms financed them with the fees they recovered in auto accident cases.

17. IS THERE SOME EDUCATION IN THE SECOND KICK OF A MULE?

1. James M. Anderson, Paul Heaton, and Stephen J. Carroll, "The U.S. Experience with No-Fault Automobile Insurance: A Retrospective" (Santa Monica, CA: RAND Institute for Civil Justice, 2010), xvi.

2. In no-fault, since the insurer is responsible for injury to its insured, if its insured is driving a safer car, it can offer premium reductions because safer cars will reduce the likelihood of injury and the degree of any injury. An insurer cannot do so in the tort system because the BI portion of the premium covers its insured only for the losses of some unknown third party. Thus, the safety of its insured's car is meaningless to the insurer when it comes to setting personal injury premiums.

3. Lee Drutman, "How Corporate Lobbyists Conquered American Democracy," *Atlantic*, April 20, 2015.

4. Mark Twain appears to have been the source of the quotation in its original form: "There is nothing to be learned from the second kick of a mule."

5. See Appendix 5.

6. All state no-fault laws have thresholds that permit such suits in cases of serious injury, as did the earlier federal no-fault bills.

7. The outcome of legislation can also be affected by more personal matters. In this case, two of the key players had been staffers on the House Commerce Committee at the same time as I was in the 1970s and worked together on the Health Subcommittee. Jeff Schwartz, whose child had been grievously injured by a DPT vaccine shot and ultimately would die from it, created Dissatisfied Parents Together (DPT), an organization of parents that advocated for legislation. Steve Lawton represented the American Academy of Pediatrics. Their good personal relationship helped facilitate passage.

8. Most of the bill's Democratic supporters were from a wing of the party that was much larger then than now. Today, you would find moderate to conservative Democratic senators only in small, rural states.

AFTERWORD: DOES NO-FAULT HAVE ANOTHER TURN ON THE FEDERAL AGENDA?

1. Margy Waller and Mark Alan Hughes, "Working Far from Home, Transportation and Welfare Reform in the Ten Big States" (Philadelphia and Washington, DC: Progressive Policy Institute and Public/Private Ventures, 1999), executive summary.

2. Stanford Law School Professor Nora Engstrom has put forth an interesting argument as to why no-fault lost its allure, suggesting that it was because changes in the no-fault and liability systems brought them closer together in practice, thereby making it a harder sell to abandon tort for no-fault. Nora F. Engstrom, "An Alternative Explanation for No-Fault's Demise," *DePaul Law Review* 61 (2012): 303–382. Let me make three points about this argument. First, the main reason no-fault came to look more like the tort system—increased litigiousness—was its trial lawyer opponents' success in undermining no-fault to protect their fee income. It is the thresholds that the trial lawyers weakened that resulted in motorists in no-fault states such as New York and Florida still paying half their premiums for liability coverage. If those litigious states were to adopt the kind of tight threshold the creators of no-fault intended, as was done in Michigan, the reduction in premiums would be dramatic. Second, some large insurers do not use computerized programs to try to standardize recoveries for the same kind of injuries. Even for companies that use such programs, their ability to standardize payouts is limited by the involvement of lawyers and the likely unwillingness of the courts to accept insurer-imposed amounts. Third, no changes to the fault system would ever pay people injured in single-car crashes (because no one was at fault), as no-fault does. Such payments can come only from non-fault/no-fault-equivalent coverages, either MedPay auto insurance or one's health insurance. The tort system should not get credit for these no-fault payments. If a truer no-fault system were adopted in any state—with a tight threshold and health insurance–like cost controls—it would likely fulfill no-fault's promise of not only better and faster compensation but much lower premiums. Then, no-fault would look very different than tort, and that might spark renewed interest in no-fault. Of course, a state would have to demonstrate the political will to stand up to the trial bar to test that proposition.

3. Stephen Carroll and Allan Abrahamse, *The Effects of an Enhanced Choice Auto Insurance Plan on Auto Insurance Costs and Premiums* (Santa Monica, CA: RAND Institute

for Civil Justice, April 2002), 10, 14–19 (not cleared for open publication). The memorandum contains estimates for multiple scenarios. Steve later e-mailed me an update for PIP drivers that showed that an increase in PIP from what was essentially $25,000 in the bill to $50,000 would have reduced savings for PIP drivers from 62 percent to 57 percent.

4. Anderson, Heaton, and Carroll, "The U.S. Experience with No-Fault," xv.

5. Jeffrey O'Connell, Peter Kinzler, and Dan Miller, "No-Fault Insurance at 40: Dusting Off an Old Idea to Help Consumers Save Money in an Age of Austerity," *Issue Analysis* (Indianapolis, IN: National Association of Mutual Insurance Companies, December 2011), 12.

6. O'Connell, Kinzler, and Miller, 6, 8–10.

7. Anderson, Heaton, and Carroll, "The U.S. Experience with No-Fault," 131.

8. Insurance Research Council, *PIP Claiming Behavior and Claim Outcomes in Florida* (Malvern, PA: Insurance Research Council, February 2011), 1.

9. Insurance Research Council, *New York's No-Fault System: Preliminary Findings from Closed Auto Injury Claims* (Malvern, PA: Insurance Research Council, December 2010), 1, 2, 11, 12, 18, 20. For a more detailed discussion of the Florida and New York PIP experience, see also O'Connell, Kinzler, and Miller, "No-Fault Insurance at 40," 7–9.

10. Statement by August D'Aureli, supervising investigator of the Insurance Frauds Bureau, New York State Insurance Department, before the New York State Senate Standing Committee on Insurance (February 9, 2004); see also New York Insurance Frauds Bureau, *No-Fault Fraud in New York State*, 2n166; and *The 2000 Report to the Governor and the Legislature of the State of New York on the Operations of the Insurance Fraud Prevention Act* (January 15, 2001).

11. *McCormick v. Carrier*, 2010 WL 3063140 (Michigan Supreme Court, July 31, 2010).

12. O'Connell, Kinzler, and Miller, "No-Fault Insurance at 40," 9–10.

13. O'Connell, Kinzler, and Miller, 10–11.

14. O'Connell, Kinzler, and Miller, 9–10.

15. O'Connell, Kinzler, and Miller, 5.

16. Anderson, Heaton, and Carroll, "The U.S. Experience with No-Fault," 69.

17. Anderson, Heaton, and Carroll, 79.

18. Anderson, Heaton, and Carroll, 82.

19. As roughly 85 percent of the population carries auto insurance, making auto insurance primary would avoid having the people who don't carry auto but carry the national health care coverage subsidize the cost of health care for auto accidents.

20. As you may recall, the collateral source doctrine prohibits the admission of evidence that the injured plaintiff has received compensation for the same injury from another source—most typically, his or her health insurer.

21. The latest available DOT data found the economic impact of motor vehicle crashes to be $242 billion in 2010, with $23.4 billion of that amount for medical costs. Medicare and Medicaid combined paid 23.1 percent of those costs. NHTSA, "The Economic and Societal Impact of Motor Vehicle Crashes, 2010 (Revised)" (Washington, DC: US Department of Transportation, May 2015), 1–2, 237. Updated for medical cost inflation to 2018, some 40 percent (see Centers for Medicare and Medicaid Services, "National Health Expenditure Data, Table 2, National Health Expenditures; Aggregate, Annual Percentage Change, Per Cent Distribution and Per Capita Amounts, by Type of Expenditure: Selected Calendar Years, 1960–2018") would raise total medical costs for auto accidents

to approximately $32.76 billion for 2018. If Medicare and Medicaid still paid 23.1 percent of the costs, moving those costs into the auto insurance system would have saved those programs $7.57 billion.

22. Congressional Budget Office, *Federal Subsidies for Health Insurance Coverage for People under 65: 2020 to 2030* (Washington, DC, September 29, 2020), 17.

23. In addition to the Medicare and Medicaid payments to auto accident victims, 56.4 percent of the medical costs of auto accidents was paid by private insurance (from a combination of private health insurance and private auto insurance), and another 12.13 percent was picked up initially by self-pay and charities that DOT indicated may ultimately shift to Medicare and Medicaid (NHTSA, 237). Just adding the self-pay and charity costs, were they to ultimately shift to Medicare and Medicaid, as the DOT study indicated was possible, would add an additional $4.3 billion in savings. It's impossible to estimate how much of the cost paid by private health insurance might wind up being paid by auto insurance because DOT does not break out the percentage. If more states were to enact no-fault laws, more of the money that private health insurers pay for auto accidents would move into the auto insurance system because the health insurers would not have to keep track of auto accident cases that can sometimes take years to resolve before they can recover through a process called subrogation the monies they paid to auto accident victims in the first place.

24. *Hearings before the Committee on the Judiciary, United States Senate, Ninety-Third Congress, First and Second Sessions, on No-Fault Insurance*, December 4, 1973 (Washington, DC: US Government Printing Office), 130.

SELECTED BIBLIOGRAPHY

American Bar Association. "Automobile No-Fault Insurance: A Study by The Special Committee on Automobile Insurance Legislation." Chicago: American Bar Association, February 1978.

Anderson, Jack, and Les Whitten. "White House vs. no-Fault." *Washington Post*, April 1976.

Anderson, James M., Paul Heaton, and Stephen J. Carroll. "The U.S. Experience with No-Fault Automobile Insurance: A Retrospective." Santa Monica, CA: RAND Institute for Civil Justice, 2010.

"Automobile Insurance Reform and Cost Savings." *Hearings before the Committee on Commerce, US Senate, Ninety-Second Congress, First Session, on S. 945, Uniform Motor Vehicle Insurance Act*, Part 3, Serial No. 92-18.

Blum, Walter J., and Harry Kalven. *Public Law Perspectives on a Private Law Problem: Auto Compensation Plans.* Boston: Little, Brown, 1965.

Bureau of Justice Statistics. "Civil Trial Cases and Verdicts in Large Counties, 2001." Washington, DC: US Department of Justice, April 2004.

Cannon, James M., Files, Gerald R. Ford Presidential Library, box 23, folder "No Fault Insurance (1)," https://www.fordlibrarymuseum.gov/library/document/0039/1515888.pdf.

———, Files, Gerald R. Ford Presidential Library, box 23, folder "No Fault Insurance (2)," https://www.fordlibrarymuseum.gov/library/document/0039/16988092.pdf.

———, Files, Gerald R. Ford Presidential Library, box 24, folder "No Fault Insurance (3)," https://www.fordlibrarymuseum.gov/library/document/0039/1515889.pdf.

———, Files, Gerald R. Ford Presidential Library, box 24, folder "No-Fault Insurance (4)," https://www.fordlibrarymuseum.gov/library/document/0039/16988094.pdf.

Carroll, Stephen J., and Allan F. Abrahamese. "The Effects of a Choice Automobile Insurance Plan on Insurance Costs and Compensation: An Updated Analysis." Santa Monica, CA: RAND Institute for Civil Justice, 1998.

Carroll, Stephen, Allan Abrahamese, and Mary Vaiana. "The Costs of Excess Medical Claims for Automobile Personal Injuries." Santa Monica, CA: RAND Institute for Civil Justice, 1995.

Carroll, Stephen J., James S. Kakalik, Nicholas M. Pace, and John L. Adams. "No-Fault Approaches to Compensating People Injured in Automobile Accidents." Santa Monica, CA: RAND Institute for Civil Justice, 1991.

"Carter's Cabinet—How It Rates." *U.S. News & World Report*, October 16, 1975.

Columbia University Council for Research in the Social Sciences. "Report by the Committee to Study Compensation for Automobile Accidents." Philadelphia: Press of International Printing Co., 1932.

Common Cause. "The Political Money Tree Blooms." *In Common: The Common Cause Report from Washington* 9, no. 2 (Spring 1978).

Cummins, J. David, Richard D. Phillips, and Mary A. Weiss. "The Incentive Effects of No-Fault Automobile Insurance." *Journal of Law & Economics* 44, no. 2 (October 2001).

Cummins, J. David, Mary Weiss, and Richard D. Phillips. "The Incentive Effects of No-Fault Automobile Insurance." Philadelphia, PA: University of Pennsylvania, Wharton School, 1999.

Detlefsen, Robert R. "Escaping the Tort-Based Auto Accident Compensation System: The Federal Auto Choice Reform Act of 1997." *Journal of Insurance Regulation* 17 (1998): 186–212.

Devlin, Rose Anne. "Liability Versus No-Fault Automobile Insurance Regimes: An Analysis of the Experience in Quebec." In *Contributions to Insurance Economics*, ed. G. Dionne (Boston, MA: Kluwer Academic Publishers, 1992).

"Federal Standards for No-Fault Motor Vehicle Accident Benefits Act." *Hearings before the Subcommittee on Consumer Protection and Finance of the Committee on Interstate and Foreign Commerce, Ninety-Fifth Congress, First Session, on H.R. 6601, et al.*, March 18, April 7, 8, 23, and June 13, 1977, Serial No. 95-55.

Havens, Sarah. "A Legislative History of No-Fault Insurance." Unpublished paper, Hampshire College, 1978.

Insurance Information Institute. "Auto: Background on Compulsory/Uninsured Motorists." April 29, 2019.

Insurance Services Office. "Product Liability Closed Claims Survey: A Technical Analysis of Survey Results." Jersey City, NJ: Insurance Services Office, 1977.

Keeton, Robert E., and Jeffrey O'Connell. *Basic Protection for the Traffic Victim: A Blueprint for Reforming Automobile Insurance.* Boston, MA: Little, Brown & Co., 1967.

Kinzler, Peter. "Auto Insurance Reform Options: How to Change State Tort and No-Fault Laws to Reduce Premiums and Increase Consumer Choice." *Issue Analysis: A Public Policy Paper of the National Association of Mutual Insurance Companies.* Indianapolis, IN: National Association of Mutual Insurance Companies, August 2006.

Landes, Elizabeth. "Insurance, Liability, and Accidents: A Theoretical and Empirical Investigation of the Effect of No-Fault Accidents." *Journal of Law and Economics* 25, no. 1 (1982).

Loughran, David. *The Effect of No-Fault Automobile Insurance on Driver Behavior and Automobile Accidents in the United States.* Santa Monica, CA: RAND Institute for Civil Justice, 2001.

Moynihan, Daniel Patrick. "Next: A New Auto Insurance Policy." *New York Times Magazine*, August 27, 1967.

National Conference of Commissioners on Uniform State Laws. "Uniform Motor Vehicle Accident Reparations Act." Chicago: National Conference of Commissioners on Uniform State Laws, 1972.

National Highway Transportation Safety Administration. "Traffic Safety Facts 2017: A Compilation of Motor Vehicle Crash Data." Washington, DC: US Department of Transportation, 2017.

Nixon, Richard Milhous. "Changing Rules of Liability in Automobile Accident Litigation: Financial Protection for the Motor Vehicle Accident Victim." *Law and Contemporary Problems* 3, no. 4 (October 1936).

"No-Fault Motor Vehicle Insurance—1975." *Subcommittee on Consumer Protection and Finance of the Committee on Interstate and Foreign Commerce, House of Representatives, Ninety-Fourth Congress, First Session, on H.R. 265, etc.* (No-Fault Motor Vehicle Insurance bills), June 17, 19; July 8, 14, 17, 22, 24, 25, 1975, Serial No. 94-42.

O'Connell, Jeffrey. *The Injury Industry and the Remedy of No-Fault Insurance.* Urbana, Chicago, London: University of Illinois Press, 1971.

O'Connell, Jeffrey, and Robert Joost. "Giving Motorists a Choice between Fault and No-Fault Insurance." *Virginia Law Review* 72, no. 1 (February 1986).

O'Connell, Jeffrey, Peter Kinzler, and Dan Miller. "No-Fault Insurance at 40: Dusting Off an Old Idea to Help Consumers Save Money in an Age of Austerity." *NAMIC Issue Analysis.* Indianapolis, IN: National Association of Mutual Insurance Companies, December 2011.

O'Connell, Jeffrey, Peter Kinzler, and Hunter Bates. "A Federal Bill, with Commentary, to Allow Choice in Auto Insurance." *Connecticut Insurance Law Journal* 7, no. 2 (2000–2001): 511–584.

Office of the Secretary of Transportation, "Compensating Auto Accident Victims: A Follow-up Report on the No-Fault Auto Insurance Experience" (Washington, DC: US Department of Transportation, May 1985).

"State No-Fault Automobile Insurance Experiences." *Hearings before the Subcommittee on Consumer Protection and Finance of the Committee on Interstate and Foreign Commerce Committee, Ninety-Fifth Congress, First Session, on the Experience of Various States with No-Fault Automobile Insurance Laws,* Serial No. 95-41 (Washington, DC: US Government Printing Office, 1977).

"The Ultimate Hill Climber." *Roll Call,* September 20, 1993.

US Department of Transportation. "Motor Vehicle Crash Losses and Their Compensation in the United States, A Report to the Congress and the President." Washington, DC: US Government Printing Office, 1971.

———. "State No-Fault Automobile Insurance Experience, 1971–1977." Washington, DC: US Department of Transportation, June 1977.

US Joint Economic Committee. "The Benefits and Savings of Auto-Choice: A Joint Economic Committee Report," Washington, DC: US Congress, April 1997.

———. "Auto Choice: Impact on Cities and the Poor: A Joint Economic Committee Report, Prepared at the Request of U.S. Representatives Dick Armey (R-TX), Jim Moran (D-VA), U.S. Senators Rod Grams (R-MN), Joseph I. Lieberman (D-CT), Mitch McConnell (R-KY), Daniel Patrick Moynihan (D-NY) (March 1998)."

———. "Auto Choice: Relief for Businesses and Consumers, Prepared at the Request of U.S. Representative Dick Armey (R-X), House Majority Leader and U.S. Sen. Mitch McConnell (R-KY)." Washington, DC, July 1998.

———. "Choice in Auto Insurance: Updated Savings Estimates for Auto Choice." Washington, DC, July 2003.

Waller, Margy, and Mark Alan Hughes. "Working Far from Home: Transportation and Welfare Reform in the Ten Big States." Philadelphia and Washington, DC: Progressive Policy Institute and Public/Private Ventures, 1999.

Young, Leah. "A Chink in Ralph Nader's Armor?" *New Republic,* September 2, 1971.

INDEX